Luminos is the Open Access monograph publishing program from UC Press. Luminos provides a framework for preserving and reinvigorating monograph publishing for the future and increases the reach and visibility of important scholarly work. Titles published in the UC Press Luminos model are published with the same high standards for selection, peer review, production, and marketing as those in our traditional program. www.luminosoa.org

THE FLETCHER JONES FOUNDATION
HUMANITIES IMPRINT

The Fletcher Jones Foundation has endowed this imprint to foster innovative and enduring scholarship in the humanities.

The publisher and the University of California Press Foundation
gratefully acknowledge the generous support of the Fletcher Jones
Foundation Imprint in Humanities.

The Emergence of Modern Hinduism

The Emergence of Modern Hinduism

Religion on the Margins of Colonialism

Richard S. Weiss

UNIVERSITY OF CALIFORNIA PRESS

University of California Press
Oakland, California

Suggested citation: Weiss, R. S. *The Emergence of Modern Hinduism: Religion on the Margins of Colonialism*. Oakland: University of California Press, 2019. DOI: https://doi.org/10.1525/luminos.75

Library of Congress Cataloging-in-Publication Data

Names: Weiss, Richard (Richard Scott), author.
Title: The emergence of modern Hinduism: religion on the margins of colonialism / by Richard S. Weiss.
Description: Oakland, California : University of California Press, [2017] | Includes bibliographical references and index. | This work is licensed under a Creative Commons [CC-BY-NC-ND] license. To view a copy of the license, visit: http://creativecommons.org/licenses. |
Identifiers: LCCN 2019010309 (print) | LCCN 2019012915 (ebook) | ISBN 9780520973749 (Epub) | ISBN 9780520307056 (pbk. : alk. paper)
Subjects: LCSH: Hinduism—History—1765- | Ramalinga, Swami, 1823–1874—Influence.
Classification: LCC BL1153.5 (ebook) | LCC BL1153.5 .W45 2017 (print) | DDC 294.509/034—dc23
LC record available at https://lccn.loc.gov/2019010309

28 27 26 25 24 23 22 21 20 19
10 9 8 7 6 5 4 3 2 1

CONTENTS

List of Illustrations vii
Acknowledgments ix
Note on Diacritics and Italics xi

1. Introduction: Rethinking Religious Change in Nineteenth-Century South Asia 1
2. Giving to the Poor: Ramalinga's Transformation of Hindu Charity 27
3. The Publication of *Tiruvaruṭpā:* The Authority of Canon and Print 52
4. Ramalinga's Devotional Poems: Creating a Hagiography 73
5. The Polemics of Conflicting Modernities 97
6. The Modernity of Yoga Powers in Colonial India 122
7. Conclusion 148

Glossary 155
Notes 159
Bibliography 185
Index 199

ILLUSTRATIONS

FIGURES

1. Ramalinga Swami *12*
2. Title page of *Tiruvaruṭpā,* *63*
3. Velayuda Mudaliyar *65*

MAP

1. South India and Sri Lanka *3*

ACKNOWLEDGMENTS

I would like to thank the Royal Society of New Zealand for their generous financial support in the form of a Marsden Grant (VUW1006), which funded much of the research and writing of this book. The Faculty of Humanities and Social Sciences at Victoria University of Wellington supported this research in numerous ways, providing financial support and approving periods of leave in India, Germany, and Singapore. The Asia Research Institute at the National University of Singapore provided a vibrant scholarly setting as I began the project, and the South Asia Institute at Heidelberg University gave me an intellectual home in Germany as I wrote the latter parts of the book.

I am very pleased to see the book appear with University of California Press in its Luminos Open Access series. I would like to thank Reed Malcolm for taking it on. Reed was very enthusiastic about the work from the time I brought it to him, and he supported its transformation from manuscript to book form in a variety of ways that have improved it considerably. Archna Patel at UC Press provided expert assistance in preparing the manuscript for publication.

My colleagues in Religious Studies at Victoria University, Michael Radich, Geoff Troughton, Paul Morris, Joe Bulbulia, Philip Fountain, Eva Nisa, and Aliki Kalliabetsos, always have been collegial, inquisitive, and challenging, providing a stimulating environment in which I wrote much of the book and subjected them to frequent research seminars about it. G. Sundar at the Roja Muthiah Research Library in Chennai provided support and guidance in locating valuable works that enriched the book. Mr. Sundaramurthy at the Maraimalai Adigal Library directed me to original editions of a number of works central to this study, including the

1867 edition of *Tiruvaruṭpā.* Ms. Subhulakshmi at the U.V. Swaminatha Iyer Library helped me find relevant secondary literature.

V. Rajesh provided crucial help in a number of ways. He oriented me to Tamil scholarship on Ramalinga; we read nineteenth-century Tamil prose works together; and we discussed much of the content and ideas in the book. The work benefited greatly from his interest, collegiality, and scholarly acumen. R. Ilakkuvan helped me read Toluvur Velayuda Mudaliyar's "History of *Tiruvarutpa.*" Among many others who commented on the work in various ways, I would like to thank Darshan Ambalavanar, Sekhar Bandyopadhyay, Michael Bergunder, Nola Cooke, Wendy Doniger, Prasenjit Duara, Sascha Ebeling, Stephen Epstein, Peter Friedlander, Rafael Klöber, Michael Linderman, Layne Little, Thomas Nagy, Indira Peterson, V. Rajesh, Srilata Raman, Bo Sax, Ben Schonthal, Amiya Sen, David Shulman, Will Sweetman, McComas Taylor, Torsten Tschacher, Ravi Vaitheespara, Peter van der Veer, and A.R. Venkatachalapathy. Finally, Susann Liebich read and commented closely on many of the chapters here, and she helped me develop the sections that focus on print culture. She, and our daughters Clio and Leni, are my most treasured companions, and I dedicate the book to them.

An earlier version of chapter 2 was published as Richard S. Weiss, "Accounting for Religious Change: Ramalinga Adigal's Transformation of Hindu Giving in Nineteenth-Century India," *History of Religions* 56, no. 1 (2016): 108–38.

An earlier version of chapter 3 was published as Richard S. Weiss, "Print, Religion, and Canon in Colonial India: The Publication of Ramalinga Adigal's *Tiruvarutpa,*" *Modern Asian Studies* 49, no. 3 (2015): 650–77.

NOTE ON DIACRITICS AND ITALICS

I have not used diacritical marks in rendering Tamil personal names or places. I have used diacritics when referring to titles of texts and also for important South Asian words that I frequently use, such as *dāna*, *Tirumuṟai*, et cetera. In cases where South Asian words have a form that is commonly used in scholarly literature in English, I use those conventional renderings (e.g., Veda, Agama, Shaiva, yoga, shastra, bhakti, matha, rather than the Tamil *vētam, ākamam, caiva, yōkam, cāstiram, patti, maṭam*). I have used italics when referring to South Asian words that are not commonly rendered in English (e.g., *dāna, camayam*).

1

Introduction

Rethinking Religious Change in Nineteenth-Century South Asia

For millennia, one of the most consistent characteristics of Hindu traditions has been variation. Scholarly work on contemporary Hinduism and its premodern antecedents ably captures this complexity, paying attention to a wide spectrum of ideologies, practices, and positions of authority. Studies of religion in ancient India stress doctrinal variation in the period, when ideas about personhood, liberation, the efficacy of ritual, and deities were all contested in a variety of texts and contexts. Scholarship on contemporary Hinduism grapples with a vast array of rituals, styles of leadership, institutions, cultural settings, and social formations. However, when one turns to the crucial period of the nineteenth century, this complexity fades, with scholars overwhelmingly focusing their attention on leaders and movements that can be considered under the rubric "reform Hinduism." The result has been an attenuated nineteenth-century historiography of Hinduism and a unilineal account of the emergence of modern Hinduism.

Narratives about the emergence of modern Hinduism in the nineteenth century are consistent in their presumptions, form, and content. Important aspects of these narratives are familiar to students who have read introductory texts on Hinduism, and to scholars who write and teach those texts. At the risk of presenting a caricature of these narratives, here are their most basic characteristics. The historical backdrop includes discussions of colonialism, Christian missions, and long-standing Hindu traditions. The cast of characters is largely the same in every account, beginning with Rammohan Roy and the Brahmo Samaj, moving on to Dayananda Saraswati and the Arya Samaj, and ending with Swami Vivekananda's "muscular" Hinduism. These narratives focus on expressions of Hindu reform that emerged out of an encounter between Hindu leaders and Western ideas and models. They assume a narrative that is dominated by colonial, cosmopolitan settings, that is national in scale, that is concerned with elite leaders and movements, and that posits a radical break between this new, modern Hinduism and prior traditions. At their most successful, these studies contribute insightful accounts of cosmopolitan processes within which Hindu leaders transformed their traditions through engagement with diverse actors, institutions, and sensibilities. However, as I will show, these accounts also reinforce dichotomies between Western modernity and Indian tradition, emphasizing the role of the West in Hindu innovation and consigning expressions of Hinduism that were largely untouched by Western ideas to the realm of static tradition.

In this book, I present a narrative of the emergence of modern Hinduism that challenges these conventional accounts. I do this through a close study of the writings, teachings, and innovations of Ramalinga Swami (1823–1874). Ramalinga was a Shaiva leader who spoke and wrote in Tamil in a local setting, was marginal to colonial and Hindu institutional authority, was grounded in Hindu traditions, and did not engage the West in any visible way. I argue that Ramalinga's teachings were modern because they displayed an acute awareness of challenges of the present, innovated in ways that addressed those challenges, were founded on a desire to transform the world in specific ways, and presaged later developments in Hindu traditions. He drew on Shaiva tantric, devotional, and literary traditions in developing creative responses to contemporary challenges such as poverty, famine, and caste discrimination. He attacked social hierarchy, developed rituals of food-giving to the poor, founded a voluntary community, and promised ordinary householders yogic powers and immortality. When he gained popularity among a wide range of caste and class communities, leaders of the established Tamil Shaiva elite attacked his teachings and initiatives. By examining Ramalinga within broader narratives of Hindu modernization, I present a new model for Hindu modernity that emphasizes the capacity of Hindu traditions to provide inspiration for new forms of Hinduism that remain influential today. In a broader context, my findings have important implications for the ways that scholars think about the impact of colonization and Westernization on non-Western religious traditions.

Ramalinga provides a fascinating case study of a Hindu leader who was actively transforming Hindu traditions outside of cosmopolitan colonial centers. The phrase "colonial modernity" does not comprehensively account for the conditions in which he wrote and lived, because his world was much more than a "colonial" one. He carried on his work in the town of Vadalur, near the village of his birthplace and about twenty kilometers from the colonial outpost of Cuddalore. He was also about twenty kilometers from Chidambaram, home of the famous Shiva Nataraja temple, and sixty-five kilometers from Tiruvavadudurai, home of one of the most powerful Shaiva institutions in South India. This location suggests a number of important relationships that I will explore in this work. That is, he was close to, but also removed from, colonial centers as well as established centers

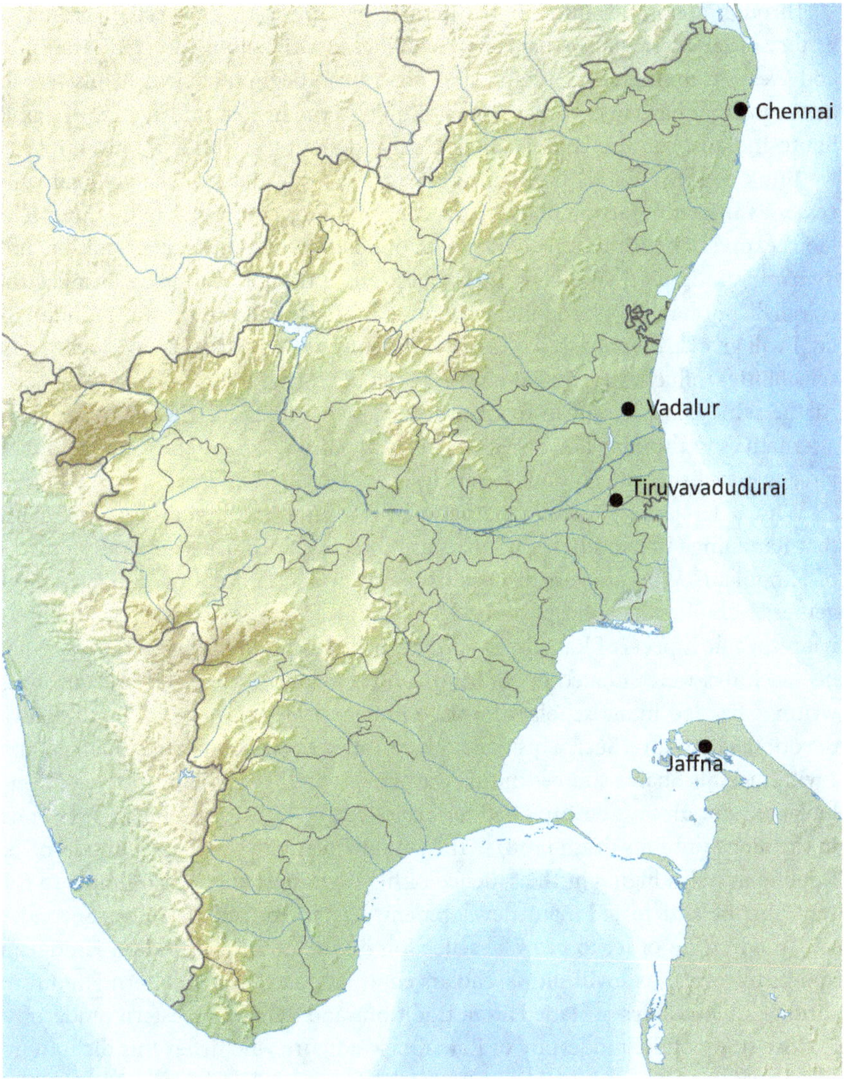

MAP 1. India and Sri Lanka. Credit: Wikimedia Commons.

of Shaiva devotional and scholarly activity. His relationship with powerful Shaiva monasteries was at times strained, a result of his middling caste status and the critical spirit of his writing. His position on the periphery of colonial activity and Shaiva institutional power provided an ideal space in which he advanced a critical and creative reformulation of Shaiva traditions. In the last years of his life, he attempted to transform Vadalur into a "northern Chidambaram" that would provide an institutional alternative to existing Shaiva centers of power.

Through a close examination of Ramalinga's innovative projects, I present a history of religious change that is not beholden to a dichotomy of Hindu tradition and Western modernity. In doing so, I hope I can begin to articulate answers to questions that have urgent relevance not only to the history and agency of Tamil South Indians, but also colonized people throughout the world. That is, how can we think about religious modernization in ways that do not take colonial processes as the only starting point? How can we discuss creative, South Asian religious expressions without recourse to an opposition between static tradition and dynamic modernity? In raising these questions, I do not overlook the impact of colonialism on religious and literary culture, because this impact was monumental. I will give due emphasis to the ways that European cultures, technologies, and sensibilities influenced religious changes even in settings far from colonial centers. At the same time, I want to focus on other inspirations for change to consider alternatives to thinking about religion in *colonial* India, where the term "colonial" already establishes the grounds for analysis.

Why, if I reject the dichotomy between tradition and modernity, do I insist that Ramalinga was modern, and that his projects helped usher in modern forms of Hinduism? Why not just dispose of the term and concept of "modern" altogether? I employ the concept of modern for at least two reasons. First, it illuminates specific aspects of Ramalinga's project by focusing attention on the ways that his teachings were situated in his historical present. The literary character of his writings has led many scholars to place him in a *longue durée* of Tamil Shaiva devotional literature. Such a history explains much about Ramalinga's sources, and I will trace his Shaiva sources in this way. However, this sort of history can overlook the relevance his writings had for his followers in the time of his rise to fame in the 1860s until his death in 1874. The employment of a concept of "modern," as I define it, helps highlight the salience of his teachings, and it also points to the ways that he anticipated many developments in pan-Indian Hinduism. Second, I use "modern" in order to provoke reflection on the notion of modern Hinduism and its histories. As I will show, scholars continue to examine modern Hinduism through dichotomies of static Hindu traditions and dynamic Western modernity. A close study of the modernity of Ramalinga, a figure who defies this dichotomy, challenges us to expand the histories we tell of modern Hinduism, and reflect on the character of modernity itself.

REFORM HINDUISM, MODERN HINDUISM, AND THE WEST

Scholars usually trace the beginning of modern Hinduism to the emergence of Hindu reform movements in the nineteenth century. Much of this work is outstanding, documenting and analyzing the myriad ways that Hindu leaders reshaped their traditions as a result of colonial encounters. The dominance of these studies is such that, taken together, they provide an inescapable point of reference for any scholarly study of nineteenth-century Hinduism, including this one. In this section I present some of the major debates and presumptions of this scholarship, necessarily simplifying a large body of varied literature on diverse authors and movements. My primary aim is not to contribute to, nor to comprehensively critique, this literature on reform Hinduism but rather to highlight what it misses. I hope to open up space for a broader consideration of Hindu innovation that goes beyond a focus on reform Hinduism. In subsequent chapters, I show how a close study of Ramalinga suggests a narrative for the emergence of modern Hinduism that differs in crucial ways from cosmopolitan reform accounts.

I use the phrase "reform Hinduism" to refer to the range of novel cosmopolitan expressions of Hinduism in the nineteenth century that were clearly influenced by European ideas and models. I have chosen to use "reform" because it retains the resonances of both the Protestant Reformation and Victorian-era European reform. Both of these European "reform" projects had a significant influence on nineteenth-century cosmopolitan Hindu leaders and their reimagining of Hindu traditions. These European and Hindu projects shared a number of concerns, including debates about the status and accessibility of texts; the efficacy and ethics of ritual practices; priestly mediation of devotion; the centrality of personal faith; the status of women; class relations, often extended to caste; new charitable practices; and the accessibility of education. "Reform Hinduism" has become the most recognizable shorthand to describe these new expressions of Hinduism, and it has attracted the interest of scholars for more than a century.

Hinduism is a contested category, with many scholars arguing that it was only in the nineteenth century that the notion of a single Hindu tradition emerged. The scholarship on the "invention of Hinduism" is large, demonstrating that scholars have taken to heart the hegemony and distortions wrought by Western categories of religion.[1] I am convinced by much of this scholarship but continue to find the term "Hinduism" useful for discussing a range of nineteenth-century traditions. When I use the term "Hindu" or "Hinduism," I do not posit a single, unified "World Religion," but a range of traditions and expressions that broadly share ritual and theological orientations.[2] In the following pages, I describe a variety of ways of being Hindu and of being modern, and I posit diverse genealogies for those expressions of modern Hinduism. If reform Hinduism is one such expression, Ramalinga's teachings are another. The diversity of modern Hinduism thus includes tendencies toward a Protestant rationality that characterized Hindu reform, but also a range of other features that do not fall into this framework, including apocalypticism, revelation, and miracles. Such features continue to find resonance among Hindus, responding in important ways to contemporary challenges.

Hindu reform leaders and movements were elite, urban, and cosmopolitan, leading Brian Hatcher to characterize such projects as "bourgeois Hinduism."[3]

Their teachings resonated most strongly in colonial contexts, and they had little impact beyond them. For example, in the 1881 census, only the Brahmo Samaj was important enough to merit distinct consideration. Of a Hindu population of 187,937,450, only 1,147 Hindus counted themselves as Brahmos.[4] That is, only one in every 160,000 Hindus identified with the Brahmo Samaj. The authors of an 1883 Report on the Census note that they believe the numbers of Brahmos were higher than reported, but they also cite A. Barth's *Religions of India* (1882) on the group: "it is more than 60 years since the Brahma Samaj was founded; and how many adherents can it reckon up? In Bengal, its cradle, among a population of 67,000,000, some thousands, all in the large towns; in the country districts (and India is an essentially rural country), it is hardly known."[5] Given that the few who formally declared their affiliation to the Brahmo Samaj were elite figures, it may be that their influence, and that of other reform groups, was greater than these numbers suggest. Outside of those bourgeois circles of educated urban Indians, however, it is doubtful that reform Hinduism had much impact on the traditions of devotion and ritual that most Hindus were practicing in the nineteenth century.

Reform leaders were cosmopolitan not only in their utilization of Indian and Western cultural frameworks, but also in their awareness of pan-Indian and even global social and political processes. Their cosmopolitanism was often implicit, sometimes veiled, and certainly partial and "rooted."[6] That is to say, they did not see themselves as global citizens but as Indians first and foremost. They were fiercely loyal to Hindu traditions, even if, at the same time, they were highly critical of these traditions. Theirs was a colonial cosmopolitanism that, as Peter van der Veer points out, emerged not as "a liberating alternative to ethnic and nationalist chauvinism," but as part of nationalist, colonial, and anti-colonial projects.[7] It is not accidental that it was Calcutta, the administrative capital of British India, that was also the most important center of Hindu reform.[8] Many reform leaders themselves acknowledged their debt to Western models, such as Keshab Chandra Sen, who noted that "Pure English education and pure religious reformation commenced almost at the same time in Bengal and have since gone on parallel lines."[9] Not all Hindu reformers had an English education, with Dayananda Saraswati being the most prominent reform leader without knowledge of English. Even Saraswati's Arya Samaj, however, incorporated many of the features of Protestant models of religion, emphasizing scriptural authority, conceiving of religions as distinct and unified entities, and attempting to reshape Hinduism according to Protestant notions of rationality.

Scholars have focused on this cosmopolitan character of reform Hinduism, increasingly refining models of interactions between Hindu and Western traditions. J.N. Farquhar's classic study (1915) of nineteenth-century movements describes Christian "seeds" of inspiration, planted in the fertile "soil" of India's "old religions."[10] Farquhar's gendered, biological metaphor assumes Western agency and Indian passivity; Christianity supplies the active, male seed that instigates change, while India's traditions are female, receptive, and provide continuity. In an essay published in 1978, Paul Hacker argues that the "one common trait" of Neo-Hindus is that "their intellectual formation is primarily or predominantly Western. It is European culture, and in several cases even the Christian religion, which has led them to embrace certain religious, ethical, social, and political values." Neo-Hinduism "presents Western or Christian ideas in a Hindu garb."[11] For Hacker, Neo-Hinduism owes more to Western sources than it does to Hindu traditions.

More recently, idioms of exchange have emphasized the agency of Hindu reform leaders, their strategic decisions in reformulating their traditions, and the role of Hindu traditions in instigating religious change. Amiya Sen criticizes "impact-response" models that characterize Hindu reform innovations as reflexive responses to Western challenges. He instead describes the "Indo-British encounter . . . as being quite dialogic and dialectical in nature."[12] Hatcher prefers the idiom of "convergence," in which Western and Indian models, values, and ideas interact in complex ways. Convergence does not ascribe hegemony to either Indian or Western cultural forms, and it recognizes the active role played by Hindu leaders, languages, and traditions.[13] Elsewhere, Hatcher develops "eclecticism" as an analytical tool to think about the ways that reform authors drew from a range of sources to develop new formulations of Hinduism. He emphasizes that the eclecticism of Hindu reform does not undermine the "authenticity" of these emerging traditions, but rather it indicates the creativity of their authors in fostering pride among Indians. Indeed, Hindu reformers employed Western models and ideas at least in part to resist Western cultural imperialism.[14]

I will not weigh in on these debates on the character of the colonial-Indian encounter. Rather, I want to raise two series of questions about this scholarly literature on Hindu reform that have important implications for my study of Ramalinga, and also implications more generally for the study of modern Hinduism.

First, why has there been relatively little scholarship on non-reform Hindu change in the nineteenth century? Given that discussion of the Brahmo Samaj was relegated to a footnote and an afterthought in the 1881 census, why has there been a disproportionate amount of scholarly work on the group and others like it? Answers might point to a persistent Eurocentrism or, perhaps, to scholarly inertia. One important reason, certainly, is the relative inaccessibility of rich data. As Hacker noted, "traditional Hinduism . . . has one serious drawback. Unlike Neo-Hinduism, it has scarcely any publicity abroad. It does not produce any remarkable literature, least of all in English."[15] Hacker was wrong about "traditional," non-reform Hinduism not producing important literature in the nineteenth century, but he was right about the high profile of reform writings. Hindu reform figures enjoyed some fame among elite Hindus and Europeans, so the sources for studying their projects have been in front of Western eyes from at least the beginning of the nineteenth century, when Rammohan Roy wrote editorials for English newspapers. These leaders were well known to colonial administrators, and even if they did not move in the same circles as the British, they occupied overlapping worlds of discourse, debate, and, to some degree, ideology and sensibility. They are attractive figures to study at least partly because of these overlapping worlds.

Evidence that would support detailed, layered studies of non-cosmopolitan forms of Hinduism is harder to find, especially for scholars who work in English. However, Hatcher rightly notes that "there are literally worlds of material in the regional vernaculars awaiting scholarly attention."[16] Such literature provides extensive resources for the study of Hindu change that does not clearly fit into reform models, even if these are literary expressions that do not represent a sort of "subaltern" Hinduism. Ramalinga, for example, was a celebrated Tamil poet, but he worked largely outside cosmopolitan contexts. There are other Tamil poets like him, such as his contemporaries Minakshisundaram Pillai and Dandapani Swamigal, who were producing religious literature that was not clearly inflected with colonial concerns. I expect that there were similar authors writing in other vernacular languages. Sources for the study of non-reform Hindu change are available: they are in vernacular languages, written by people who worked outside the purview of a cosmopolitan public eye.

To be fair, some scholarly work of this sort has already been done. One important example is the Swaminarayan movement.[17] Also important is work on Mahima Dharma, a group that emerged in Orissa in the latter quarter of the nineteenth century. Mahima Dharma emphasized low-caste empowerment but had "no intrinsic, direct Western influence."[18] Closer to Ramalinga's Tamil world, there have been a handful of studies on the Ayyavazhi movement.[19] This movement originated at the southern tip of India in the 1840s, its leaders articulating a new and complex theology and critique of caste. Regional experts in other South Asian languages could certainly expand this list. The emergence of these movements cannot be described as a dialogue between Hindu and Western discourses, even if they also did not arise in a vacuum of tradition, sealed off from any Christian or colonial influence. They were highly innovative and popular in their appeal, often centering on a founding, charismatic figure. What is noteworthy is that these studies, and the leaders and movements that they portray, feature neither in accounts of nineteenth-century Hinduism nor in narratives of the emergence of modern Hinduism. They remain marginal histories in that narrative, because they do not fit the model of reform Hinduism, with its links to the West and Protestant notions of rationality. I argue here that the inclusion of these sorts of examples of non-reform Hindu innovation would enrich our accounts of the sources of modern Hinduism. What I offer in this book is an extended study of Ramalinga Swami as one important example of non-reform Hindu innovation and modernization, which I consider in the broader historiography of nineteenth-century Hinduism.

Second, what are the implications of this inordinate attention to reform expressions of religious change? What distortions in the study of Hinduism has it engendered? There are undoubtedly a number of answers to this question. I want to emphasize just one here: the prevalent tendency among scholars to give a historical account for the emergence of modern Hinduism by referring only to reform Hinduism. Scholars consistently equate three terms that should rather be distinguished: reform Hinduism, modern Hinduism, and Hinduism as a larger rubric. The slippage between these terms may be common among middle-class Hindu apologists who seek to define their tradition in specific ways to fulfill any number of agendas. It is not acceptable, I think, for scholars to engage in similar slippage, which goes at least as far back as Farquhar's 1915 study of "modern" reform movements across several traditions. Farquhar concludes his study with the hopeful assertion that "The most prominent characteristic of the long series of religious movements we have dealt with is *the steady advance of the ancient faiths*. . . . Hinduism, Islam, Buddhism, Jainism, and Zoroastrianism each leaped up into new vigorous activity, every prominent sect experiencing a mysterious awakening."[20] Even though Farquhar's focus was only on urban, cosmopolitan reform movements, he takes these to represent the whole of Hinduism, Buddhism, etc. He attributes Christian influence to their advance and modernization, expressing optimism that these reform movements are the vanguard of broader changes in their respective traditions.[21] What escaped Farquhar's attention were the myriad projects of Hindu modernization, like that of Ramalinga, that were also transforming Hinduism in enduring ways.

Contemporary scholars rightly reject Farquhar's Christian apologetics, but they continue to stress an inevitable and usually exclusive link between Christianity/European culture, reform movements, and modern Hinduism. Wilhelm Halbfass, picking up on Hacker's delineation of "Neo-Hinduism," characterizes the India-Europe encounter as one between "tradition and modernity." Reform leaders produced "modern Hindu thought" by incorporating Western elements.[22] Arvind Sharma, with reference to Keshab Chandra Sen, a Brahmo Samaj leader, writes that "modern Hinduism has tended to accept Christ, but not Christianity."[23] Hatcher's work is generally sensitive to Indian agency and appreciative of the complexity of Indian-Western interactions, and several of my arguments in the book draw from his excellent work. However, he also insists that the encounter with the West and the development of reform Hinduism mark the origin point of modern Hinduism, positing that "Modern Hinduism is thus best viewed as the product of a rich and extended conversation between India and the West."[24] Elsewhere in a discussion of colonial Hinduism, he characterizes Hinduism as a "joint project" of European and South Asian actors.[25]

A look at titles of important books on Hindu reform further clarifies this assumed link between the West, reform Hinduism, and modern Hinduism, and even modern Indian thought: David Kopf's classic *The Brahmo Samaj and the Shaping of the Modern Indian Mind* (1979); William Radice's edited volume *Swami Vivekananda and the Modernization of Hinduism* (1998); Arvind Sharma's collection of writings by prominent reformers, *Modern Hindu Thought: The Essential Texts* (2002); and Torkel Brekke's work on Hindu, Sikh, and Buddhist reform leaders, *Makers of Modern Indian Religion in the Late Nineteenth Century* (2002). Scholarly introductions to Hinduism repeat this narrative and introduce it to university students. For example, Gavin Flood's excellent and widely used *An Introduction to Hinduism* (1996) includes a chapter on "Hinduism in the Modern World." There Flood presents an account of Hindu innovation in the nineteenth century that is limited to reform leaders and movements. He cites a genealogy of Hindu modernization—Rammohan Roy to Dayananda Saraswati to Swami Vivekananda—that is followed by nearly every other scholarly overview and sourcebook of Hinduism.[26] These works continue to focus on expressions of Hinduism that emerged from colonial urban centers, and they stress the role of the West as an ever-present, necessary, and even equal player in the transformation of Hinduism.

The equation of modern Hinduism and reform Hinduism assumes a dichotomy between modernity, defined as Western in origin and character, and tradition, which in this case includes all expressions of non-reform Hinduism. David Smith exemplifies this position: "Modernity, product of the Enlightenment, is generally brought into sharper focus by the contrast with what are called 'traditional societies.'" Further, "Hinduism and modernity are opposite poles . . . ."[27] In this case, Smith means "traditional" Hinduism, which he distinguishes from a reform Hinduism or "Neo-Hinduism" that "seeks a national revival through modernization of Hinduism."[28] Sudipta Kaviraj likewise contrasts Hindu reform and "traditional Hinduism." He equates reform Hinduism with "indigenous religion," asserting that "the most significant fact was that indigenous religion, on which the entire intellectual life of society depended, did not decline, but rather restructured itself by using the European critique."[29] This dichotomy between a static, traditional Hinduism and dynamic, Westernized, innovative reform Hinduism is one that continues to shape the study of modern Hinduism in explicit and subtle ways. By limiting modern Hinduism to those forms that incorporate Protestant and other Western ideas, discourses, and institutions, it reinscribes a dichotomy between tradition and modernity.

I will argue throughout the book that the use of a tradition versus modernity dichotomy in thinking about modern Hinduism makes questionable assumptions and has distorting consequences. It gives us a narrative in which Hindu innovation was one, a response to colonial domination, and two, due to the Westernization of urban elite Indians. This "colonist's-eye view" of religious history assumes that Hinduism outside cosmopolitan discourses was traditional and static. It discounts the possibility that Hindu innovations that were not directly beholden to colonial influence may have contributed to the shape of modern Hinduism. Hatcher has succinctly summarized the issue: "Linking our understanding of Hinduism in this way to the legacy of European colonialism and European self-understanding is one of the best ways to begin wrestling with the question of Hinduism and modernity."[30] He is certainly right that it is *one* of the best ways, but is it the *only* way? Is it possible to consider a history of the emergence of modern Hinduism that does not begin, and end, with colonialism?

This is precisely what I attempt to do in this book, through a close study of Ramalinga. I highlight the ways that Ramalinga's teachings and innovations diverged from reform Hinduism, in his sources for inspiration, and also in the ways that he redefined tradition, community, charismatic leadership, and devotion. His articulations of Hinduism cannot be explained by a reform model of cosmopolitan engagement between Hindu and European ideas. At the same time, I argue that his teachings were modern ones, presaging developments that have come to characterize contemporary Hinduism, namely, charismatic leadership, employment of new technologies, new forms of charitable outreach, assertion of miracles, and emphasis on choice in community affiliation, to name just a few. To account for Ramalinga's creativity, timeliness, and impact, we need to go beyond definitions of modern Hinduism that emphasize Western influence and distinguish it from traditional forms of Hinduism. Ramalinga helps us in the project of provincializing Europe or, in this case, provincializing the most European of Hindu traditions, reform Hinduism, in accounts on nineteenth-century Hinduism.[31] His case highlights the limits of the equation of modern Hinduism with reform Hinduism, and suggests a much more varied landscape of Hindu change, one that includes miracles, devotional poetry, claims to new revelation, and the transformative potential of tradition.

A BRIEF BIOGRAPHY OF RAMALINGA SWAMI

Ramalinga Pillai (1824–1873) was later called Ramalinga Swami, Ramalinga Swamigal, Ramalinga Adigal, or simply Vallalar.[32] He is renowned for his devotional poetry, his protests against caste, and his mystical experiences. He claimed to have received miraculous powers through his close relationship with Shiva, and legends of his extraordinary abilities circulated among his followers in his lifetime. He wrote thousands of verses in traditional meter, collected together in several volumes under the title *Tiruvaruṭpā*.[33] Those poems remain central to his legacy and have been sung in private and in temples since at least the 1860s. His critiques of ritual orthodoxy, caste, and canon made him a target of attacks by established Shaiva figures. He was highly innovative, founding a religious community with a number of remarkable features, including burying the dead and waiting for Shiva's physical appearance. He sponsored the construction of a temple where Shiva is worshiped in the form of a flame. He developed a ritualized practice of giving food to the anonymous poor, departing from established Shaiva traditions of giving to esteemed recipients. He drew from a variety of diverse Shaiva traditions in developing his projects, including canonical devotional works as well as tantric and siddha traditions. He used Shaiva ideas, symbols, and idioms in formulating his

FIGURE 1. Ramalinga Swamigal. Credit: From the collection of Layne R. Little and Archana Venkatesan.

teachings, but he did not live in a nostalgic world of tradition. His projects sought to address the social inequality and poverty that characterized his world.

There are many sources that present biographical details of Ramalinga's life. His poems themselves are highly autobiographical, communicating important life events and everyday activities. He wrote letters to his disciples that contain valuable details about his life. One of his senior followers wrote a short history of events leading up to the first significant publication of Ramalinga's verses, providing a sketch of some details of his life.[34] P. Ramasami Mudaliyar published the earliest comprehensive account of Ramalinga's life in a preface to the first full edition of his verses in 1892, eighteen years after Ramalinga's death.[35] Since then, there have been many biographies.[36] Below I present a composite summary of major events in his life. Subsequent chapters will fill out these details and, especially, will discuss his motivations and concerns.

Ramalinga was born in a village called Marudur, just twenty-five kilometers from the major Shaiva shrine of Chidambaram. His family was of the Karuniga community, a non-brahman caste of scribes and bookkeepers.[37] Their caste status was somewhat ambiguous. They were considered *vellalars,* pure castes that enjoy ritual privileges and status, but they were of somewhat lower status than other *vellalar* castes. Ramalinga's father died soon after Ramalinga was born, and the family moved to Chennai, where Ramalinga would live for most of his youth. In 1857 he moved back to his area of birth, where he spent the remainder of his life.

Ramalinga's family appears to have emphasized education. His father was a village accountant, and he served as a teacher in Marudur.[38] Ramalinga's older brother, Sabhapati Pillai, studied under the famous Kanchi Sabhapati Mudaliyar, who was a Tamil scholar, pandit of Pacchaiyappa School in Chennai, and a leading figure in the publication of much of the Tamil devotional canon.[39] Sabhapati Pillai himself became a Tamil pandit, and he was Ramalinga's primary teacher. Ramalinga began his studies when he was five years old, learning literary Tamil works from his brother. Ramasami Mudaliyar describes Ramalinga as a keen and capable learner, able to master texts with one reading and appearing to understand works even without instruction. Ramalinga aspired to follow the path taken by his brother, who was initiated into Shaivism and earned his living giving discourses on Shaiva texts. As Ramalinga matured in his learning, he studied works of Vedanta and Siddhanta and tried to find common ground between them.[40]

In his writings, Ramalinga demonstrates detailed knowledge of canonical Shaiva texts, as well as other well-known Tamil works such as the *Tirukkuṟaḷ*. He appears, then, to have received a conventional Tamil Shaiva education. He had no knowledge of English and makes no explicit mention of contact with European peoples or knowledge. Ramalinga did not know Sanskrit, even expressing gratitude that he never had any interest in the "Aryan or other languages," calling them "pompous," "obscure," and "tumultuous."[41] However, it would be a misreading to ascribe to him the sort of anti-brahman, anti-Sanskrit, or anti-Aryan sentiment that would later dominate the ideologies of the Dravidian movement.

Ramalinga is famous today for his verses that vigorously critique caste and ritual orthodoxy, but most of his poems are conventional Shaiva devotional works, proclaiming the power and benevolence of Shiva and Murugan. Many of his poems to Shiva were published in 1867, and poems to Murugan appeared in print in 1880. It was only in 1885 that some followers decided to publish his radical poems, polemical works that criticized caste and Shaiva elitism.[42] Further writings appeared in the coming years, including a number of letters and prose works collected by A. Balakrishna Pillai in his edition of Ramalinga's collected writings, published in twelve volumes between 1931 and 1958.[43]

Ramalinga's efforts to articulate a new vision of religious community went beyond his writings: he established innovative institutions that embodied his ideals. These institutions were novel in his Tamil Shaiva context. The first of these, and the basis for the others, was an association of devotees that would put his ideas into action. He had begun to speak of his path as the *caṉmārkkam,* the "True Path," and in 1865 he formed a society that would advance the goals of this path.[44] His society set up an almshouse to feed the poor, and they built a temple to worship god in the form of light.

In 1870, Ramalinga moved his residence to a site a few kilometers from the town of Vadalur, the location of his almshouse and temple. Ramalinga's new home provided him some distance from the crowds of the town and his institutions. It became the location of his personal activities and the place where he gave lectures to his followers in the last years of his life. He called this residence "Citti Vaḷākam," the "House of Siddhi." "Siddhi" has a number of meanings, including the extraordinary powers gained through yoga that Ramalinga claimed to have attained. It also refers to final liberation, the term often given to the place of death and liberation of Tamil saints, perhaps most importantly the Tamil siddhas, to whom Ramalinga is often compared. It is in the latter sense that the name for the residence proved prophetic. Ramalinga's followers testify that he entered the "House of Siddhi" on January 30, 1874, and disappeared. He was never seen again.[45]

Ramalinga's writings and projects enjoyed significant popularity and patronage in his lifetime. The *Madras Mail,* in its July 5, 1871 edition, reported that "Ramalinga Pillai, a Tamil Scholar of some repute, it appears has set himself up for a god. . . . Thousands throng there daily; and a Pandal (temple) is being erected at the cost of 15,000 Rs. !!!"[46] He attracted followers across a range of castes and classes, and his poems addressed the plight of the poor. For example, he expressed his fear, empathy, and distress when he saw "mothers, companions, relatives, those who are dear to me, and others afflicted by hunger and disease . . . the elderly and the young alike suffering because of poverty."[47] In part because of the success of his populist message, he found himself subject to the critiques of Shaiva leaders who promoted a more elite, caste-based vision for Shaivism. As we will see, the scholar Arumuga Navalar considered Ramalinga's challenge to established Shaivism important enough to warrant a vigorous written attack in 1869. In his polemic, Navalar notes that Ramalinga's verses were being sung in Shaiva temples at the expense of the traditional *Tēvāram* verses that had been sung for centuries.[48] Ramalinga's fame made him a significant force in the changing character of Tamil Shaivism, and his influence continues to this day. This influence is most visibly effected through the dozens of groups that work to establish his True Path in their local communities, most importantly through charitable outreach to the poor.

STUCK BETWEEN TRADITION AND MODERNITY

The dichotomy between tradition and modernity has served as the general problematic for scholarship on Ramalinga. Scholars have tried to place him in one or the other, or to show how he mediates between the two categories. Luba Zubkova recounts that when she and her co-author A. Dubiansky were writing a history of Tamil literature, Ramalinga was the "most controversial in view of a need to draw a border line between tradition and modernity."[49] Different commentators have indeed made varying decisions about his place, apparently feeling the need to judge whether Ramalinga was traditional or modern, and often struggling to decide which better characterizes his teachings. I will review some of this scholarship to argue that the "problem" arises because scholars reject the possibility that "tradition" can also be "modern." I will then detail my own approach, which reconsiders the concepts of modernity and tradition.

Those who place Ramalinga within "tradition" generally emphasize his literary debts to Shaiva bhakti poetry and his miraculous claims. Charles Heimsath writes that Ramalinga, Swaminarayan, and Ramakrishna "were much closer in inspiration, character, and message to the traditional saints of the pre-modern period than to any of the religious leaders of the modern Westernized reform movements."[50] For Ramachandra Dikshitar, Ramalinga is not the first in the lineage of modern Tamil authors but the last of the Tamil "Mystic Poets." Dikshitar begins this lineage with the poets of the canonical *Tēvāram*, which we will return to often in the following chapters. He does not mention Ramalinga's anti-caste writings but instead focuses on his constant devotion to Shiva and his miraculous disappearance. Dikshitar credits mystic poets like Ramalinga with "Keeping alive the religious life of the masses in this world . . . thanks to these mystics, our religion and our religious faith were saved from extinction during many an hour of peril and crisis."[51] Kamil Zvelebil largely agrees with this assessment, asserting that "Irāmaliṅka Cuvāmikaḷ (Ramalinga Svami, 1823–1874), a controversial figure as a religious leader, was unquestionably the greatest Tamil poet of the 19th century. He was also the last great poet in the line of the Śaiva bhakti poet-saints."[52] N. Subramanian likewise situates Ramalinga in prior Shaiva traditions: "Saintly persons like Ramalinga Swami were traditionalists who continued the mystic teachings of earlier saints though he occasionally spoke of anti-Brahmanical communal reform."[53] Subramanian equates Ramalinga's innovations with "reform" but stresses the "traditional" features of his writings. These scholars understand Ramalinga primarily as the inheritor and propagator of prior Shaiva traditions.

They attach specific characteristic to tradition, namely, mysticism, devotion, miracles, saintliness, and the poetic.

Contrary to these depictions of Ramalinga as the last great traditional bhakti poet and saint, other scholars emphasize the novel character of his teachings. For R. Balachandran, Ramalinga is one of the "Pioneers of Tamil Literature" who were responsible for "the transition of Tamil literature into its modern phase."[54] C. Jesudasan calls Ramalinga "a powerful force in the revival and strengthening of modern Hinduism."[55] Neela Padmanabhan begins his survey of modern Tamil literature with Ramalinga, focusing on his anti-caste writings and charity. According to Padmanabhan, Ramalinga is "a rebel, decrying religious fanaticism and the tyranny of caste. He champions an ideal, egalitarian society breaking the barriers of caste and religion." Here Ramalinga appears to fare well as modern, but Padmanabhan also notes that "in modern Tamil literature, tradition and modernity necessarily constitute a continuum." Ramalinga appears at the beginning of the section on "The Nineteenth Century: Sparks of Modernity," so we are probably justified to conclude that he is one of the more "traditional" of modern Tamil poets.[56] Sascha Ebeling, in his work on nineteenth-century Tamil literature, suggests that Ramalinga deserves consideration in any reassessment of modern Tamil poetry. Ebeling credits Ramalinga and his primary foil, Arumuga Navalar, with a "transformation of the traditional Tamil Śaivite religious milieu."[57] For these authors, Ramalinga's importance to nineteenth-century literature and society was not that he kept past traditions alive, but that his innovations proved influential to literary, social, and religious changes. They consider him to be modern because he stressed change and transformation, advanced egalitarian ideals, and taught social responsibility to the poor and marginalized.

Other studies place him somewhere between tradition and modernity, or with one foot in each. The *History of Indian Literature* includes an entry on Ramalinga in its volume on nineteenth-century literature, entitled *Western Impact: Indian Response.* Here Sisir Kumar Das calls Ramalinga "a great saint and a man of traditional learning . . . who initiated a new religious movement and created a new body of religious lyrics."[58] Das's discussion of Ramalinga is in a section on "Traditions and Innovations," suggesting that these are opposing categories, and that Ramalinga embodies both in different ways. Jean-Luc Racine and Josiane Racine refer to Ramalinga's innovative "reforms" as a rejuvenation of "the siddhar mysticoascetic tradition."[59] In Peter Heehs's *Indian Religions: A Historical Reader of Spiritual Expression and Experience,* Ramalinga appears as the first of the "Mystics of Modern India" in a section titled "Continuity and Innovation (1850–1990)." Heehs understands Ramalinga in the context of "modern religious movements." Such movements "situate themselves in a line going back untold ages, yet give themselves the freedom to depart from tradition when modern circumstances require it." Leaders of such movements use scripture and "their own inner experience" to "justify their innovations."[60] Heehs characterizes Ramalinga as both a traditional poet and a modern innovator, attributing his capacity for creation to the accounts of revelation that dominate his poems. For Heehs, innovation comes primary from "modern circumstances," while tradition legitimates these changes, reminiscent of Hacker's assertion that Neo-Hinduism "presents Western or Christian ideas in a Hindu garb."[61] These accounts of Ramalinga complicate his placement in either tradition or modernity, but they maintain the dichotomy itself, positing tradition as continuity and stability, and associating modernity with Western intervention, dynamism, and change.

The difficulties scholars have in placing Ramalinga on the axis between tradition and modernity make him an excellent figure through which to question this dichotomy. He appears to be a "traditional" character, drawing clearly on Shaiva materials, with little apparent influence of Western ideas. At the same time, he innovated in ways that align with conceptions of modernity, for example, stressing the accessibility of ritual and promoting egalitarianism. If we view tradition as static or as incompatible with modernity, his placement is unclear. Some scholars have tried to resolve this dilemma by suggesting an invisible source of Western influence that provided the creative spark for Ramalinga's innovations. For example, Eugene Irschick describes Ramalinga as a proto-Tamil nationalist, suggesting that this nationalist sentiment, and Ramalinga's teaching that his followers should bury, not cremate, their dead, are signs of Christian influence.[62] In a study of Ramalinga's charitable outreach to the poor, Srilata Raman credits Christianity with providing the inspiration for Ramalinga's new ideology of food-giving.[63] I cannot disprove Christian influence and, indeed, in some cases, I posit that his innovations drew on multiple sources, including Western ones. However, it seems to me that his writings overwhelmingly indicate that the primary inspiration for his innovations were Shaiva traditions. When we acknowledge that Hindu traditions provided rich resources for modernization, the dichotomy between tradition and modernity disappears, as does the impulse to characterize Ramalinga as one or the other.

In suggesting that Shaiva traditions, not Western ones, provided the primary sources for transformation, I follow scholarly literature in Tamil on Ramalinga. These works pay close attention to tensions within Tamil Shaivism and to the ways that Ramalinga's ideological orientation challenged established Shaivism. Raj Gautaman describes Ramalinga's position outside established, powerful Shaiva institutions, which was most dramatically demonstrated in the long conflict between Ramalinga and his followers, on the one hand, and Arumuga Navalar and his supporters, on the other.[64] R. Venkatesan points to the caste tensions between, on the one hand, Ramalinga and his closest disciples, who were from middle-caste groups, and the relatively higher caste *vellalar* communities that dominated established Shaiva institutions and literary production. He also discusses the heated debates between Tamil Nadu scholars and those from Sri Lanka, like Navalar.[65] Work of P. Saravanan focuses on the conflict between Ramalinga and powerful, non-brahman Shaiva monasteries, providing important primary resources through which to examine these polemics.[66] I follow these scholars in considering Ramalinga's principal foils and interlocutors to be other Tamil Shaivas, not European Orientalists or missionaries. I pay particularly close attention to the tensions between Ramalinga's teachings and those more established, caste-based practices that prevailed at the Shaiva monasteries that dominated Tamil temple culture and literary production through much of the nineteenth century.

RAMALINGA, HINDU MODERNITY, AND HINDU TRADITIONS

Throughout this book, I seek to demonstrate a number of connected things. First, I argue that Ramalinga's main source of inspiration came from Shaiva traditions, not from Christianity or the West, although he was certainly not entirely removed from colonial processes. Second, I show that Shaiva traditions did not just provide Ramalinga with stability and continuity, but they also supplied the sources and models for his innovations. Third, I suggest that these changes were just as "modern" as those implemented in Hindu reform movements. By analyzing Ramalinga as a leader who developed modern innovations within Shaiva traditions, I challenge two aspects of the dichotomy of tradition versus modernity. The first is the equation of modernity with the West, and the other is the characterization of tradition as premodern and unchanging. At the same time, I do not dispense with the terms tradition and modernity, because both serve to illuminate the material I present here. Rather, I deliberately define them in ways that foreclose drawing them into a dichotomy. It seems to me that they are not similar sorts of things that can be poles on a single axis.

Dipesh Chakrabarty notes the imperializing effects of the equation between modernity and the West. "If a language, as has been said, is but a dialect backed up by an army, the same could be said of the narratives of 'modernity' that, almost universally today, point to a certain 'Europe' as the primary habitus of the modern." This leads Chakrabarty to propose a project of "provincializing Europe," which begins with "the recognition that Europe's acquisition of the adjective 'modern' for itself is an integral part of the story of European imperialism within global history."[67] This equation of modernity and the West has played out in specific ways in narratives of Hindu modernization. Such narratives insist that Hindu modernity began with a dialogue between Hindu and Western ideas, thereby privileging a specific, cosmopolitan brand of Hindu reform. They relegate figures who do not fit into Hindu reform, like Ramalinga or Sahajanand Swami, the founder of the Swaminarayan movement, to the margins, or to past tradition.[68] Or, when Ramalinga has been considered an innovator, there has been a tendency to equate him with cosmopolitan reformers and assume significant Western influence on his teachings, which misses the most important sources of his inspirations.[69] In speaking of the source of modern Hinduism as a dialogue between India and Europe, such narratives continue to posit a Western origin for expressions of Hinduism that are relevant, forward-looking, or novel, opposing these to "traditional" expressions that are survivals of a past.

Rajeev Bhargava urges us to recognize "alternative modernities that lie unnoticed because of the hold on our imagination of a simplistic, dichotomous framework that bifurcates our world into western modernity and indigenous tradition."[70] I agree with Bhargava's critique, but he does not, in my opinion, go far enough, since he still insists on a single, Western source of all modernity. S. N. Eisenstadt, in his important statement on "multiple modernities," notes that as modernity develops throughout the world, it is shaped in decisive ways by local cultures, traditions, and histories. Thus, he stresses that "modernity and Westernization are not identical; Western patterns of modernity are not the only 'authentic' modernities."[71] However, like Bhargava, Eisenstadt posits a single, "original Western project" as the "common starting point" and "reference point" of all modernities.[72] But what if we imagine a more radical notion of multiple modernities, one that does not locate the origins of all modernity in Western history? What if Hindu traditions were the starting point of projects of Hindu modernization, in which Western influences were only experienced obliquely or vaguely?

One way to begin to define modernity in ways less reliant on Western discourses is through a model of "convergence." In his study of "modern monks" such as Rama Tirtha (1873–1906), Timothy Dobe follows Hatcher in proposing that "the modern and the premodern might share enough to overlap or 'converge,' raising questions about how different they were in the first place."[73] For example, Dobe notes that Rama Tirtha's promotion of individuality displays features of Western modernity but also of Hindu ascetic ideals. Dobe proposes that the particular salience and power of Tirtha's formulation lay in the convergence of Hindu and Western ideas.[74] Such a notion of convergence enables a position in which modernity is not exclusive to the West, with Hindu traditions providing sources for modern religious expression. However, this model still runs the risk of allowing Western modernity to set the agenda for all modernity, if we consider as modern only those aspects of Hindu traditions that have parallels in Western modernity.

Sanjay Subrahmanyam presents a somewhat different possibility, one that accounts for such convergences not in terms of affinity or accidental parallels, but through historical influence. He seeks to "delink the notion of 'modernity' from a particular European trajectory . . . and to argue that it represents a more-or-less global shift, with many different sources and roots, and—inevitably—many different forms and meanings depending on which society we look at it from."[75] He argues that "modernity is historically a global and *conjunctural* phenomenon, not a virus that spreads from one place to another."[76] By "conjunctural" Subrahmanyam has in mind "supra-local" continuities between ideas that suggest "that what we are dealing with are not separate and comparable, but connected histories." If "convergence" stresses synchronic affinities, "conjucture" highlights historical interactions. Convergence is then an instance of conjuncture at a single point of time. Subrahmanyam presents the example of "millenarian conjuncture" in the sixteenth century, in which millenarian ideas took hold across the "Old World," southern and western Asia, and North Africa, concerning Christians and Muslims alike.[77] For Subrahmanyam, these parallels in far-flung and apparently unconnected places indicate that ideas traveled more fluidly in the premodern era than we would be led to believe by scholarship that is shaped by national boundaries and Eurocentrism. He posits the far-reaching, global exchange of a number of social, political, and imaginative features that have come to shape modern sensibilities, including "a new sense of the limits of the inhabited world"; conflict between settled and nomadic peoples; "political theology"; and "historical anthropology," which includes considerations of individuality. He typifies these shifts as "early modern," and he posits that they are not only, or even primarily, of European origin.[78]

In their volume *Textures of Time,* Subrahmanyam, David Shulman, and Velcheru Narayana Rao pursue these ideas with a close study of narrative literature of South India, arguing that this literature displays "the arrival of a certain kind of 'modernity' in the far south" between 1600 and 1800.[79] In his review of this volume, Sheldon Pollock notes that the implication of such a position is that modernity would not be the same everywhere. He warns against searching for the West in India's modernity, arguing that "newness" would be experienced differently throughout the world. Pollock concludes that "it seems that modernity across Asia may have shown simultaneity without symmetry."[80] In other words, comparative history may demonstrate that the modern world emerged not through a single model that spread from its European source, but through the simultaneous development, in a multitude of places, of a variety of ways of being modern. These authors are generally concerned with early modern India, but their point is relevant for nineteenth-century Hindu innovation and the emergence of modern Hinduism. While the West was probably the most influential "external" source of influence on Hindu traditions in the nineteenth century, to consider it the main source of Hindu change, even in the idiom of dialogue, overlooks the capacity for Hindu agency; ignores the cosmopolitan character of Hindu traditions prior to colonialism; and neglects the "newness" that defined Hindu change in the centuries prior to the nineteenth century.

The notion of modernity that I pursue allows for diverse content, depending on historical context, making it impossible to identify a canon of characteristics that are quintessentially modern. Rather, focusing on certain stylistic features of modernity seems to me a more promising way to begin. Thus, Eisenstadt follows Nilüfer Göle in asserting that "one of the most important characteristics of modernity is simply, but profoundly, its potential for self-correction, its ability to confront problems not even imagined in its original program."[81] Following this characterization of modernity, we find that modern Hinduism emerged from a variety of sources and in myriad ways, not just in a single, Western encounter. As Hatcher notes, "The goal, therefore, in thinking through the origin and nature of modern Hinduism is to look for evidence of its continual emergence as a process of 'reiterative imagining.' When we do this, we may be better able to appreciate all the times and places it (re-)emerges."[82] Here I suggest that Ramalinga's teachings and projects, though distant from reform Hinduism, nevertheless provide an important case of Hindu modernization. Such a move posits a multiplicity of Hindu modernities and a variety of genealogies that produced them.

I describe as "modern" teachings that one, innovate in strategic ways that respond to contemporary challenges; two, view the present as unique and malleable, that is, as a time of unparalleled opportunity for significant transformation; and three, presage future processes and developments. Accordingly, there are plural configurations of "newness" that characterize the modern in different times and places. These varied formulations of modernity have diverse genealogies, but their trajectories are not unilinear or isolated. They share some of the conditions of other formulations, and they at times interact and compete with other modernities. As Bjorn Thomassen points out, positing diverse origins and histories for multiple modernities does not preclude recognizing cultural contact, the global spread of ideas, and the "frictions" that come with encounters between diverse agendas of modernity.[83]

According to this definition of modernity, traditions can also be modern when actors reshape their traditions to respond to shifting contexts. I describe Ramalinga's teachings as modern because they challenged established Shaivism, engaged with current social and economic challenges, articulated a new ethical vision for community, viewed the present as offering a unique opportunity for transformation, and sought to initiate epochal change. In many ways Ramalinga presaged later developments in contemporary Hinduism better than did nineteenth-century Hindu cosmopolitan reformers. One only needs to consider a figure like Sathya Sai Baba to see the importance of personal charisma and authority, and the salience of the miraculous, in the landscape of modern Hinduism. In the chapters that follow, I focus on features of Ramalinga's teachings that served to make his agenda and vision "modern" in this sense. These include the wielding of a new technology, print; the development of a new ideology of charity, based on compassion to the poor; a call for egalitarianism and a critique of caste and Shaiva elitism; an emphasis on the accessibility of ritual; the founding of a new, voluntary society; the delineation of an audience that cut across class and caste lines; and the promise of supernatural powers and immortality to those who joined him.

Nearly all these "modern" features have precedents in Shaiva traditions. Many of these also match up with Western notions of modernity, suggesting that processes of (synchronic) convergence and (diachronic) conjuncture were at play. In

Ramalinga's case, the mechanism for convergence was not a direct encounter with Western discourses but indirect, filtered through his devotees, Shaiva adversaries, and colonial and Hindu institutions that were themselves "hybrid." Some of the parallels between Western modernity and Ramalinga's teachings can also be explained through longer historical processes of conjuncture in Subrahmanyam's sense. In Ramalinga's case, such instances of conjuncture signal complex and ambiguous histories of institutional and discursive interactions of a sort that Shalini Randeria has described as "entangled histories." Randeria focuses on complex historical exchanges that characterized the colonial experience, arguing that these interactions played an important role in shaping features of Western modernity.[84] One consequence of her position is that "the idea of a homogenous Western modernity travelling, more or less imperfectly, to the rest of the world must be replaced by a messier and complex picture of . . . uneven and entangled modernities."[85] Peter van der Veer has argued that histories of cosmopolitanism and modernity should reject "both center-periphery models and the identification of originary movements," and instead should describe "historical entanglements."[86] Therefore, when we note instances of convergence or conjuncture between Ramalinga's teachings and Western modernity, it may be that Ramalinga was drawing on Shaiva traditions that had already been influenced by Western ideals, but also that Western modernity and its institutional agents in South India were themselves shaped in part by local concerns. I argue that we need to resist the temptation to view such processes in terms of distinctive, "pure" religious or ideological positions that come into contact.

Aside from these points of apparent convergence, important features of Ramalinga's teachings that proved crucial to the success of his agenda do not find a place in a list of features of Western modernity or Protestant rationality. He maintained the efficacy of simple rituals, including mantras; spoke of direct revelation from Shiva; and claimed to have miraculous powers, which he, in turn, promised to those who joined his Society. I maintain that these features are modern because they satisfy my definition of modernity. Ramalinga's articulation of miracles was innovative, breaking from past conceptions; his description of revelation was vital in drawing people to him; his stress on the efficacy of accessible Shaiva rituals found broad resonance and presaged later expressions of Hinduism. We can speak of multiple modernities without requiring that all elements of these modernities originate from the West. In this study I focus on two versions of modernity that were opposed in crucial ways, namely, Ramalinga's modernity and that of Hindu reform. Rather than characterizing this tension as a clash of tradition and modernity, I suggest that we view it as the clash of competing visions of modernity.

My reformulation of modernity also compels us to reconsider tradition. The notion of traditions as premodern, static, unified entities grounded in scripture is itself a discursive and ideological construction that was formed in opposition to ideas of modernity. Frederick Cooper notes "the dangers of modernity's invention of 'universal man' to be the model for the entire world, erasing the colonial origins of that man and the invention of his traditionalist, non-European 'other' as his foil."[87] Hindu reformers, such as Ramalinga's adversary Arumuga Navalar, subscribed to many features of this notion of tradition. They idealized a static, systematic Hindu (or Shaiva) tradition, and they described their work as preserving that tradition through a reconstruction based on ancient texts. Their projects were of course innovative, but reformers tended to obscure this innovation by describing their work as returning to a golden age enshrined in a revered canon.

My sense of tradition is not this colonial, reform notion. In my delineation, tradition neither opposes modernity nor persists or "survives" alongside it, nor does it simply "condition" modernity through the stubborn force of its inertia. Tradition affirms continuity, but it is not primarily an orientation to the past or an idealization of stasis. Traditions are in constant flux, responding to a variety of influences and challenges. Importantly, traditions themselves provide resources for change, and sources for inspiration and innovation. With this view of tradition, one not need posit Christian or colonial influence to explain Hindu change. I will discuss traditions primarily in the plural; most important, I will speak of diverse Shaiva traditions upon which Ramalinga drew. This notion of tradition is similar to Ramalinga's conception of Shaivism as flexible, living, and a source of inspiration and transformation. He demonstrated no consciousness that Shaiva traditions were under threat or imperiled, or in need of preservation, and here he differed crucially from Hindu reform writers. He did not view canon as fixed in the past, but he spoke of devotional poets speaking to him in the present and even sought to add to the Shaiva devotional canon. He deliberately pursued change, but he did not consider his innovations to be departures from Shaiva tradition. For Ramalinga, Shaiva traditions were not obstacles to modernity, but they provided conceptual, ritual, and literary frameworks through which he created new ideologies of food-giving, community, and accessible ritual practices that served to respond to contemporary challenges in his social and historical milieu. He expressed a Shaivism that was already modern, that contributed to current debates, and that addressed local concerns, especially the social and material suffering of his lower caste and poor neighbors.

Saurabh Dube calls modernity an "idea, ideal, and ideology."[88] I would argue that the same is true for tradition, and that my delineation of both terms is all of these things. I have tried to articulate notions of tradition and modernity that take into account the historical complexity of cultural interactions. I am critical of analytical models that emphasize Western sources for all Hindu modernization in the nineteenth century. Here my project shares much with Anne Blackburn's "microhistorical immersion" into the life and projects of the Sri Lankan Buddhist leader Hikkaduve Sumangala. Blackburn convincingly highlights the limitations of a model of "Protestant Buddhism" in explaining Hikkaduve's work, which drew most strongly from Buddhist traditions. She advances a plea for further such "human-scale" studies, which will "restore a richer sense of local agency to the record of colonial-period South Asians."[89] Like Blackburn, I present here a microhistory that, although highly compressed in its subject matter, asks questions about wide-ranging and crucial processes in colonial India. It is thus less a biography of Ramalinga than a study of processes of religious change, agency, and innovation in nineteenth-century India. Ramalinga presents such a significant case study because his innovative projects exemplify a number of crucial historical shifts. By focusing on Indian enterprise instead of colonial settings, I highlight the creative work of Hindus that has been obscured by investigations that assume that change is driven by Western agency. Where Blackburn emphasizes continuity and stability in Buddhist practice, however, I emphasize Ramalinga's ingenuity and innovations. Considering my work alongside hers, it is clear that Protestant bias among scholars has not only obscured the continuities of traditions, but it has also distorted the sources of change.

In the chapters that follow, I build on my argument that Ramalinga's reconfiguration of Shaivism was modern by focusing on a number of his innovations. I highlight the ways that he departed from reform Hinduism, that bearer of Western modernity. I carry out this analysis through the close reading of a corpus of texts written between 1860 and 1874. Most important are Ramalinga's own writings, including his poems, prose compositions, and letters to his followers. I also examine writings of his followers, including letters, verse compositions, and responses to critiques by their adversaries. Additionally, I analyze Arumuga Navalar's 1869 polemical attack on Ramalinga, which I argue represents a reform critique of Ramalinga's teachings. Each chapter focuses on a specific set of primary sources and on a distinct area of religious change. In each case, I have sought to illuminate features of Ramalinga's work that reflect broader historical processes of colonialism and religious transformation.

Chapter two analyzes Ramalinga's ideology of ritual food-giving to the hungry poor. His novel ideology of giving marked a radical departure from established South Indian Shaiva ritual processes, which excluded poor, lower-caste participants. A recent study traces his project of food charity to Christian influence. I take a different position, demonstrating that Ramalinga drew primarily from prior Shaiva traditions, especially tantra and siddha, and also from institutions that emerged out of complex interactions between Western and Indian sources. More broadly, the chapter demonstrates the importance of traditional Shaiva precedents and ideas in shaping this modern practice.

Chapter three looks at the impact of print technology on Hinduism in the middle of the nineteenth century, the period when print began to proliferate in South Asia. Hindu reformers, often directly influenced by Christian publishing in India, employed print in order to extend the audiences and influence of established canons through accessible publications in prose. Ramalinga and his followers used print differently, challenging established Shaiva authority and scripture by publishing a compilation of his poems as a new contribution to canon. Since published books were becoming the physical form and medium of canon, Ramalinga viewed the shift to print as an opportunity to advance at least two claims: that his verses were the equal of revered devotional literature, and that he was worthy of a place in the pantheon of Shaiva saints.

The fourth chapter examines Ramalinga's views of authority and tradition through a close reading of his devotional works. Scholars have noted that Hindu reformers emphasized the authority of the written text, and also that they relegated scripture and revelation to the distant past, expressing nostalgia for a golden age of Hindu tradition. Ramalinga diverged strongly from these views, asserting that Shaivism was a living, oral tradition based on direct experiences of Shiva's revelation that continue into the present. The chapter stresses the autohagiographical character of Ramalinga's writings to argue that new notions of the literary past were emerging in nineteenth-century South Asia outside of reform Hinduism.

Chapter five presents a detailed scholarly account of an important debate between Ramalinga and the Tamil Shaiva reform leader Arumuga Navalar. Like Ramalinga, Navalar worked to transform Tamil Shaivism, but his vision of tradition closely conformed to cosmopolitan expressions of Hinduism. He sought to limit Shaiva canon to a specific corpus of revered texts, and he advanced a rationality that denied the possibility of modern miracles and new scriptural revelations. He strongly criticized Ramalinga's supernatural claims and the use of Ramalinga's verses in Shaiva ritual contexts. His resistance to Ramalinga's influence underscores the disparity between Ramalinga's vision of Hinduism and those of cosmopolitan leaders. This chapter thus highlights the diversity of Hindu approaches to modernization.

Chapter six considers Ramalinga's claim to have acquired extraordinary powers. Most studies of Hindu modernization describe processes of rationalization, with Hindu reformers distancing themselves from miraculous claims. Ramalinga, on the other hand, claimed to possess supernatural powers, and he promised his followers that they, too, could acquire these powers by joining his community. He embraced tantric and siddha expressions of Shaivism to challenge reform models of an increasingly rational Hinduism. The chapter argues that his promotion of the miraculous has endured, leading to the conclusion that his vision of an enchanted Hinduism is as modern as that of a rational, reform Hinduism.

The conclusion challenges the scholarly tendency to locate the origins of modern Hinduism only in cosmopolitan reform Hinduism and, by extension, dialogue with the West. I demonstrate that Ramalinga's innovations aligned with, and contributed to, new trends in Hindu expression, including the extension of ritual to lower castes; the use of new technologies to increase accessibility and challenge established authority; and the sustained "enchantment" of Hinduism and its emphasis on charismatic leadership. I argue that because Ramalinga drew inspiration from Shaiva traditions in articulating these innovations, any consideration of Hindu modernity must take seriously the role of Hindu traditions in not just forging continuity with the past, but also with providing sources of innovation and change. I call for further studies that examine regional leaders working in vernacular languages, and for frameworks that consider multiple modernities with diverse genealogies.

Through these detailed chapters of Ramalinga's innovations, this study argues that even though his work departs radically from that of Hindu reformers, his project is no less modern than were theirs. Indeed, if one considers his continuing popularity, the sustained emphasis on the miraculous, use of print media, and outreach to the poor, Ramalinga was at the forefront in processes of Hindu modernization. I hope that this work will open up the study of modern Hindu history to the countless projects of religious change that were occurring on the margins of European empire. By including Ramalinga, and figures like him, in this history, we can develop new ways of thinking about modern Hinduism that more accurately reflect its diverse ways of being modern. More broadly, I hope that my study may provide a model that can be instructive in other area contexts, in which a dichotomy between Western modernity and traditional religion continues to shape scholarship on religious modernization in non-European societies.

2

Giving to the Poor

Ramalinga's Transformation of Hindu Charity

Gifts of food to the poor in India are commonplace today, often proceeding under the auspices of organizations that identify themselves in a general way as Hindu.[1] In South India, groups that carry on Ramalinga's legacy consider the distribution of food to the poor to be central to their public mission. These efforts appear to be nothing out of the ordinary in contemporary India, a fact that conceals the novelty of Ramalinga's project to feed the poor in his own time. Ramalinga's outreach to the hungry poor, in acts of ritual giving that disregarded the caste purity of its recipients, was an important instance of modern innovation. I consider it to be modern because it departed from past practices; responded to contemporary challenges, in this case widespread hunger; sought to transform social and ritual practices; and presaged future developments in Hinduism.

It is not that Hindu institutions did not make food gifts prior to the nineteenth century. The distribution of food by temples, monasteries, and other religious institutions has a long history in South Asia. Inscriptional and textual evidence indicates that gifts of food to specific groups—pilgrims, ascetics, eminent people, caste groups, sectarian groups, et cetera—have been central to ritual transactions in South Asia for at least a millennium. This food-gifting enhances the status of the receiver, and at the same time it enables temples to reestablish, consolidate, or extend social, economic, and political networks with specific groups of people. The giving of food in South Asia thus supports social, political, and ritual agendas. Where Ramalinga departed from prior forms of giving was in distributing food to poor, not esteemed, recipients within a Hindu ritual context.

Reform Hindu leaders and organizations did not make charitable outreach to the poor a central part of their projects until after Ramalinga's death. In 1870,

Keshab Chandra Sen, a Brahmo Samaj leader, advocated uplift of the poor through education and moral instruction, rather than through measures of immediate charitable relief.[2] Dayananda Saraswati stressed the importance of moral character, not poverty, in considerations of giving. In his 1875 work *Satyarth Prakash,* he asserts that a worthy recipient of charity has the refined qualities of "chastity, control over the senses, love to study and teach the Vedas and other systems of knowledge."[3] Reform organizations, including Hindu reform groups, would later engage in charitable relief to the poor, part of a shift from traditional modes of giving to public, associational philanthropy that Carey Watt traces to the 1890s.[4] The associations that proliferated at the turn of the twentieth century were critical of more traditional forms of Hindu giving, claiming their new, philanthropic giving "to be on the side of modernity and efficiency."[5] In this case, however, their projects of modernity, strongly influenced by European notions of philanthropy, came decades after Ramalinga's innovation, one that he described in Shaiva, not European, idioms. This suggests that we might profitably examine the sources of Ramalinga's innovation in order to think more clearly about the emergence of this "modern" practice of charity to the poor.

This chapter presents details of Ramalinga Swami's ideology of food-giving, expressed in his prose work *Jīva Karuṇya Oḻukkam, The Path of Compassion for Living Beings* (hereafter JKO). In particular, I examine his ideology's continuities and discontinuities with earlier forms of religious giving, or *dāna.* I pay close attention to Ramalinga's efforts to situate his novel practice in Shaiva traditions. Recently, Srilata Raman has argued that Ramalinga's gift-giving innovation occupied a "border space" between Tamil literary expressions of hunger and Christian practices of giving.[6] I reach a somewhat different conclusion here, namely, that his project is best understood in a framework of Shaiva innovation and transformation. I advance this argument through close attention to local material conditions, most importantly a famine that preceded his project of food outreach; Ramalinga's Shaiva context; and institutions of food distribution that may have influenced him. My broader goal is to examine the range of sources that potentially conditioned and inspired the emergence of modern Hindu practices, in order to argue that scholars must expand the genealogy of modern Hinduism to sources beyond reform Hinduism or Protestant intervention.

PROTESTANTISM AND OTHER SOURCES OF MODERN HINDUISM

The term "Protestant Hinduism" has never enjoyed the popularity of the often used and sometimes maligned "Protestant Buddhism."[7] Nevertheless, much scholarly writing on the emergence of modern Hinduism shares a basic assumption of Protestant Buddhism: simply, that Christianity was a central influence in the development of modern Hinduism, providing not only the impetus for change, but also theologies and institutional models that Hindu modernizers took from Christian interlocutors. While this assumption has merit, especially in describing religious change in cosmopolitan settings, I argue here that scholarship on modern Hinduism has underestimated the degree to which Hindu religious change occurred apart from Christian projects and influences.

J. N. Farquhar's 1915 study provides an important reference point for the scholarly study of religious change in colonial India. He begins the work by acknowledging "two great groups of religious facts" that set the stage for his study: the "old religions of India" and "Christian Missions." He advances a model of religious change in which "the old religions are the soil from which the modern movements spring; while it will be found that the seed has, in the main, been sown by Missions."[8] Farquhar gives place to "ancient faiths" in the emergence of these new movements, namely, in the force of tradition. However, it is Christianity that is the instigator of change. "While the shaping forces at work in the movements have been many, it is quite clear that *Christianity has ruled the development throughout.* Christianity has been, as it were, a great searchlight flung across the expanse of the religions; and in its blaze all the coarse, unclean and superstitious elements of the old faiths stood out, quite early, in painful vividness."[9] Farquhar's language is highly gendered: Indian traditions provide the feminine, generative soil, while the missions sow the seed and rule over the emergence of modern Hindu movements. He conceives of cultural engagement in biological, copulative metaphors, understanding the process as a creative if unequal union of traditions.

Because Farquhar defines modern Hindu movements by their engagement with European civilization, the Hindu leaders and groups he discusses are cosmopolitan, most importantly Rammohan Roy and the Brahmo Samaj; Dayananda Saraswati and the Arya Samaj; and Swami Vivekananda. This account of Hindu modernization remains the primary genealogy in scholarly narratives of the emergence of modern Hinduism. However, recent scholarship presents a more nuanced account of this vital period of religious change, recognizing greater agency on the part of Hindu leaders. In his discussion of the emergence of "modern Hindu thought," Brian A. Hatcher rejects a model of historical interaction that emphasizes that modern Hinduism arose out of the "impact" of the West on India, "where 'Western' may be taken to mean European Protestantism."[10] His critique is that such models minimize the importance and continuities of prior Indian traditions, and allow little space for Indian creativity. He instead proposes a model based on convergence, on "the basic premise that any number of previously existing ideas, values, and practices from precolonial India converged in the modern period with those ideas, values, and practices that made their way into India as a result of colonial rule."[11] Hatcher's model is certainly an improvement over Farquhar's assertion that Christianity has driven the emergence of modern Hinduism, yet it continues to focus on colonial centers, maintaining the West as an ever-present, necessary, and equal player in the transformation of Hinduism. Indeed, Hatcher concludes that "modern Hinduism is thus best viewed as the product of a rich and extended conversation between India and the West."[12]

Hatcher's explanatory model illuminates religious change in the urban centers of colonial cosmopolitanism, where Hindus engaged Christians in well-documented public debates that shaped Hindu reform movements. However, such models are less salient in describing religious innovations of Hindus who had little direct engagement with Christianity and colonial ideologies. There were Hindu leaders like Ramalinga who were not ensconced in the colonial milieu but who nevertheless engaged in projects of religious change that influenced modern Hinduism in important ways. What did "conversation" entail for someone like Ramalinga, who was not in direct dialogue, as far as we know, with colonial or Christian leaders? What does it mean to assert that Indian and colonial ideas, values, and practices "converged," when one's focus is on the margins of colonial cosmopolitanism?

In addressing these questions, it will become clear that although Ramalinga was not directly engaging in conversation with Europeans, neither was he working in a context that was untouched by colonialism. How, then, can we account for his new religious vision? What were his sources of inspiration? My argument is somewhat different than Raman's "border space" characterization of Ramalinga's sources. I suggest that Ramalinga modeled his almshouse on private and colonial institutions that distributed food to the hungry in times of famine. His primary ideological foils, against which he developed his innovative ideology of food-giving, were not Christian missionaries or colonial authorities, but leaders of a network of non-brahman mathas or monasteries that dominated South Indian Shaivism in the nineteenth century. While Raman analyzes JKO as a literary representation of hunger with Christian theological overtones, I will pay more attention to Ramalinga's immediate material and religious context, and to the Shaiva sources of his project, which will lead me to different conclusions. Our work might be read together, an exercise that should highlight the way that distinct approaches to context can result in very different interpretations of religious texts.

FOOD-GIVING IN TAMIL SHAIVISM

The sharing of food has always been complicated in Hindu culture. If, as Katherine Ulrich points out, the boundaries of the body are often analogized to social boundaries, then bodily interactions that cross these boundaries bring bodies, and groups, into particular relationships. The sharing of food between groups is especially important, as food travels from the hand of one person to the plate of another, and then it is taken into that body where it becomes part of the consumer.[13] The relative purity of the giver and recipient of food are of vital concern, and for this reason the sharing of food among Hindus has often proceeded along the lines of caste. When inter-caste sharing of food does occur, the giving of food by one group to another brings these groups into some sort of relationship, often based on social, economic, or political concerns. Configurations of food exchange can have a greater impact on social status than the purity of what is actually eaten.[14] Disparate ideologies of food-giving such as those presented below, the well-established South Indian Shaiva view and the radical formulation of Ramalinga, both assume the power of food to bring disparate groups into productive relations.

The major institutions that have engaged in ritualized food-gifting in South India in the past millennium have been temples and mathas. Mathas are institutions that have been established by ascetic lineages of particular caste and sect groupings. Besides fostering religious devotion and learning among initiates, the major roles of Hindu mathas have been temple management, scholarly activities, and ritual giving. I will focus on non-brahman Tamil Shaiva mathas, since these were the institutions that dominated the liturgical, theological, and literary world that shaped Ramalinga's writings and institutional projects. From medieval times to the present day, these mathas have consistently engaged in ritual and economic exchanges with powerful individuals, groups, offices, and institutions.[15]

The initiates and leaders of the non-brahman centers are drawn from a few high-caste *vellalar* landholding communities.[16] Most of the lay following that supports the mathas and participates in their ritual activities are drawn from these same *vellalar* groups.[17] These are exclusive institutions that garner prestige for a limited number of high-caste, non-brahman communities that are eligible to associate with them. They have long-standing relationships with a variety of caste groups, such as local ruling families, merchant groups, and brahmans who serve as priests in temples under the administration of the mathas. Their associations with these groups are pragmatic but maintain a certain distance. After initiation, members of the order retain their caste identities, and the rituals they perform aim to benefit their order and the lay following of the matha, that is, their caste communities.[18]

One of the most important activities of the mathas from medieval times to the present has been the feeding of pilgrims, ascetics, and the orders' own members at festival and other occasions. It was, and remains, a form of *dāna*, or ritual giving, that has been a common form of exchange among South Asian groups for millennia. In her study of medieval Hindu literature on ritual giving, Maria Heim points out that *dāna* "provides a site for idealizing and formalizing certain social relationships and interactions, and a locus for moral reflection." Gifts "reveal a hierarchical social order, and . . . may be grounded in discourses riddled with power."[19] Heim characterizes giving as reflecting an "ethics of esteem" based on social hierarchy, which she contrasts to an ethics of respect that assumes the equality of human beings.[20] Giving in South Asia, according to the material analyzed by Heim, cements social relationships, but these are vertical relationships of reverence and admiration.

Ritual feeding at non-brahman Shaiva mathas in South India reflects this ethics of esteem, with the recipients of gifts occupying varying positions of prestige in the matha and in the broader community. For example, for centuries mathas have distributed food at a ritual called *mahesvara puja.* According to medieval inscriptions, the recipients of food in this ritual setting include *maheswaras* (devotees), *sivayogis* (yogis devoted to the Hindu god Shiva), *tapasvis* (those practicing austerities), and *paradesis* (wandering mendicants).[21] The various classes of ascetics lend auspiciousness to the occasion, and the benefits of proper ritual performance include prosperity and goodness. Non-ascetics, such as lay supporters of the matha, politicians, and prominent local figures, are also fed, consolidating the matha's ties with these groups.[22] The patrons of the ritual are the head and initiates of the matha, but the matha itself is supported through donations by wealthy, influential lay leaders. In the eighteenth and nineteenth centuries, these patrons included Sethupati and Tondaiman chiefs who cemented important political and economic allegiances with powerful *vellalar* families via the mathas.[23] Ritual meals such as those at the *mahesvara puja* reflect and affirm these complex relationships.

I have found little evidence of matha efforts to feed the anonymous, non-eminent poor in premodern times or even in the latter half of the nineteenth century. Heim points out that gift-giving to the poor is not proscribed but occupies an uncomfortable place for Hindu, Jain, and Theravada medieval commentators and, indeed, it is rarely mentioned by them. The moral worthiness of the poor cannot be guaranteed and, in fact, by the logic of karma and rebirth, poverty in South Asia is often viewed as a sign of unworthiness.[24] *Dharmashastra* texts, when they do refer to charitable giving, distinguish gifts to worthy recipients from gifts to the poor and do not usually classify the latter as *dāna.*[25] David Brick, in his study of the *Dānakāṇḍa* and *dānanibandha* literature, more generally, notes that while gifts to the poor were "marginal," the poor might be legitimate recipients in times of necessity. He cites a line from the *Dānavivekoddyota* to affirm that such giving can even have soteriological benefit, a view that we will also see Ramalinga express: "A gift that is given out of compassion to those who are dejected, blind, and indigent—even if they are improper recipients—brings about endless reward." Such gifts should be limited, however, to those that offer only temporary support, most notably, gifts of food.[26]

Ritual feeding in non-brahman Shaiva mathas in premodern times appears to conform closely to these shastric ideals, stressing the feeding of recipients who are worthy of esteem in a range of ways: economically, socially, politically, and ritually. When they did feed the poor, it appears to have been a secondary activity. R. Champakalakshmi, discussing the charitable activities of mathas in the medieval and Vijayanagara periods, mentions the feeding of ascetics and pilgrims, and also the "daily feeding of the poor," though she does not cite her source.[27] Koppedrayer makes an offhand comment that "the feeding of Brahmins, sadhus and the poor, have historically been done in matas."[28] Elsewhere she cites an inscription dating to 1162 C.E. that lists a number of activities of a particular matha, including providing "a place where food is always given to the poor, the helpless, the lame, the blind, the deaf . . . to the naked and the crippled . . . to mendicants . . . to ascetics . . . and to all other beggars from many countries [desa]."[29] Michael Linderman notes that a thirteenth-century inscription of the Goḷaki Maṭha in the Andhra region mentions charities that offered food to everyone, "from Brahmaṇas to Chandalas."[30] It may be, then, that mathas of a variety of traditions did at times endeavor to feed the poor. However, the paucity of references to such charitable acts suggests that it was not a primary concern, and it appears that when it was done, it was outside important ritual settings.

Non-brahman mathas today certainly make it their concern to feed the poor. K. Nambi Arooran cites a 1972 publication of endowments of the Tiruppanandal matha that includes a large sum for "feeding the poor and pilgrims."[31] A 1955 publication of the Dharmapuram Adhinam states—probably overstates—that "The Adhinam is trying to be helpful to the town at large . . . So the entire resources of the mutt [matha] are being utilized for the general welfare of the public, particularly the poor and the needy."[32] Yocum observed that the Tiruvavadudurai Adhinam fed "especially its ascetics and its employees, but also school children who attend Mutt-run schools, the poor."[33] This stress on outreach to the poor seems to be a modern shift in focus for the mathas. Evidence overwhelmingly suggests that the primary concern of mathas prior to the twentieth century was to feed the specific caste and sectarian groups that provided their personnel, as well as the various corporate groups with which they maintained social, political, and economic relations. The centrality of Shaiva charity to the poor appears to be a modern development.

RAMALINGA SWAMI AND THE FEEDING OF THE POOR

Ramalinga made feeding the poor one of the primary activities of the society that he founded. His divergence from *dāna* practices at Shaiva mathas was consistent with his general rejection of the ritual and caste strictures of Shaivism that prevailed at non-brahman mathas. His relationship with these mathas was at times strained. After the publication of *Tiruvaruṭpā*, a book of poems, in 1867, Ramalinga was subject to numerous polemical attacks by scholars based at Tiruvavadudurai Adhinam, led by the famous Shaiva leader Arumuga Navalar, which I detail in chapter five. Ramalinga claimed a direct relationship with Shiva as the source of his authority, and he drew on this authority to articulate new expressions of Shaiva theology, ritual, and community. These new Shaiva forms, and his ever-increasing popularity from the late 1850s until his death in 1874, posed a critical challenge to the Shaiva non-brahman mathas, which was exacerbated by the fact that Ramalinga took up residence near the influential Tiruvavadudurai matha in the heart of Tamil Shaivism.

Ramalinga sought to establish a religious community through the publication of his poetry and the founding of a number of groups and institutions. In 1865, he assembled the "Camaraca Vēta Caṉmārka Caṅkam" (Society of the True Path that is Common to all Scripture), hereafter the "Society of the True Path."[34] He reflected on his hopes for his Society in a verse sung to the goddess: "Oh, my mother, see my desire! I want to establish a Society of the True Path, that brings together people who are like gold; I want to found a holy temple that is linked to the Society; I want this True Society to achieve great heights and be illustrious for eons; I, a servant in that Society, want to sing and dance to you, my body refreshingly cool."[35]

In February 1867, Ramalinga and his followers published the first major volume of his poems as *Tiruvaruṭpā*. Three months later they opened a house for the distribution of food, the "Camaraca Vēta Tarumaccālai" (Almshouse of the Unity of Scripture), hereafter the "Almshouse of Unity." The temple that he spoke of to the goddess, the "Cattiya Ñāṉa Capai" (Temple of True Knowledge), was finished in 1872.[36]

By calling his almshouse a "Tarumaccālai," he situated this new institution in the pan-Indian tradition of *dharmashala,* rest houses that provide food and accommodation to pilgrims. His use of "Veda" in the title does not specifically refer to works of the Sanskrit Vedic corpus, but it is a general term that invokes established scripture.[37] I understand "camaraca" according to the Shaiva usage of one of Ramalinga's bhakti predecessors, Tayumanavar, who used the term to refer to an ideal reconciliation of diverse scriptures.[38] Thus, the name Ramalinga chose for his almshouse indicates that it would embody the ideals of all scripture and doctrine, beyond specifically Shaiva understandings.

Ramalinga established the Almshouse of Unity in 1867, on the heels of a significant famine in South India in 1866. It is clear from some of Ramalinga's verses that he observed hunger and poverty firsthand. "Whenever I saw plants, withering and dried up, I also withered. I saw poor people, emaciated with hunger and terribly weary, going to every house, yet their hunger was not removed, and my heart suffered intensely. Those who suffer with relentless disease, I saw them in front of me and my heart trembled. I saw those people, poor and of unmatched honor (*īṭil-māṉikaḷ*), their hearts weary, and I grew weak."[39] This verse is extraordinary for Ramalinga's expression of empathy for the poor, weary, diseased, and hungry whom he encountered. He emphasizes that the poor he sees have "unmatched honor," a clear departure from the cold logic of karma that we observed at work in longstanding Hindu considerations of food-giving. Ramalinga addressed his concern for these hungry poor in his founding of the Almshouse of Unity.

Ramalinga and his followers opened the Almshouse of Unity in grand fashion on May 23, 1867. The Society of the True Path made all arrangements and bore all costs for the event, with expectations of three thousand guests. A permanent structure for the almshouse was not yet in place, so a temporary one of mud walls thatched with darba grass was constructed to feed attendees.[40] In conjunction with the opening of the almshouse, the Society of the True Path distributed an announcement that summarizes the ideas contained in JKO. The announcement outlines the basic principles of "Jīva Karuṇya Oḻukkam," "The Path of Compassion for Living Beings," to all "those who have taken a human birth. This is a high birth characterized by wisdom and rationality gained through study and eagerness to learn." It urges "compassionate people" to make donations to the almshouse and share in the benefits of giving.[41]

The book-length text JKO, probably the best known of Ramalinga's prose compositions, presents in detail the ideology of giving that animated the opening of the almshouse. The work focuses on compassionate action and its benefits, especially the giving of food to the hungry and poor. It was first published in 1879, printed with the subheading "the path of compassion to living beings is the first duty of the Pure True Path."[42] The "True Path" is the ethical and soteriological vision that he set out for members of his new Society. Given that the opening of the Almshouse of Unity was orchestrated by the Society of the True Path and considered an important act of outreach, it is clear that Ramalinga meant for this work to be a statement of moral action for members of his association, who were the primary audience for the text. However, the public reading of JKO and the announcement of the work's message to all those who have "taken a human birth" indicate that he wanted his innovative ideology of giving to be widely publicized.[43] The public character of his outreach to the poor became an important feature of Ramalinga's mission in his day, and it remains central to Ramalinga organizations. In the detailed discussion of the JKO that follows, I consider the relationship of Ramalinga's ideology of giving to established Shaiva practices of *dāna*, which provided the point of reference for his innovation. I focus particularly on the Shaiva sources that shape Ramalinga's logic, legitimate his claims, and inspire his innovations. These include bhakti (devotional) poetry, notions of karma and rebirth, mythologies and temple practices, Shaiva Siddhanta doctrinal categories, and siddha/yoga traditions.

Ramalinga begins JKO by stating that the goal of human life is to obtain god's "full natural bliss." This bliss can be attained only through god's grace (*aruḷ*), which, in turn, is achieved by showing compassion to all living beings. This is because grace is god's natural manifestation, and compassion is the natural manifestation of living beings, so god will only bestow his nature on those who realize their own nature by showing compassion.[44] He asks: "What is the path of compassion towards living beings? It is to live worshipping god with an attitude of tenderness (*urukkam*) of the soul towards other beings."[45] The word Ramalinga uses here to describe the attitude of compassion, *urukkam*, is from the root *uruku*, to melt, which in Shaiva devotional contexts commonly refers to the melting of the heart in devotion toward god. This word appears frequently in the *Tēvāram*, for example, to describe the melting of the hearts of devotees when they think of Shiva.[46] Ramalinga also stresses here the worship of the divine, referring to the everyday rituals of worship in temples and homes. Thus, he is defining this ethic of compassion not according to philosophical or doctrinal strands of tradition, but to emotional, devotional ones with roots in bhakti and everyday practice. However, Ramalinga extends the usual object of melting, the divine, to the ordinary beings of this world, and particularly those who are suffering.

This "tenderness" or "melting" of the soul arises when one sees or hears about the suffering of others due to hunger, thirst, disease, unsatisfied desire, poverty, fear, and killing. Ramalinga then asks, "what is the duty (*urimai*) for compassion for all beings?" His answer contrasts markedly to the long history of Hindu gift practices, which emphasize the caste, sectarian, economic, and political bonds between givers and recipients. Ramalinga proposes a very different logic of duty and rights (both terms are designated by *urimai*) based on a universal bond between beings. "Because all beings are created by all-powerful god as parts of true nature which has a singular quality, they are all brothers. When a brother suffers some calamity, another brother will see that his brother is suffering, and he will feel tenderness. This is the bond and duty of brotherhood. Likewise, when seeing the suffering of another, a living being will feel sympathy and will understand the ancient bonds of souls."[47] By connecting all beings to god's creation, Ramalinga asserts the bonds of responsibility and compassion between beings. His use of kinship terminology to describe a universal human connection disposes of caste distinctions and emphasizes responsibility toward all beings. Those who lack compassion toward suffering beings are hard-hearted, their wisdom clouded.

This is not to say that Ramalinga does not share certain assumptions of Hindu gift-giving logic. Considerations of karma and rebirth underlie many of Ramalinga's ethical assertions. He asks, for example, why some beings suffer from hunger, thirst, et cetera, while others do not, and his answer is precisely that of medieval texts on *dāna:* they suffer because of actions in past lives. For Ramalinga, chief among such actions is the lack of compassion due to hard-heartedness in a past life, which has led to hunger and suffering in the current one.[48] He interrogates the very notion of rebirth: "Did beings have previous bodies?" He addresses the question with an analogy of a man renting a house: one assumes that he had a house prior to the current one, and if he runs into trouble in the current house, he will move to another. Likewise, living beings had prior bodies and will have bodies in the future. Ramalinga extends the analogy to argue that karma is sustained across births, so karma in past lives is carried into the current one. This is why those who lacked compassion in their previous lives suffer with hunger in their current lives.[49] By invoking karma and rebirth to explain suffering, Ramalinga seeks to establish his novel ideology of giving within a conventional Hindu doctrinal framework.

Where he differs from shastric traditions on *dāna* is not in the etiology of hunger but in the ethics of giving. Ramalinga asks whether it is against god's mandate to show compassion to the hungry, because their hunger signals the working out of their karmic destiny. He rejects this argument, reasoning that a king employs servants to feed even the worst criminals, and god (*kaṭavuḷ*) feeds sinners in hell through subordinate deities. Similarly, god will be happy with those who give food to suffering beings, and he will respect such donors as people with compassion. Indeed, without compassion, knowledge and affection will disappear, the character of both the strong and the weak beings will suffer, and uncompassionate beings will have wicked rebirths.[50] Ramalinga's reference to god feeding the wicked (*pāpikaḷ*) through subordinate deities refers to hierarchies of Hindu deities that are expressed in Hindu mythologies and in South Indian temple practices. For example, many South Indian temples house a hierarchy of deities, where minor deities fulfill subordinate or even impure duties, such as consuming animal sacrifices.[51] Such practices are especially important in village temples, and roughly reflect relational and purity considerations of caste.

The length and detail of this passage indicate that Ramalinga's argument for feeding the poor was unconventional, even controversial, in South Indian Shaivism in the 1860s. This justification of his novel ideology is interesting in a number of ways. First, he places the poor alongside "the worst criminals" and "sinners in hell," revealing a tension between his regard of the poor as having honor, as we have seen in a verse cited earlier, but also as sinful. Second, he sets kings and god side by side as authoritative figures who approve of compassionate feeding. Third, he cites contemporary temple practice and mythologies as evidence that god sanctions compassionate giving. It is symptomatic of his eclecticism that in this instance he justifies his controversial ideology not through any shastric or literary source, but through popular rituals and narratives that extend across a range of practices, including those of low-caste communities. His willingness to take popular religiosity as a basis for authoritative statements is consistent with his objective to bring together disparate communities into relationships of food-giving.

Ramalinga next returns to the theme of unity between beings. He emphasizes that compassion is a vital aspect of civilized ethics, and he asserts that knowledge, helpfulness, and unity will not be found in a world without compassion. He speaks in broad terms of the unity between different types of beings, but he clearly has in mind social unity, adding that in the absence of compassion, the good treatment of weak beings by the strong will be destroyed by such emotions as envy. As an example, he notes that the forest is uncivilized, full of animals like tigers and lions that lack any compassion for other beings. Places where people lack compassion are similarly devoid of a civilized ethics.[52] While above we saw Ramalinga uphold the shastric consideration of the hungry as unworthy sinners, here he transforms the relationship between the worthy and unworthy into one between the strong and the weak. Virtue emerges from compassion and entails the cooperation—indeed, unity—between the weak and poor. Although he does not explicitly mention class and caste at this point, it seems clear that he has in mind social divisions of the sort that were reinforced by established Shaiva practices of giving, and so this passage can be read as a subtle critique of Shaiva orthodoxy.

Ramalinga was concerned not only with the character of the giver and the recipient, but also with the qualities of the gift, emphasizing that food gifts must be vegetarian.[53] He asks whether one might feed meat to a carnivorous animal to assuage its hunger, but rejects this notion, as "killing a being to satisfy the hunger of another being with meat is not the path of compassion towards living beings, and god does not approve of this."[54] He utilizes Shaiva Siddhanta categories to assert that vegetarianism is an essential aspect of compassion. He expands on the character of the individual being (*cīvaṉ*), a category that is in the title of his work and which has been a focus of Shaiva Siddhanta reflection.[55] Shaiva Siddhanta works often debate the nature of the relationship between beings and god, and Ramalinga does likewise here, asserting that all beings manifest grace, which is god's natural form. The production of meat requires the killing of beings suffused with god's grace, and its consumption clouds the clarity of the soul, because meat has dense, sluggish qualities. With this clouding of the clarity of the soul, the soul becomes bound (*pacu*), characterized by the three impurities of arrogance, illusion, and karma.[56]

Ramalinga's commitment to compassion for living beings leads him to ask whether the acquisition of vegetarian food also requires killing. He argues against this, as long as food is produced only from the "seeds, vegetables, fruit, flowers, roots, and leaves" of plants, without killing the plant. Showing his concern for Hindu purity considerations, Ramalinga asks whether food that is acquired from the cuttings or products of plants would have the same impurities as the cuttings or products of the human body, such as nails, hair, or semen. He rejects this argument on the basis that such cuttings do not have any vital energy or creative power.[57] In considering these issues of concern for his co-religionists, he appears to be appealing to a high-caste Shaiva audience. Alternatively, we might view this as a sort of "Sanskritization," in which a high-caste practice, in this case vegetarianism, is advanced as a universal ideal. What is clear is that in addressing Shaiva concepts and ethics through the work, Ramalinga seeks to give his formulation of food-giving a Shaiva doctrinal basis.

Ramalinga drew on shastric and devotional sources in formulating his ideology of giving, but also from sources with less conventional and widespread acceptance, most importantly siddha, yoga, and tantric traditions. Several times in the text he mentions the *siddhis*, or supernatural powers, that yoga and siddha texts promise as the fruit of intense discipline. For those who ease the hunger of others, Ramalinga offers the incentives of "pleasures of this world, the unlimited pleasures gained through the *siddhis,* and the pleasure of eternal liberation . . . as god ordained in the Vedas."[58] Grace, it seems, is not sufficient enticement for compassion, so he employs a tantric tactic of offering pleasure and powers. It is not entirely clear to me what he means here by "the Vedas," but his knowledge of Sanskrit was limited, at best. I believe that he uses "Veda" as a synecdoche for ancient, orthodox tradition. Aware that the *siddhis* and pleasures might have questionable status in the view of established Shaivism, it may be that he links these enticements to the Vedas in order to give them more legitimacy.

Elsewhere he presents a detailed list of the material benefits that come with "taking as a vow the practice of appeasing the hunger of the hungry poor." These include a long lifespan, education, knowledge, wealth, and enjoyment. Householders who feed the hungry will be impervious to the heat of the summer sun, storms, wind, snow, and thunder. They will be free of dangerous diseases like malaria and typhoid, profit in their businesses, and be well respected in their vocations.[59] The benefits are many and similar to those that siddha medical practitioners promise their clientele.[60] The proposal that feeding the hungry can increase one's lifespan and prevent disease points to the influence of siddha and yoga traditions. Elsewhere in JKO, Ramalinga's discussion of the transformative effects of bliss highlights his familiarity with traditional medical concepts.[61] This bliss, which is achieved through grace, which is attained through compassion to all living beings, will transform one's body into high-quality gold. The bodies of compassionate receivers of grace cannot be harmed by mud or stones; when immersed in water, their bodies will not sink; when immersed in fire, they will not burn. Those who feed the poor will acquire certain *siddhis,* such as the ability to see through mountains, and indeed to see everything in the universe, and the ability to hear all spoken words, no matter how far away. They will be free of gray hair, wrinkles, old age, and death, the effects of aging that siddha medical practitioners frequently claim to overcome.[62]

Srilata Raman notes the absence of references to other texts in Ramalinga's work and convincingly argues that we can detect "literary echoes" that suggest the influence of medical literature and Tamil literary representations of hunger.[63] I would add to these the influence of bhakti and shastric literature, popular mythologies and practices, and siddha yoga traditions. Ramalinga consistently draws on these Shaiva elements to situate his new ideology of gift-giving within established Hindu traditions, and his eclecticism allows him to speak to a broad cross-section of people. The text is thus strongly grounded in Shaiva traditions, and indeed it could and should be considered a Shaiva text, despite an absence of any direct mention of Shiva. Instead, he refers to the highest god in the text as "kaṭavuḷ," a more general term that has considerable ecumenical potential. This is thus a text of a Shaiva leader working to elaborate an ideology of giving that is more inclusive than the established Shaivism of the mathas. In the next section, I will examine more closely the basis, shape, and limits of Ramalinga's inclusivity.

HUNGER, SOCIAL UNITY AND THE LIMITS OF RAMALINGA'S SHAIVA COMMUNITY

Ramalinga's extension of giving to all social groups, animals, and even plants signals an innovative widening of Shaiva gift-giving traditions. Hunger was central to his unifying project for a number of reasons. First, hunger was a common and vital concern in South India in Ramalinga's lifetime. Second, he considered the effects of hunger to be the same for all beings. Finally, as Shaiva traditions of food-giving affirm, appeasing hunger by sharing food was an important way that disparate groups established links and confirmed social relationships.

For Ramalinga, relieving hunger and saving a being from being killed are the most compassionate types of action, and also the most heavily rewarded. His focus on hunger is pragmatic, because one can practice the alleviation of hunger more easily than preventing the killing of other beings. He considers hunger to be the most debilitating affliction, worse than disease, thirst, or fear.[64] It also seems clear from vivid descriptions in the text that hunger, and perhaps even famine, was an all-too-common reality in Ramalinga's world. "When beings get hungry, their wisdom becomes confused; knowledge of god is clouded. . . . The eyes become sluggish and sunken, and the ears buzz with the sound 'kum.' The tongue becomes dried and parched . . . the skin becomes weak and loses sensitivity, the arms and legs become languid and limp; the voice changes and falters; the teeth loosen. . . . These sorts of conditions appear because of hunger, and they are common to all beings."[65] The portrayal of hunger is sympathetic, and the anatomical detail supports Ramalinga's reputation as a *vaidya* or doctor.[66] It also suggests that Ramalinga encountered hunger, especially in the village setting in which he lived, surrounded by people of a variety of castes and classes. It is perhaps no coincidence that the composition of the text and the establishing of the almshouse came on the heels of a widespread famine in South India in 1866. I will consider more closely the possible effects of this famine on Ramalinga's ideology of giving in the final section of the chapter.

For Ramalinga, hunger destroys the spiritual, intellectual, and physical achievements of all beings, reducing them to beings whose only object is food. It is a leveler, because it affects all living things, regardless of species, gender, caste, and social status. "For all human beings, of both types, men and women, the destruction and suffering brought on by hunger, and the benefits and pleasures that occur by satisfying that hunger, are generally the same."[67] All people are susceptible to hunger. "Even a king, who rules over the entire world, when hungry, will leave aside his powerful position and, with humble words, will complain to his ministers, 'I'm hungry, what can I do?'" Likewise, a great warrior, when hungry, will become weak and will not be able to fight. Sages, yogis, and siddhas, when hungry, abandon their meditation and move around looking for food. Ramalinga even takes what is perhaps a swipe at orthodox Shaiva leaders, writing that "even the *acharyas* (religious leaders), who adhere to [divisions of] caste (*jāti*), sect (*camayam*), and orthodoxy (*ācāram*), when they're hungry they forget orthodoxy and wait for food."[68] His list of eminent persons in this passage—ascetics, kings, warriors, and religious leaders—are the same esteemed figures that medieval shastric texts considered worthy recipients of gifts. Ramalinga, clearly cognizant of such distinctions, seeks to overcome them by emphasizing that hunger afflicts all people equally, regardless of gender or position.

He does make one important distinction between these powerful social figures and the poor, however. Appealing to the reader's sense of compassion, he asks, "if all these [eminent] people suffer in this way, when poor people who are without any support are hungry, how much more will they suffer? When the poor receive food at that time, how much joy will they feel? How much benefit will accrue to those who create such happiness [by providing food]? This can't be expressed in words."[69] For Ramalinga, altruistic giving is not sufficient motivation for giving, so he follows other South Asian traditions of *dāna* by offering very specific benefits, material and spiritual, to the generous giver. However, he also appeals to the readers' sense of compassion by giving a vivid account of the suffering of the hungry poor. I will quote this moving passage at length.

> Compassion towards living beings means removing the panic of the poor, who are despondent, thinking, "that wicked sinner called hunger, that nearly killed us yesterday and last night, has come again today! What can we do?" . . . Compassion towards living beings is removing the anxiety of the poor, who are immersed in worry, thinking "it has become dark. Now where will we go for food? Whom will we ask? What will we do?" Compassion towards living beings is giving food and dispelling the tears of the poor, who cry thinking "after walking endlessly [searching for food], our legs are exhausted. After asking constantly [for food], our mouths too are tired. Thinking incessantly, our minds are tired. What can we do to satisfy this wretched stomach?" There are those who have great dignity, silent but distressed like the dumb who have had a nightmare, their minds and faces expressing their thoughts: "The day has gone, and hunger pains us. Shame prevents us from going elsewhere [to beg for food], pride makes it difficult to beg openly, yet the stomach burns. It isn't clear how we can escape this life—why did we take birth in these bodies?" Compassion for living beings is feeding these people and preserving their dignity. . . . Compassion for living beings is giving food and removing the suffering of the poor, who lament, "How can I go without food today, like I did yesterday? Since I'm young, I can dare to go without food today, but what can we do about the stomach of my poor wife, who can't bear to be without food? Yet her hunger is not a big thing, when our mother and father, exhausted because of their age, will die if they go without food today! What can we do about that? How can we look at the faces of our children, who are weary of constantly crying because of hunger?[70]

While the poignancy of this passage seems obvious, the novelty of it is perhaps less so. Ramalinga is seeking to evoke the empathy of the reader through an appeal to a shared sense of compassion. The poor, as he presents them here, are not only helpless and so worthy of pity, but they also have dignity and honor, a criticism of the karmic logic of the immoral poor who are unworthy of gifts.

It is notable that his account is in prose, an emerging Tamil literary form in the nineteenth century. Raman cites the prose form of the JKO as a primary indicator of Christian influence on Ramalinga.[71] This may be right, but it is important to acknowledge that Christian works were neither the only examples of Tamil prose writing in the nineteenth century nor the first. Kamil Zvelebil points out that modern Tamil prose is modeled on medieval Tamil commentaries, and he argues that Christian prose writing had an "impact" on the development of modern Tamil prose rather than a "direct and absolutely decisive influence."[72] Ramalinga's first published work was in prose styled on medieval commentaries in Tamil, underlining Zvelebil's point. That work, a commentary on the Shaiva philosophical work *Oḻivil Oṭukkam,* appeared in 1851, about fifteen years before his composition of JKO.[73]

Ramalinga's prose in JKO, unlike that of his 1851 commentary, uses common speech, presenting the thoughts and words of the poor in everyday language to evoke the empathy of the reader. JKO is not a poetic or scholastic work, unlike most of Ramalinga's writing, but an accessible text suited for a broad readership. It may be that Ramalinga deliberately employed an emerging literary form—modern prose—because it suited his innovative message. By the time he wrote JKO, there was a rich Tamil literature in modern prose, including Tamil journalistic writing.[74] Closer to Ramalinga's Shaiva world, his primary foil, Arumuga Navalar, had been writing Tamil prose works for at least a decade and a half. Navalar's works included accessible renderings of Shaiva classics, educational tracts, newspaper editorials, and polemical pamphlets.[75] He worked with the Jaffna-based missionary Peter Percival for many years and was clearly influenced by Methodist modes of writing and preaching.[76] After he broke from Percival, he spent his life resisting Christian evangelization, and many of his prose writings were polemics against Christianity. Navalar was certainly in conversation with Europeans, though in this case the conversation usually took the form of acrimonious argument. It is possible that it was contemporary Shaiva works in prose, such as those of Navalar, that inspired Ramalinga's use of accessible Tamil prose. If this is the case, the influence of Christianity on Ramalinga's writing was not direct but mediated through more cosmopolitan Shaiva authors. This indicates that the lineages of influence on Ramalinga were complex, and they certainly were not ethnically or religiously pure, exhibiting complex interactions between diverse cultural expressions.

Although hunger is, for Ramalinga, one of the basic sources of suffering of all beings, it also presents an opportunity to practice compassion. Without hunger, beings would not help one another, there would be no compassion toward others, and therefore no occasion to receive god's grace. Hunger is an instrument provided by god to bring beings into compassionate relationships with one another.[77] Ramalinga emphasizes that the giving of food must be universal, and so hunger offers the opportunity to cut across distinctions of caste, religion, gender, status, and species through charity. Those in a position to alleviate hunger should do so without inquiring into the afflicted person's caste (*jāti*), home place (*tēcam*), religion (*camayam*), or deeds (*ceykai*), and should give food to all equally, knowing that god's manifestation to all beings is the same.[78] The caste of the giver is irrelevant: "Those who practice compassion to all living beings, shielding those beings from the danger of hunger, those generous givers are esteemed people, no matter what caste, religion, or deeds, and they should be honored as gods, sages, siddhas, yogis, etc. One should know that this is true with the all-powerful god as witness."[79] These comments on caste are perhaps the most radical of the text, and clearly put Ramalinga at odds with established Shaiva traditions of the mathas of his day. He advances the notion that worthiness is based on compassion and not on birth, and he opens the possibility for a community of the worthy that cuts across caste.

The primary audience of JKO appears to have been the members of his Society of the True Path. The compassion he outlines in the work was central to his "True Path," which he insisted all members of his society follow. Who were these members of his society? An 1867 list of members who contributed money to support the Society's new journal indicates a diverse caste membership, including *vellalars* (Pillais, Mudaliyars), Nayakars, a brahman (Rama Iyer), Chettis, Naidus, Nairs, and at least one Muslim (Katar Sahib). The list also includes single names without a caste marker that may indicate people of Dalit caste groups.[80] Most members would have been householders, even though Ramalinga called them "sadhus." Ramalinga himself was married but lived alone for the entirety of his career as a teacher and leader. His married status would nevertheless have disqualified him from leading a Shaiva matha, and his householder following clearly distinguishes his community from Shaiva ascetic lineages.

Accordingly, JKO is addressed to householders. Married people who practice compassion toward living beings "do not need the aid of the paths of worship (*cariyai*), service (*kiriyai*), yoga (*yōkam*), and wisdom (*ñāṉam*)," and they will attain the "house of bliss," where they will live forever as liberated ones.[81] Ramalinga here subordinates the traditional four paths of liberation of South Indian Shaivism to his new path of compassion. He describes the limited efficacy of the four paths: those who lack compassion will not receive salvation even if they follow the paths of worship and service, which include popular practices like going on pilgrimage, bathing in holy rivers, chanting mantras, and worshiping images. Even yogis who control their senses and practice other austerities, siddhas with supernatural powers, sages, and wise people of deep knowledge will not attain liberation without compassion toward living beings. Householders, on the other hand, who practice compassion and enjoy worldly pleasures like eating and sex, are worthy of god's grace.[82] Echoing the Hindu shastric literature, Ramalinga speaks of the worthiness of the giver, but he defines worthiness by compassionate action, not by caste, gender, sect, spiritual attainment, adherence to the shastras, ascetic discipline, or status.

Given Ramalinga's insistence on the brotherhood of all beings, and the unity fostered by compassion, we might expect both donor and recipient to be part of an idealized religious community, joined in acts of compassion and in a common experience of truth and of god. However, Ramalinga frequently distinguishes between the giver and receiver, the provider and the poor. Members of his society are the compassionate givers of food, while the poor are the grateful recipients. The hungry poor, because of their past karma, do not have "the wisdom or freedom to avert dangers like hunger and being killed, resulting from destiny and carelessness," and so those who have adequate wisdom should help them.[83] When fed, the hungry poor are happy, and "the mind cools, knowledge shines, the radiance of beings and of god glows in their hearts and faces, and unlimited satisfaction and pleasure appears." Here Ramalinga seems to suggest some potential for the poor to participate in his Society of the True Path, which is based on the reception of god's grace. However, in the next line he points out the merits that the giver derives from such benevolent action, overlooking the spiritual qualifications of the hungry poor.[84] The primary audience of his appeal was householders who had the means to give, and the benefits they received for their compassion were many.[85] Even for Ramalinga, the unity of beings had its limits.

Indeed, in JKO the unity of beings does not mean the equality of beings. Ramalinga clearly has in mind relationships between the poor and those with wealth to be based on mutual benefit, where the giver gains material and even physical benefits while the receiver gains nourishment. He does not advocate fellowship between these groups, and in other writings he warns his followers in no uncertain terms against too much interaction with the immoral hungry. "Oh god who bestows grace, you said to me: 'Those who kill beings and eat flesh, they are not close to us. They are outcasts. Until they follow your desirable true path, do no more than dispel their hunger. Don't sympathize with them or speak courteously to them. Don't give them friendly assistance. This is my command.'"[86] Ramalinga reaffirms public responsibility to the hungry, but he also highlights the limits of his community of followers. Although he does not speak here in terms of caste, meat-eating is linked to caste differences, and so there are caste implications to his statement. He did not entirely reject the ethics of esteem that shaped established Shaiva *dāna* practices. Ironically, his commitment to compassion to all living beings served as the basis for relationships that transcended caste, but it also drew rigid boundaries that reflected caste distinctions.

ENTANGLED HISTORIES OF INFLUENCE

Ramalinga drew primarily on Shaiva traditions for ideological inspiration for, and legitimation of, his novel project of giving food to the poor. However, we might ask in a critical spirit, were there other, unspoken, historical processes that inspired his new ideas? Here I trace a genealogy of diverse, "entangled" institutional and ideological sources that potentially exerted an influence on Ramalinga as he developed his ideas of compassion. I hope to show that it is impossible to untangle those influences into pure ethnic or religious lineages. The assumption of distinct cultural influences suggested by terms like conversation, dialogue, and encounter is perhaps legitimate in describing processes of close, direct contact between Europeans and Indians. However, in provincial centers, in the absence of direct engagement with missionaries or colonial authorities, the language of encounter or dialogue is inadequate to account for the emergence of new religious expressions. I argue here that Ramalinga developed his ideology of giving in a context shaped by complex, entangled histories of diverse ideologies and institutions, which were themselves characterized by hybridity, not cultural purity.

Ramalinga's focus on charity to the poor suggests the possibility of Christian influence. Srilata Raman has proceeded along these lines, arguing that Ramalinga's emphasis on personal conviction and description of the suffering of the hungry "all point to an unmistakable Christian influence, if not directly on his terminology, then most definitely on his theology in the last phase of his life."[87] His poignant account of the suffering of the hungry "leads us also to see that the suffering and dying person becomes a source of grace, the sole means through which one might attain salvation—leaving one to speculate and consider how deeply and intimately the Passion of Christ might have worked its way into the very core of Ramalinga Swamigal's theology."[88] He saw "all around him a religious continuum that could be appropriated in different ways. This enabled the emergence of certain kind of 'subaltern knowledge' in the border space between Christianity and Hinduism."[89]

Raman acknowledges that these claims are speculative, recognizing that Ramalinga was not directly drawing on ideas from Western sources in any obvious way. He did not read English, and although there were English works being translated into Tamil by the middle of the nineteenth century, he never mentions any work in English, as far as I have seen. He also does not make reference to Christianity in JKO, and he is clearly not in "dialogue" with Christian missionaries in the manner of cosmopolitan reformers. There were, as Raman points out, active missions in the vicinity of Vadalur, the base of Ramalinga's activities.[90] There do not appear to have been any missions in Vadalur, but in the 1860s there were several Protestant missions within about twenty miles of it, including a Danish mission at Melpattambakkam and, most important, Leipzig mission stations at Cuddalore and Chidambaram.[91]

Although we cannot rule out Christian influence, there are other ways to account for Ramalinga's transformation of Shaiva food-giving practices. Here I will focus on other possible influences, namely, Hindu institutions of charity and relief houses that distributed food to the poor during the 1866 South Indian famine. I will not address other possibilities, including Islamic charity, Jain and Buddhist approaches to giving, and the long history of representations of hunger in Tamil literature that Raman skillfully discusses.[92]

While ritualized giving to the poor is largely absent in the non-brahman mathas that dominated Shaivism in the region of Ramalinga's activities, there were other Hindu models for giving that Ramalinga might have encountered. As we have seen, the term he uses for his almshouse, *dharmashala,* refers to pilgrimage houses that distribute food and provide accommodation to pilgrims. More immediate to Ramalinga's geographic and historical context were networks of *chattrams* that served pilgrims and travelers. These institutions, the subject of a fascinating study by Michael Linderman, were established by royal patrons such as the Maratha kings in the Thanjavur region, just south of Ramalinga's almshouse.[93] In the early nineteenth century, the most famous of these kings, Raja Serfoji II, built *chattrams* that offered a variety of services, including the distribution of food to a wide range of people including the poor.[94] Serfoji took the practice of establishing *chattrams* from the Nayaka kings, and he extended their food-distribution practices to include the poor. "By the late Maratha period, the scope of *annadāna,* or 'feeding charity' to a set number of Brahmins and mendicants, the targeted constituencies of the medieval feeding grants, had broadened to include distribution of aid or hospitality to the indigent poor, students of schools, and even European guests."[95] *Chattrams* were numerous in Ramalinga's district of South Arcot, with the 1885 *Imperial Gazetteer of India* noting that there were 210 "chaultries" there. These, along with 76 Hindu temples and 243 mosques, were the "only institutions worthy of note" in the district.[96]

It is conceivable that Ramalinga's almshouse was inspired by South Indian *chattrams,* not by Christian missions, or perhaps by both. The possibility of multiple sources of inspiration highlights the complexity of questions of causality. Moreover, Serfoji himself was highly cosmopolitan, a king who advanced projects that brought together European and Indian medicine, music, education, and art.[97] Linderman points out that in letters to British correspondents, Serfoji emphasized his charity to the poor, perhaps influenced by British criticisms that Hindu *dāna* practices ignored the poor in favor of, in their minds, unworthy brahmans.[98] It may be that his *chattrams* do not present a wholly "indigenous" model from which Ramalinga drew inspiration. This suggests that it is as problematic to posit continuity within a pure Shaiva tradition as it is to assume a clear line of influence from the West to India. On the colonial margins, diverse cultural influences were at play that are not easily captured by a model of distinct cultures coming into conversation or contact.

Are we on stronger grounds in suggesting that Ramalinga's critiques of caste were influenced by Christianity? This is also not clear. Of the missions in South Arcot in the 1860s, the most active was the Leipzig Lutheran mission. M.A.

Sherring and Edward Storrow note that the growth of the Leipzig mission in Cuddalore from the 1850s to the 1880 came at the expense of the Society for the Propagation of the Gospel, whose numbers decreased over the same period. They attribute the Leipzig mission's success to its acceptance of caste hierarchy, lamenting that the mission's leaders permitted caste distinctions within its congregation.[99] It appears, therefore, that the missions that were most dominant in South Arcot in the 1860s were not actively protesting against caste. This does not mean that Ramalinga was unaware of critiques of caste advanced by other missions or by British commentators, but it does indicate that Christian missions propagated divergent messages about caste.

Ramalinga mentions caste in three important instances in the text: to emphasize that food should be given to all, with no regard for caste; to state that all those who give with compassion should be held in high esteem, regardless of their caste; and to comment that *acharyas,* or religious leaders, are concerned with caste.[100] The combination of these three highlights that his ideology departed from orthodox concerns and advanced criticism of those concerns. Ramalinga may have been aware of British and missionary critiques of caste, but as with charity to the poor, he also had non-Western sources to draw upon. Most importantly, the writings of the Tamil siddhas express disregard for caste and critique of orthodoxy. In JKO he frequently draws on siddha traditions, as I have pointed out earlier. Ramalinga not only demonstrates familiarity with siddha works, but his medical writings hint that he may have practiced medicine based on siddha texts.[101] It appears we have the same conundrum of influence in explaining his views on both caste and charity.

In addition to institutional models and theological ideologies, any historical account of the JKO must also consider the immediate material and social context in which Ramalinga was working. Most importantly, he established his almshouse just months after a severe famine affected a wide swath of South India. His descriptions of hunger in JKO indicate that he had personally encountered debilitating hunger, and his outreach to the poor addressed certain social processes that accompany famine. In particular, famines in colonial India most severely affected poor, low-caste laborers and often engendered social conflict. David Arnold, in his work on the catastrophic Southern Indian famine of 1876–78, points out that the wealthy Indians had the means to overcome famine, and some rich merchants even profited from increases in food prices.[102] Landlords and laborers would sometimes join forces to address famine by patronizing and performing collective rites.[103] More often, however, *vellalar* landholders, or ryots, would suspend their customary relationships of employment and support of low-caste laborers, increasing the vulnerability of the poor and accentuating caste and class divisions.[104] Laborers perceived this break as a failure of landholders to honor their responsibilities toward their workers, a failure that must have looked especially unjust when storehouses of grain were guarded by British authorities. Collective action of these disenfranchised communities often took the form of looting in bazaars.[105]

Various authorities and organizations worked to provide relief during the 1876 famine. Private measures involved wealthy *zamindars,* who owned much larger tracts of land than ryots; local princes keen to fulfill their royal duties (*rājadharma*); temples and pilgrimage centers; *chattrams* in the Thanjavur region; and religious societies. These disparate groups gave in various ways, some distributing food without regard to caste or religion, while others gave on the basis of caste or just to poor brahmans, or to Hindus or Muslims only. Government efforts included setting up relief centers that would distribute food according to British ideals of a worthy recipient, primarily the hungry poor. The British also established relief camps and employed the poor in government work schemes, dalits composing the largest number of camp residents and laborers.[106]

A government report confirms that many of the same social tensions and relief efforts were present in the 1866 famine, which struck South India just months before Ramalinga established his almshouse. The author of the report, R. A. Dalyell, noted that in early 1866 prices began to skyrocket, with the price of raggy, the staple food for working class and low-caste communities, rising much faster than the price for rice, indicating that food stress was especially acute for the poor. Merchants profited from the high prices, but often sold their grain in neighboring districts, "where the excessive prices enabled them to make large profits, rather, than [sic] increase the prices much beyond the present high rates in their own towns and villages. They fear popular indignation and riots ending in attacks on the grain shops."[107] By February, some poor were living on wild plants and roots, and looting by the "very low castes" became common.[108]

Wealthy people from the Muslim community began to purchase food at market rates and resell it at affordable prices, and "the principal Hindu gentlemen" of Madras city also began to raise funds for relief efforts.[109] *Zamindars* gave generously, with a *zamindar* from Madurai establishing four relief houses, each of which fed one thousand people daily "irrespective of caste and creed." Dalyell notes that these private relief houses ran on the same principles established by a government committee for public relief houses.[110] In August 1866, the government began employment projects and opened relief depots in South Arcot, Ramalinga's district, which provided some aid to the "poorer classes." There were twenty relief houses in South Arcot operating during the famine, feeding 1,436 people per day in August.[111] Government camps and employment schemes primarily engaged the lower castes, and the government delivered food directly to the upper-caste poor who refused to eat at relief houses. Thus, government relief efforts were themselves shaped in part by long-standing caste considerations, again undermining any notion of culturally "pure" institutions operating in, and modernizing, a "traditional" context. Dalyell estimates that two hundred thousand people died in

Madras Presidency from the effects of the famine.[112] One interesting absence in Dalyell's work is any reference to Christian relief efforts. It could be that the missions were not active in addressing the famine, which seems unlikely, but I am not sure how to explain this omission.

Ramalinga appears to directly address this context in JKO. When he defines compassion to living beings as "satisfying the hunger of those who suffer from hunger, without distinguishing or inquiring into their native place, religion, caste or deeds," we should understand this against the backdrop of the 1866 famine.[113] Faced with local divisions between those with means and the hungry poor, distinctions that were exacerbated by famine, he urges people not to abandon the poor but to feed them with compassion. He addressed *vellalar* landholders who were chief among his followers, affirming the perspective of the poor that the wealthy have a responsibility in times of famine to feed the hungry, basing this responsibility on the shared brotherhood of beings.

Unlike the relief houses that were founded to address the famine, Ramalinga's almshouse was not temporary but would, along with the temple he established, serve as the center of his community for decades. He routinized the temporary empathy and compassion inspired by the famine. We might see his project in terms of Erica Bornstein's distinction between the impulse of philanthropy and regulated giving based on rights and responsibilities. "Although rights-based regimes of social welfare respond to organized attempts to address social need, rights are not always afforded to those whose circumstances warrant immediate, perhaps fleeting, attention. Philanthropy, as an impulse, addresses the relational, affectual, and dynamic aspects of the gift, which is perhaps its enticement."[114] Ramalinga announced on April 25, 1867, that the Almshouse of Unity would open less than a month later in a temporary structure of mud walls and a thatched roof, indicating a certain urgency to get his institution working to distribute food to the hungry in the wake of the famine. If this indicates an impulse to ease hunger, his plan to build a brick structure with a well that would serve as a more permanent institution suggests that he wished to turn this impulse into an enduring project for his Society of the True Path.[115] When Ramalinga wrote about the responsibilities we have toward other beings and the "right" (*urimai*) to have compassion, he laid the ideological groundwork for an institution that creatively transformed the impulse to give into a Shaiva institution that has endured for almost a century and a half.[116] In so doing, he founded a new form of Shaiva giving, one that made giving to the hungry poor a central ritual transaction.

CONCLUSION

Ramalinga's ideology of giving aimed to unify beings in compassionate relationships organized around the giving and receiving of food. His poignant portrayal of the hungry poor showed empathy for their suffering and aimed to arouse compassion in his audience. He acted on an impulse to ease suffering, but in this he was not alone, as he founded his institutions in a context in which relief houses for the hungry poor were common. His innovation was in making this the enduring and central activity of his religious community, which demanded a convincing ideological framework that would reassure his Shaiva audience and perhaps also himself. The danger to his new Society of the True Path was clear, because their primary group of ritual transaction was to be the hungry poor not the usual eminent recipients of Shaiva *dāna*. He addressed the concerns of his followers by arguing within a Shaiva framework that the donor will be rewarded, not punished, by giving to the poor. He also, one suspects, lessened the potential for negative social repercussions for his followers by maintaining distinctions between the donor and the recipient. The success of his Almshouse of Unity and JKO is clear from the proliferation of institutions that distribute food to the poor in his name today. More generally, he was on the leading edge of modern Hindu institutions that make giving to the poor a central feature of their public outreach.

In trying to account for possible inspirations for his novel ideology, I have pointed to complex, entangled sources of potential influence. While questioning any straightforward assumption of Christian influence on Ramalinga, I hope I have been clear that I am not suggesting that he developed his innovative ideology in some pure Hindu realm untouched by Western influences. I doubt that there was any such realm in his day. Nor have I sought to retrieve Ramalinga's food-giving project from Christian attribution in order to restore its proper Hindu provenance. As Michel Foucault has shown, genealogies of complex phenomena do not reveal pure identities. "What is found at the historical beginning of things is not the inviolable identity of their origin; it is the dissension of other things. It is disparity."[117] In this case, there are numerous elements that might contribute to a genealogy of Ramalinga's novel ideology of food-giving, including Tamil literary representations; Christian theologies; colonial and private institutions of famine relief; and Shaiva tantric, siddha, and devotional traditions. Despite this complex lineage, Ramalinga frames his ideology only in Shaiva terms, grounding his innovation in long-standing Shaiva idioms and ideas in order to imbue it with Shaiva authority and then to challenge elite, caste-based Shaivism. It is perhaps this aspect of the work, the crafting of a diverse and eclectic lineage into a unified Shaiva framework, which was his most creative act.

On the margins of colonialism, the influences that inspire religious change are more complex than suggested by models of the meeting of two distinctive, pure cultures. By pointing to multiple historical possibilities, my account allows for a creative process that is not ultimately dependent on any single tradition, whether Christian or Hindu. Admittedly, it gives a less certain explanation for the emergence of modern Hindu expressions, allowing more scope for multiple and alternative explanations, which may better account for processes of religious innovation. Scholarly accounts of the emergence of modern Hinduism will benefit by going beyond notions of dialogue between Western modernity and Indian tradition, and instead embrace the possibility that a variety of sources with complex histories, including Hindu traditions, inspired the emergence of modern Hinduism.

3

The Publication of *Tiruvaruṭpā*

The Authority of Canon and Print

The publication in 1867 of Ramalinga's *Tiruvaruṭpā,* a book of his devotional poems in Tamil, was a landmark event in the history of his legacy and community. At the time, Ramalinga's writings and teachings were enjoying increasing fame in the metropolis of Chennai and also in the provincial area in which he lived, the eastern regions of the Kaveri Delta, which had been the literary and institutional heartland of Tamil Shaivism for at least a thousand years. His students had worked for years to publish his poems on a grand scale, which they finally achieved with the 1867 edition. They presented the work as an authoritative Shaiva text that should stand alongside established Shaiva literary classics. The audacity of their publication was perhaps best indicated by the vitriolic attack on *Tiruvaruṭpā* by Arumuga Navalar, the well-known Tamil pandit and polemicist from Jaffna, and a staunch advocate of Shaiva ritual and textual orthodoxy.[1] Focusing on the choices that Ramalinga and his followers made regarding the material form, organization, and content of the 1867 publication, I argue that they used print as a tool to garner religious and textual authority. As a technology new to mass religious communications in South Asia, print provided novel possibilities for canonical claims, especially for religious leaders like Ramalinga, who was without the backing of long-standing and powerful Shaiva institutions that dominated Tamil literary production and status through at least the end of the nineteenth century.

Scholars of the emergence of the Protestant Reformation in early modern Europe have for some time recognized the potential of print to empower religious leaders who stand outside established halls of power. Since the publication of Elizabeth Eisenstein's *The Printing Press as an Agent of Change* in 1979, the impact of print on Christendom has been a central concern to scholars of book history and of the early Reformation.[2] For Eisenstein, print enabled religious leaders in Europe to carry "democratic and patriotic" messages to the "everyman."[3] Catholics also used print to standardize priestly goals, Church theology, and oral teaching, but Eisenstein argues that the burgeoning industry was more aligned with novel religious expression than with conservative churchmen, communicating "more democratic and national forms of worship."[4] Eisenstein has understandably been criticized for not paying enough attention to the way that the established Church employed print to its advantage.[5] Yet even if we do not accept Eisenstein's view of a natural affinity of print and heterodoxy, print remained, as Alexandra Walsham argues, a vital tool in spreading unorthodox religious messages, providing dissenters with a "powerful device for communicating with both their co-religionists and the wider world."[6] Print benefited religious groups and leaders on the margins of established power by providing an efficient and inexpensive means for the wide circulation of their messages. However, in India in the latter half of the nineteenth century, print offered other possibilities and meanings rather than just efficiency. In Tamil Shaivism, print became the medium through which Shaiva leaders and pandits reestablished their canon by producing handsome volumes of well-known Shaiva works.[7] Ramalinga and his followers exploited this use of print to make a bid for the canonicity of Ramalinga's poems, publishing them in a material form that was identical to those publications of Shaiva classics.

In South Asia, as in Europe, the spread of print technology transformed the religious landscape. However, in stark contrast to scholarship on early print in Europe, there has been little attention to the impact of print on Hindu traditions in nineteenth-century India.[8] This lapse is particularly significant if we consider that a high percentage of published works in Indian languages through the nineteenth century can be classified as religious. James Long, an Irish missionary who compiled statistics on the publication of Bengali books through the 1850s, estimated that more than 50% of Bengali books published between 1844 and 1852 were religious, with Hindu works accounting for 36% of all titles.[9] Tamil publishing was similar, with many, perhaps most, of the printed books available in Tamil in the 1860s being religious in character. John Murdoch, inspired by Long's surveys of Bengali books, produced a similar volume for works in Tamil, published in 1865 as a *Classified Catalogue of Tamil Printed Books.* Murdoch compiled a list of 1,755 publications in Tamil that were available to him, classifying about 69% as religious works.[10] Religious works dominated Tamil book publishing, and as I argue below, the emergence of print as the primary medium of Tamil Shaiva texts transformed relationships of authority, expanded the accessibility of texts, reshaped canons, and led to the emergence of new literary forms. The impact of print on Hindu traditions in the nineteenth century appears to have been no less transformative than it was of Christian traditions in Europe centuries earlier.

Reform Hindu leaders like Rammohan Roy and Dayananda Saraswati were instrumental in printing editions of Hindu canonical works. They focused their efforts primarily on the Vedas, publishing translations and commentaries that would expand the readership of these elite texts. Roy produced abridged translations of Vedic works in Hindi and Bengali, and distributed these for free.[11] He focused on Vedic texts in an effort to counter European critiques of "superstitious" Hindu myths and practices grounded in Puranic works. In a tract defending the freedom of the native press, Roy argued that the press plays a crucial role in the "mental improvement" of Indians, "either by translations into the popular dialect of this country from the learned languages of the East, or by the circulation of literary intelligence drawn from foreign publications."[12] Saraswati's editing and publishing efforts focused on the earliest strata of the Vedas, the Samhitas. He wrote prose commentaries on the Vedas in Hindi in order to make them accessible to educated readers. He acquired a press and established the "Vedic Press" in 1880 to publish his works.[13] His printed editions were available to everyone, of any caste community, who had the money to purchase them, and his publishing activities drew attacks from orthodox Hindus. These efforts earned him the title of "Luther of India."[14] The reference to Luther was not entirely misleading, since Saraswati, like Roy, utilized print to reshape Hinduism in accord with certain Protestant ideals, including critiques of image worship, priestly mediation, and narratives that did not align with natural laws.[15]

Closer to Ramalinga's Tamil Shaiva context, Kanchipuram Sabhapati Mudaliyar, Tamil pandit at the Pacchaiyappa School in Chennai, was the leading figure in editing and publishing impressive editions of the Shaiva canonical works such as the *Tēvāram*, *Tiruvācakam*, and the *Periya Purāṇam* in the 1850s and 1860s. For example, he edited and published the *Periya Purāṇam*, a twelfth-century hagiography of Shaiva saints, in 1859–62. This two-volume work, with commentary, was 802 pages long, in large octavo size, and available for three and a quarter rupees, a high price that would put the publication beyond the reach of all but the most keen readers.[16] The title page of volume one states that it was published "for everyone's easy reading." The first of several benedictory compositions in praise of the book was written by Tandavaraya Swamigal, a pandit of the Tiruvavadudurai monastery, indicating that this edition had the endorsement of this powerful Shaiva institution.[17] In 1852, after a period of working on a translation of the Bible into Tamil with the Methodist missionary Percival, Arumuga Navalar rendered the *Periya Purāṇam* in prose form. In a preface to that work, he reported that he published his prose version so that "scholars and those with just a little bit of education will be able to read and understand the work easily, and that uneducated men and women will ask others to read it to them."[18] Navalar chose this canonical work because its conservative message aligned with his support of established caste and ritual practices.[19]

These reform publishing projects addressed two sorts of missionary critiques. First, by making canonical texts available to anyone who could afford to buy them, they countered criticism of the exclusionary practice of withholding scripture from lower-caste communities. Second, publishing in prose addressed critiques that Hindu works were deliberately obscure or even incomprehensible. Reformers therefore presented classical works in translation, with explanatory commentary, and in prose renditions, in pursuit of a "Protestant literalism" that would render their scriptures accessible to ordinary readers.[20] As one member of the Brahmo Samaj put it in 1869, they used print to "emancipate minds from the yoke of a superstition."[21] In the hands of Hindu reformers, print was a tool to "rationalize" Hinduism, even if this rationalization was in line with Protestant notions of rationality. By utilizing the press in this way, reformers put into practice the colonial aspiration that the "native press" would help India become a "modern society."[22] Hindu reformers thus used the press as a crucial tool to transform Hinduism in line with European notions of modernity. These printing efforts of Hindu reformers amplified the authority of canonical scriptures, enabling them to present a Hindu corpus with an authority equal to the Bible or texts of other, emerging, world religions. If their attempts to extend the readership of classical works appear to be a sort of "democratization" of knowledge, it must also be kept in mind that these works often contained messages that supported caste privilege, ritual exclusivism, and social disparity. If we see this as a "modernization" of Hinduism, we also need to recognize that the criteria for this modernization were Protestant and European.

The specter of Protestant influence and interaction was therefore clear in the case of cosmopolitan Tamil publishing. However, print was also taken up outside of those elite settings, even if those non-elite contexts have not been considered closely by scholars. In her study of print culture in colonial Calcutta, Anindita Ghosh notes that scholarly studies of print in colonial India usually "focus on 'high' literature and perpetuate images of a Western-educated indigenous intelligentsia effecting modernization and reform."[23] She points out that in the 1860s, the period when print commercialism exploded, the output of presses publishing popular literature easily surpassed that of the more "respectable" presses in Calcutta. Murdoch's catalogue indicates that Tamils were also publishing inexpensive printed books for devotional purposes and to address the daily needs of their clientele. He lists among many such texts *Vākkuvātam*, "a very popular work in which the wives of Vishnu and Shiva rake up stories against each other's husband." The pamphlet was only seven pages long, octodecimo size, anonymous, and cost just three pie.[24] These cheap publications differed from canonical works in content, price, size, durability, and presumably prestige. Popular works were in pamphlet form, octodecimo, a few pages long, and inexpensive, while canonical works were invariably larger octavo printings, with lengths running into the hundreds of pages, and were relatively expensive, usually costing at least one rupee. The audiences would likewise have varied, with the classics appealing to an educated public with the means to purchase these volumes.

Ghosh goes as far as to claim that publishing projects that aimed to reform, educate, and modernize Indian society were a failure, especially when compared to the commercial success of other sorts of literature. This is perhaps overstated, but I agree with her conclusion that the diversity of "Bengali readers as consumers of print engaged with it as subjects and agents, capable of affecting its impact, thickening the modernity narrative and exposing its internal tensions."[25] That is, we must question a straightforward narrative that print served to modernize Hinduism along European lines. Print advanced other sorts of projects, such as the wide distribution of non-elite texts and messages in the popular literature on which Ghosh focused. I argue here that Ramalinga's publication of *Tiruvaruṭpā* presents yet another way that print was employed by Hindus. His work was in verse, not in prose, and it was an expensive three rupees, indicating that Ramalinga was neither pursuing a project of Protestant literalism nor an inexpensive work that would circulate widely in bazaars. Rather, he and his followers presented these poems as a new contribution to Shaiva canon, at a time when his poems and teachings were becoming controversial in Shaiva circles.

Ramalinga's publication presents an instance of the use of print not only to spread messages more widely, but also as a technology for advancing claims for authority. Stuart Blackburn notes that from the time of publication of the Tamil classic *Tirukkuṟaḷ* in 1812 at the College of Fort St. George, "textual authenticity would not rely solely on the reputation of the pundit. After 1812, printing would also be used by pundits as an 'instrument' to ensure authenticity."[26] Ulrike Stark, speaking of commercial publishers in Northern India in the second half of the nineteenth century, argues that "the successful publisher's choices not only *responded* to readership tastes and reflected processes of canonization as well as current trends in literary activity, they also *shaped* these processes."[27] What is true for literary canons was equally true for religious canons, and here I argue that by the 1860s, publication in printed form was becoming a sine qua non for a work to be considered a Tamil Shaiva classic. That is, for an authoritative text to maintain its prestige, it was imperative that it make its way into print, as editors, patrons, and publishers of Shaiva literature were redefining the Shaiva canon. Likewise, the publication of a new work with the specific features of the canonical works being published at the time signaled a claim for canonicity.[28] Print thereby enabled someone like Ramalinga, on the margins of Shaiva institutional power, to make a bid for the canonicity of his writings.

THE PRE-PUBLICATION HISTORY OF *TIRUVARUṬPĀ*

Over his lifetime, Ramalinga composed a number of prose works as well as thousands of verses in Tamil. His students collected these verses and eventually published them in three volumes with the title *Tiruvaruṭpā* [Poems of Divine Grace], which records his reflections on Shiva, devotion, contemporary religious practices, and social reform.[29] The first volume appeared in 1867, by which time Ramalinga had a devoted following in and around his local village of Karunguli, as well as in Chennai. The publication of his verses was an important event in the history of this community, facilitating the establishment of a "textual community" in the sense that Brian Stock uses the term. That is, Ramalinga's followers came to use *Tiruvaruṭpā* "as a reference system both for everyday activities and for giving shape to many larger vehicles of explanation."[30] Stock argues that heretical groups in early medieval Europe used texts "to structure the internal behaviour of the groups' members and to provide solidarity against the outside world."[31] This is precisely how *Tiruvaruṭpā* came to serve the people who had gathered around Ramalinga. The status of the community would depend on the prestige of the text, so it was vital that the work be produced in such a way that it invoked authority. As we will see, his followers ensured that its material form was identical to other canonical Shaiva works being published at the time.

One of Ramalinga's primary devotees, Irakkam Irattina Mudaliyar, collected Ramalinga's verses over a period of several years. We find details of these efforts in letters that Ramalinga wrote to Mudaliyar, which also provide a fascinating picture of the relationship between Ramalinga and one of his closest devotees.[32] The dates of the letters range from 1858, just one year after Ramalinga's departure from Chennai, to 1869, covering a period when Ramalinga was in Karunguli and Mudaliyar was in Chennai. In the letters, Ramalinga gives advice to the young Mudaliyar on marriage and health, thanks him for posting books and gifts, reports on people close to him, asks about friends in Chennai, makes financial requests, and reminds him to think often of Shiva. There are also several references to the collecting of verses for eventual publication and to Ramalinga's ongoing composition of verses, which give important details of the efforts leading up to the publication of *Tiruvaruṭpā*.

A. Balakrishna Pillai had access to these letters and made them public for the first time in his edition of *Tiruvaruṭpā*, published between 1931 and 1958. The first letter of particular interest to the publication effort is one that Ramalinga wrote to Irattina Mudaliyar on the seventh day of the Tamil month of Tai, mid-January to mid-February. Unfortunately, he did not indicate the year—I will follow Balakrishna Pillai in dating it to either 1859 or 1860.[33] In the letter, Ramalinga instructs Mudaliyar to constantly meditate on the five syllables of Shiva ("nama civāya") with a clear mind, citing verses from Auvaiyar's *Nalvaḻi* and Manikkavacakar's *Tiruvācakam* that encourage this practice. He also includes one of his own verses to support his advice: "What merit have I done, that I have been blessed with a fleshy tongue that recites '*civāya nama*' (praise to Shiva)?" Ramalinga does not distinguish his verse in any way from those earlier, eminent works, quoting the three in succession as if they each reflect equal authority.

Indeed, he does not even acknowledge that this verse is his own, giving all three without citing author or text, presumably confident that Mudaliyar would know the provenance of each.[34] The verse would appear later in the *Tiruvaruṭpā*, indicating that by this time Ramalinga was composing and keeping verses that he used to instruct his followers.[35]

Ramalinga wrote down poems throughout his life. He wrote on palm leaves, paper, and in notebooks, his life bridging the period of transition from manuscript to print. For the most part, he wrote on palm leaves when he was in Chennai and on paper after he left in 1857.[36] Many of his verses ended up in the possession of his followers. One long palm-leaf manuscript of 202 leaves, with verses of devotion to Shiva at Tiruvotriyur, a temple just north of Chennai, was kept by his student Selvaraya Mudaliyar.[37] Later editions of *Tiruvaruṭpā* reproduced images of Ramalinga's handwritten verses. These verses show few signs of editing, indicating either that they were clean, final copies that Ramalinga wrote out after working through earlier versions, or that he was particularly skillful in composing verses orally before writing them down.[38] Despite writing down his verses, Ramalinga, as is common in Tamil literary traditions, generally wrote that he "sang" (*pāṭu*) these verses. This suggests that he considered his poems to be oral compositions, sung directly to Shiva. Indeed, in his verses he usually addresses Shiva using vocative forms. Ramalinga did not clearly distinguish between the written and spoken word, between literacy and orality, and here he differed in a crucial way from Hindu reformers, who consistently emphasized the authority of the written word.

In a letter written on December 30, 1860, Ramalinga writes that he had "sung" many songs since arriving back in his home at Karunguli from Chennai, where it is likely he met with Irattina Mudaliyar. He continues: "I didn't intend to write them down and collect them all together, so they lie scattered around." He promises to collect the poems and personally deliver them to Mudaliyar in Chennai.[39] Ramalinga expresses a certain disregard for collecting and looking after his writings, a sentiment that he repeats in later letters. Why did he write them down at all? Perhaps it was to share the verses with his followers, as his poems were dispersed among his closest students. For example, in this same letter Ramalinga tells Mudaliyar that Kumarasami Pillai and Shanmuga Pillai Reddiyar have about fifty of his poems.[40] Ramalinga's willingness to acquiesce to Mudaliyar's request to send verses seems to have been sparked by Mudaliyar's vow to eat only once a day until he received some poems. Ramalinga continues in the same letter:

> You who are so dear to me, I pray that you do what I ask. Earlier, you wrote, "Until I get a parcel containing these verses, I'll only eat once a day." Since seeing those words, rice isn't agreeable to me. I'm like one who is fasting. To give me peace of mind, please leave aside this vow to eat just once a day, and let me know immediately by post, or else I won't get rid of my weariness. I'm only eating once a day. This is true.

> It's my vow. You should let me know as soon as you abandon this vow. Two months from now the verses will definitely reach you.[41]

It may be that Ramalinga's indifference to prior requests for verses drove Mudaliyar to fast in order to cajole poems from his reluctant guru.

In the same letter, Ramalinga notes that many of his poems have already been published, and he asks Irattina Mudaliyar not to be angry about this.[42] Ramalinga's reference to earlier publication of his work is important, indicating that there were already some of his verses in print. His request that Mudaliyar tolerate these earlier publications hints at tensions and competition over the publication of his poems. From this letter it is not clear whether Ramalinga contributed in any way to the publication of these earlier compilations, but his reluctance to assist Mudaliyar, a close devotee, in the publication of verses indicates that these early publications were pursued independently of Ramalinga's input. It is also not clear from the letter which poems were published or in what form. I have not found any extant publications of Ramalinga's verses prior to the 1867 edition of *Tiruvaruṭpā*.

Velayuda Mudaliyar's "History of *Tiruvaruṭpā*," included at the end of the 1867 edition of *Tiruvaruṭpā*, gives more details of these earlier publications. Mudaliyar wrote that one of Ramalinga's followers by the name of Muttusami sung some of Ramalinga's verses in front of the image of Shiva at Tiruvotriyur. Other devotees, overhearing these "verses of grace" (*aruṭpā*), spoke about their desire to have them in written form. Some "people who shall remain unnamed" searched out Muttusami and copied those verses. With the intention to make a profit, they "foolishly" ignored propriety and printed them in "small publications."[43] A few of Ramalinga's followers, including Velayuda Mudaliyar, Irattina Mudaliyar, and Selvaraya Mudaliyar, approached them and asked them to stop publishing those verses and even offered a little money. However, those "unnamed" people continued to publish them, and even stole some poems for publication. It was then that Ramalinga's disciples approached Ramalinga himself to ask if they might publish his poems "in the proper way." Ramalinga initially denied their request, but Irattina Mudaliyar persisted and eventually won his guru's approval.[44]

We find a few more details of this encounter in a later biographical work on Ramalinga by S. M. Kandasami Pillai, "Biographical Details of Ramalinga Swami," which Pillai included in his 1924 edition of *Tiruvaruṭpā*. According to Kandasami Pillai's version of events, a few people were publishing Ramalinga's verses, but in "individual pamphlets [literally 'small books'] and with printing errors." Learning of these inferior publications, some members of Ramalinga's "Society of the True Path that is Common to All Scripture," including Puduvai Velu Mudaliyar, Selvaraya Mudaliyar, and Irattina Mudaliyar, approached Ramalinga and made known their desire to publish his verses. Ramalinga did not agree at first, but eventually gave in to their request.[45]

Balakrishna Pillai, in his edition of *Tiruvaruṭpā* published between 1931 and 1958, mentions that two of Ramalinga's poems to Murugan, "Teyva Maṇimālai" and "Kantar Caraṇa Pattu," were printed in a single volume, perhaps prior to 1851.[46] These two poems are together forty-one verses of eight lines each, so it is likely they would have been published as a pamphlet. However, the poems' focus on Murugan and pre-1851 date does not accord with Velayuda Mudaliyar's narrative, which suggests that the illicitly published verses were addressed to Shiva at Tiruvotriyur and were published later than 1851. It may be that prior to the publication of *Tiruvaruṭpā* in 1867, there were a number of editions of Ramalinga's verses in circulation in inexpensive formats. In any case, none of these copies of earlier works seems to be extant, and their existence is largely forgotten except in the scattered references noted above.

The concern of Ramalinga's followers was that these works contained mistakes, which Kandasami Pillai calls "accup pi̱laikaḷ," printing errors, clarifying that these errors should not be attributed to Ramalinga himself. Just as important, they worried about the publication of his verses in small and likely cheap pamphlets. Such pamphlets would not have a long life span, and probably would have circulated at the bazaars and markets alongside other cheap publications. Murdoch notes that such publications were widely available in bazaars: "Books published by natives are sold in the Madras Book Bazar, and to some extent, in every town of any size in the Tamil country. . . . The more expensive books are not kept on sale at the Bazar; but the hawkers can readily procure them."[47] Throughout India, popular works were often held in low esteem by elite authors, editors, and publishers, as well as by British administrators. For example, in 1872, in his history of Bengali literature, Ramgati Nyayaratna lamented the proliferation of Bengali books: "Books which are being churned out in this manner will not be read by ordinary people nor will they last long; they will cease to exist after a few days. There are some among these which, in fact, smell of the gutter."[48]

Ramalinga's followers wanted to distinguish their publication from precisely those sorts of works. His students seemed concerned that the ephemeral quality of these cheap publications, to be read and then disposed of, would detract from the prestige of Ramalinga's poetry. In creating a volume that would establish the authority of his words, they needed to ensure that the volume would last. Their collection of verses, when published years later, would contrast sharply from any earlier publications of Ramalinga's verses, benefiting from the careful editing of a Chennai pandit and published in a handsome, hefty, and expensive volume boasting a price out of reach of most readers. Ramalinga's disciples sought to give the physical publication the quality of timelessness that characterizes a literary classic, manufacturing a volume that would last for decades, and indeed centuries.[49] Time has justified their approach: earlier, shorter collections have been lost and forgotten, while *Tiruvaruṭpā* continues to be held in high esteem and is widely available.

After his letter of December 30, 1860, Ramalinga did not explicitly mention the publication of his verses for nearly five years. In a letter that arrived in Chennai on November 19, 1865, he refers to a registered letter from Irattina Mudaliyar that he received on November 13. "The matter that you refer to in your letter is not of much importance to me. However, as is your wish, you and Selvaraya Mudaliyar may use only those verses which speak of Shiva in my heart."[50] It seems that Ramalinga did not warm much to the idea of publishing his verses in the intervening years, or perhaps he wished to appear indifferent to a project that might be seen as vain, which would be contrary to the persona of modesty and simplicity that he usually projected. In later biographies, his indifference to the publication is generally viewed as evidence of his humility, and it shields him to some degree from the controversies that were to follow.[51]

By 1866, preparations for publication were in full swing. In a letter mailed from Chidambaram on February 14, 1866, Ramalinga appears to be more committed to the project, asking Irattina Mudaliyar to hold off on the publication of poems to Shiva at Tiruvotriyur, since he had composed a few additional poems that he would like to add. Similarly, in a letter written on March 28, 1866, Ramalinga tells Mudaliyar that since returning home to Karunguli, he has composed about two hundred poems in praise of Shiva at Chidambaram. He also promises to send a verse preface in a few days. Ramalinga ends his letter by responding to a prior request that Mudaliyar apparently made: "I don't give my permission that the work be brought out under the name 'Ramalinga Swami' [as author]. Why? Because it seems that this name is controversial, so it shouldn't be used."[52] There appears to have been some controversy at this time in referring to Ramalinga as "Ramalinga Sami," "Sami" or "Swami" being an appellation that designates spiritual authority and leadership. This controversy may have referred to Suppaiya Desikar's publication of a volume of poems to Shiva, also in 1867, "with the permission of Ramalinga Swami, renowned for his wise speech."[53] The eventual publication of *Tiruvaruṭpā* refers to Ramalinga as "Tiruvaruṭpirakāca Vaḷḷalār, Citamparam Irāmaliṅka Piḷḷai," that is, "Ramalinga Pillai of Chidambaram, the generous one who is radiant with holy grace."[54] Ramalinga's desire to avoid controversy in this case is noteworthy, because his legacy today is that of a radical critic of caste society, and the publication of *Tiruvaruṭpā* sparked a controversy that was to continue for decades.

THE ORGANIZATION AND CONTENT OF *TIRUVARUṬPĀ*

Tiruvaruṭpā was published in large octavo format in February 1867 by Asiatic Press, 292 Lingee Chetty Street, Madras.[55] Ramalinga's poems fill 406 pages of the volume. Front matter includes a table of contents, a benedictory verse, and a page with details for purchasing the publication. The back material begins with Velayuda Mudaliyar's "History of *Tiruvaruṭpā*," a composition of sixty-three verses that eulogizes Ramalinga and his poems, and narrates events leading up to the publication of the work. This is followed by another benedictory verse, a list of errors and corrections, a list of Ramalinga's poems yet to be published, and finally an alphabetical list of verses ordered by the first word of each verse. The pages are bound in a hard cover, making for an impressive volume.

An advertisement at the beginning of the work informs the reader that copies of *Tiruvaruṭpā* could be purchased for three rupees directly from a few of Ramalinga's disciples, giving street addresses in Chennai; Vellore, about 105 kilometers west of Chennai; and Cuddalore, the largest town near Ramalinga's residence. Those who lived at some distance could order copies through the post.[56] The purchase of books by post in India was not unusual; Ulrike Stark similarly notes that the distribution of books by mail was common in North India by 1870.[57] The advertisement also states that Mayilai Cikkitti Chettiyar and Somasundara Chettiyar provided financial support for the publication.[58] The printing of Tamil classics throughout the nineteenth century usually required the support of wealthy patrons and institutions, highlighting that printing books was not always a cheap way to publicize messages but rather was often an expensive enterprise.[59]

The cost of publication, three rupees, was high for a published work at the time. Murdoch's 1865 catalogue includes the prices for 127 Shaiva works. Of these, only two exceed three rupees: a two-volume edition of *Periya Purāṇam* for three and a quarter rupees, and a three-volume edition of Sambandar's *Tēvāram* verses for four rupees.[60] These are both part of the Shaiva devotional canon, esteemed company for *Tiruvaruṭpā*. Given the high price, it is doubtful that *Tiruvaruṭpā* would have been distributed in markets or bazaars, and it would not have enjoyed the sales volumes of popular religious literature. Unfortunately, there are no distribution figures for the 1867 printing, but Ramalinga's followers clearly opted for a prestigious, impressive publication rather than a cheaper one that would be more widely distributed and read. Although print in this case served to widen access to religious authority, it did so not in its capability for efficient reproduction, but because it was the new, primary medium through which editors and authors advanced claims to textual authority.

At the bottom of the title page, in English, are the words "Registered Copyright." In 1857, James Long noted the relative pricing of books marked with copyright: "The new Bengali works published by Natives are generally rather high priced when they are copy-wright, as various natives now find the composing of Bengali books profitable, and some authors draw a regular income from them. . . . Books for the masses, not copy-wright, are very cheap."[61] It is unlikely that *Tiruvaruṭpā* was subject to the Press and Registration of Books Act of 1867, which presumably would have only been enforced for books published in 1868 and after.[62] However, Murdoch noted in 1865 that "a considerable number of native books now bear on their title pages, 'Registered Copyright.' This is always printed in English, being considered much more effective in that language." In Tamil Shaiva publishing in

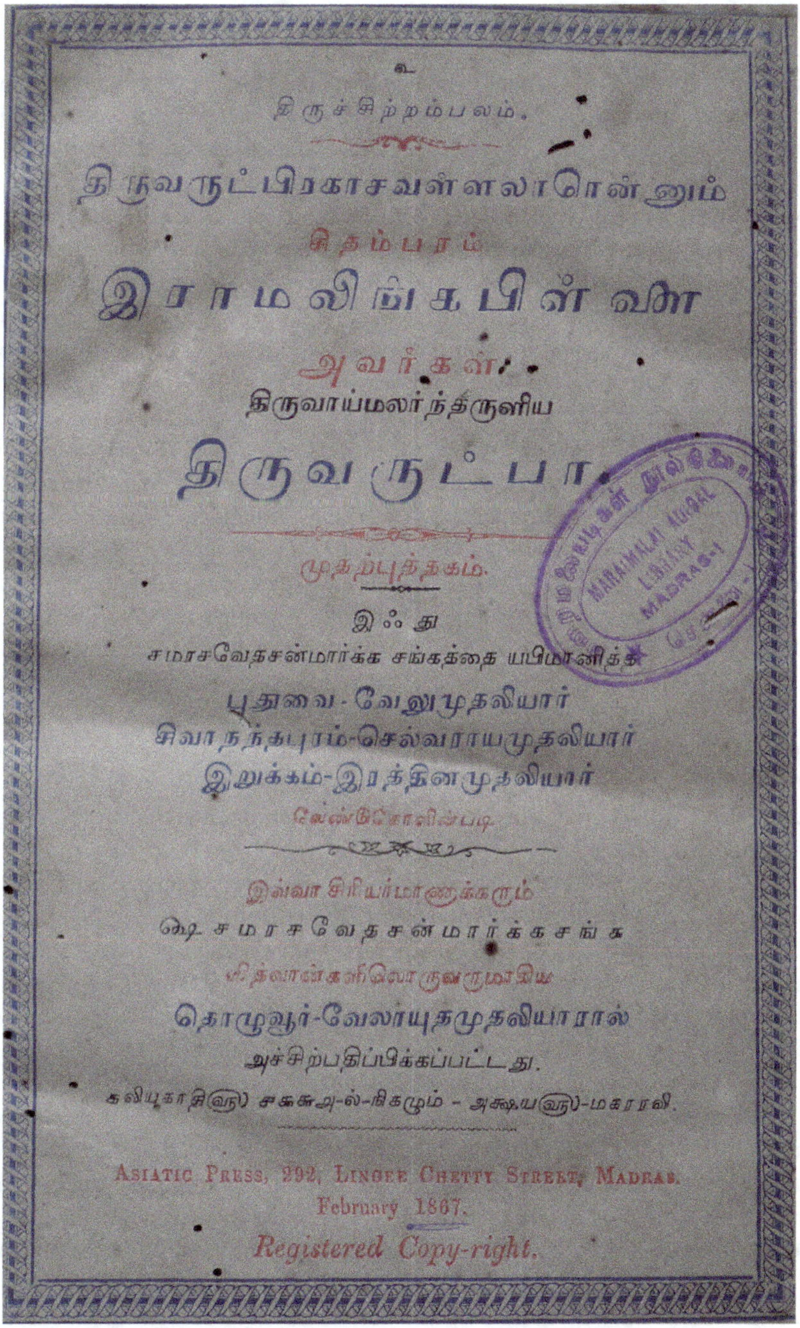
உ

திருச்சிற்றம்பலம்.

திருவருட்பிரகாசவள்ளலாரென்னும்

சிதம்பரம்

இராமலிங்கபிள்ளை

அவர்கள்

திருவாய்மலர்ந்தருளிய

திருவருட்பா

முதற்புத்தகம்.

இஃது

சமரசவேதசன்மார்க்க சங்கத்தை யபிமானித்த

புதுவை-வேலுமுதலியார்

சிவாநந்தபுரம்-செல்வராயமுதலியார்

இறுக்கம்-இரத்தினமுதலியார்

வேண்டுகோளின்படி

இவ்வாசிரியர்மாணாக்கரும்

ஷை சமரசவேதசன்மார்க்கசங்க

வித்வான்களிலொருவருமாகிய

தொழுவூர்-வேலாயுதமுதலியாரால்

அச்சிற்பதிப்பிக்கப்பட்டது.

கலியுகாதி௵ ௪௯௬௮-ல்-நிகழும் - அக்ஷய௵-மகரரவி.

ASIATIC PRESS, 292, LINGEE CHETTY STREET, MADRAS.

February 1867.

Registered Copy-right.

FIGURE 2. Title page of *Tiruvaruṭpā*, 1867. Credit: Photograph by author.

this period, prestigious canonical works were marked as copyright, setting them apart from the vast range and quantity of popular religious publications of the time.[63] Murdoch wrote that publishers told him that they could register books with the government for a fee of two rupees and suggested that some books may claim to be registered without being so.[64] Velayuda Mudaliyar wrote that *Tiruvaruṭpā* was being published in a way that "the government will know," perhaps referring to some form of official registration.[65] With the competition over the publication of Ramalinga's verses, and accusations of theft and unauthorized publication, labeling the work with "Registered Copy-right" may have offered some legal protection. Perhaps just as importantly, the note of "Copy-right" distinguished the 1867 work from prior publications of Ramalinga's verses, marking this as the authorized, and also as the authoritative, edition of his poems.

The work was edited and arranged by Toluvur Velayuda Mudaliyar, a Tamil scholar based in Chennai and a follower of Ramalinga since 1849. He later took up the prestigious position of Tamil pandit at Presidency College, Chennai. He was therefore a more cosmopolitan figure than Ramalinga, later even becoming a Theosophist.[66] The editing of the work by a pandit followed the publishing model of Tamil and Sanskrit classics. Since at least the beginning of the nineteenth century, Tamil pandits had played a vital role in publishing traditional Tamil works, editing texts and also endorsing the work of other pandits through conventional prefaces in verse or prose.[67] Blackburn notes that pandits, increasingly associated with schools and colleges modeled on British institutions, had a hand in the publication of most of the approximately two hundred Tamil works published in Chennai in the first half of the nineteenth century.[68] For example, *Tēvāram* and *Periya Purāṇam,* published just prior to *Tiruvaruṭpā,* were edited by Kanchi Sabhapati Mudaliyar.[69]

The title page of the 1867 edition describes Velayuda Mudaliyar as "a student of this master [Ramalinga] and one of the scholars of the Society of The True Path of Unity and the Vedas."[70] The link to this society, which Ramalinga established in 1865, gave the work an institutional home. It was common for institutions, especially Shaiva monasteries, to provide financial support and residency to editors of classical literature. Arumuga Navalar, U.V. Saminatha Iyer, and Damodaram Pillai, the leading editors of Tamil literature in the nineteenth century, all received patronage from the Tiruvavadudurai monastery, probably the most powerful of the Tamil Shaiva non-brahman monasteries. The influence that these institutions exerted on the editing and publishing of Tamil classics, and the prestige derived from association with such powerful institutions, prompted Damodaram Pillai to call this period of Tamil literary history "The Age of Mutts [Monasteries]."[71] Mudaliyar sought to establish Ramalinga's scholarly credentials by describing the Society of the True Path as a source of institutional prestige, albeit one that clearly stood apart from the established centers of Shaiva institutional power.

FIGURE 3. Velayuda Mudaliyar. Credit: Photograph by author.

In addition to editing the work, Velayuda Mudaliyar divided all the poems in his possession into six sections as a way of ordering the verses. He called these divisions "Tirumuṟai," the same term used to refer to the Shaiva canonical corpus.[72] He explains the rationale for this division in his "History of *Tiruvaruṭpā*."

> *Tiruvaruṭpā* is divided into six distinct sections (*muṟai*), because [1] it is a shastra (teaching) and [2] a *stottiram* (praise poem), elucidating the rituals of worship; because [3] it generates the truth of the five original, ancient syllables (*civāya nama*) that illuminate all things; because [4] it reveals that which is understood by those of the six religious systems (*aṟucamayam*), and by those outside these traditions, and because [5] it reveals that which is beyond their understanding; and because [6] it removes faults and explains that which is higher than the established paths to liberation (*attuvā*).[73]

I have translated "muṟai" here as "section," which is roughly consistent with its use in the Shaiva *Tirumuṟai* canon, where it refers to the canon as a whole, and also to each of its twelve individual parts (e.g., the eleventh *Tirumuṟai*). *Tirumuṟai* also has the sense of a holy path or tradition, drawing on the broader meaning of "muṟai" as path or way.[74] Velayuda Mudaliyar uses the term in both senses to refer to the way he divided the text into six parts and also to point to aspects of Ramalinga's verses that suggest distinct paths of religious practice. He emphasizes that *Tiruvaruṭpā* illuminates the paths taught in the six established religious traditions, which include Shaivism, while it also teaches truths that are beyond the understanding of those established traditions. Despite advancing this critique of long-standing traditions, Mudaliyar situates *Tiruvaruṭpā* within Shaivism by using the term "Tirumuṟai" to link *Tiruvaruṭpā* to the established Shaiva corpus.

One concern for the publication was the name for Ramalinga that the work would carry. We have seen that Ramalinga objected to the use of Ramalinga Swami, but it is not clear that the name that did appear on the title page, "Ramalinga Pillai of Chidambaram, the generous one who is radiant with holy grace," was much of a gesture in the direction of humility.[75] While Ramalinga clearly had some input into such details, it was probably Velayuda Mudaliyar who gave Ramalinga this title.[76] If Ramalinga was concerned about the way he would be referred to in the publication, there is no indication that he was unhappy with the title given to the work, *Tiruvaruṭpā, Poems of Divine Grace.* It would be the title, however, that would cause the most controversy in the coming years. Velayuda Mudaliyar explains the choice of title in his "History of *Tiruvaruṭpā*."

> Our Ramalinga's words, full of grace, are nectar that flows in torrents of Tamil. These words melt the hearts of great people with content minds who seize that precious grace, as well as the hearts of those sinners like me who suffer with delusion.
>
> These words, cultivating grace that provides unlimited love, are crowned with the name "*Aruṭpā*," songs of grace, because they cut through karma and enable one to

> unite with the rich, flowery feet of Shiva, whose left side has the form of a woman with laughing, fish-like eyes with golden jasmine.
>
> A few people like me, our understanding deluded with confusion, grasped the words of *Aruṭpā* as speech with divine benevolence. The words of *Aruṭpā* are imbued with grace, grace that creates auspiciousness and brings clarity to clouded minds like mine.[77]

Velayuda Mudaliyar emphasizes that because Ramalinga's poems are composed with grace, and because they reveal Shiva's grace to their readers, it is appropriate to refer to them as "songs of grace," and to Ramalinga himself as "radiant with holy grace." As Ramalinga's staunch critic Arumuga Navalar pointed out later, the term *aruṭpā* sometimes referred to the most revered Shaiva literary works.[78] Navalar, and presumably others, took the title as a claim by Ramalinga that his writings were equal to those Shaiva classics.

Two *ciṟappu pāyiram*, or celebratory verses, were included in the volume.[79] The first was written by Chidambara Swamigal, of the Madurai Tirugnanasambanda Swamigal Monastery, "the renowned seat of religious teachers of pure Shaiva Siddhanta based on the Vedas and Agamas." This is the book's only explicit link to the powerful Shaiva monastic network and indicates that Ramalinga was not entirely devoid of the support of established Shaiva institutions. Chidambara Swamigal's foreword was a single verse with the title "The Greatness of *Tiruvaruṭpā*." "Revere the greatness and dignity of the path [*muṟai*] of the fine *Aruṭpā* of our dear Ramalinga. That path creates prosperity, such that the drinking water of ordinary people abounds with power, as in the event when water had power to fuel a lamp's flame." The verse indicates that the poems of *Tiruvaruṭpā* reveal a *muṟai*, a path or tradition. The Shaiva path was often written of as the Shaiva *muṟai*, so the phrase "Aruṭpā muṟai" suggests a distinct, and novel, religious path embodied in *Tiruvaruṭpā*.[80] His use of *muṟai* here also invokes the *Tirumuṟai*, the Shaiva canon.

The mention of a lamp's flame fueled by water refers to one of the most popular legends about Ramalinga. The story is repeated in many hagiographies and is the foundational event for a popular shrine in Karunguli. Uran Adigal's extensive and knowledgeable biography, first published in 1971, gives the following narrative account.[81] Ramalinga, it seems, always had a lamp burning near him through the night. When he was staying at Karunguli, a follower named Muttiyalammal, the matron of a nearby household, would come into Ramalinga's room daily to clean, fill, and light the oil lamp. She would place a separate vessel of oil nearby that Ramalinga could use during the night to refill the lantern. One day the oil vessel broke and was replaced by another vessel, this one filled with water. Muttiyalammal was out of town so did not come to fill the vessel with oil. Legend has it that Ramalinga unknowingly filled the lamp with water through the night, and the lamp continued to burn brightly. The next day, Muttiyalammal discovered the vessel filled with water, and asked Ramalinga about it. Ramalinga confirmed that the lamp burned through the night. The story of the miraculous event spread quickly among Ramalinga's followers as a sign of his divine character.[82] Ramalinga composed a verse recounting this event, which appears in the 1867 publication.[83]

Such stories of miraculous events abound in literature on Ramalinga's life and were widely recognized when he was alive.[84] His reputation as a thaumaturge caught the attention of the urban elite, with the July 5, 1871, edition of the *Madras Mail* reporting that "One Ramalinga Pillai, a Tamil Scholar of some repute, it appears [sic] has set himself up for a god and, promises his votaries the resurrection of their relatives and friends that have departed this world. Thousands throng there daily; and a Pandal is being erected at the cost of 15,000 Rs.!!! in honor of the coming day when that glorious miracle will be wrought."[85] To his followers, Ramalinga was not only a poet whose words were filled with Shiva's grace, but he was also a powerful leader capable of working miracles. In combining poetic skill with claims of extraordinary power, Ramalinga resembled the great poet-saints of Shaivism, the celebrated authors of the most revered Shaiva devotional literature in Tamil. The *Periya Purāṇam,* for example, is replete with stories of the supernatural acts of the authors of the *Tēvāram.* Ramalinga himself frequently refers to the extraordinary powers of the *nālvar,* the four most renowned Shaiva saints, Sambandar, Appar, Sundarar, and Manikkavacakar.[86] Stories of Ramalinga's extraordinary abilities helped legitimate his place among the pantheon of Shaiva saints.

The other celebratory verse, by Ponneri Sundaram Pillai, one of Ramalinga's close disciples, made a clear claim for the divinity of Ramalinga by asserting that he was an incarnation of Shiva himself.

> God, with the highest grace, in order to destroy [the suffering of] our individual births and the bonds of our personal karma, took incarnation in a holy body out of compassion: is it eight shoulders or two? Three eyes, or two eyes of grace? A name of five syllables, or the miraculous name of grace, Ramalinga? The four Vedas, or the six Muṟais [of *Tiruvaruṭpā*]? In these ways you reapportioned yourself, ascetic [Shiva] who destroys illusion.[87]

In addition to claiming the divinity of Ramalinga, Sundaram Pillai also equates *Tiruvaruṭpā* with the Vedas, asserting the canonical status of Ramalinga's writings. The two claims are related, as a bid for canonical status is usually premised on the extraordinary insight and abilities of a work's author. Ramalinga did not claim divinity for himself in these verses, but rather emphasized his sinful nature and Shiva's grace in granting him access and wisdom. However, he did give his permission for the publication of these benedictory verses in a letter to Puduvai Velu Mudaliyar. "The preface of our Sundara Pillai is good. Go ahead and publish it. The preface of our Chidambara Swamigal is also good, so publish that one too."[88]

We can assume, then, that he did not object to Sundaram Pillai's identification of him with Shiva.

Ramalinga's verses that appeared in the 1867 edition of *Tiruvaruṭpā* run to more than four hundred pages. Most are devotional poems to Shiva in a few important temples. The verses are highly reflexive, narrating Ramalinga's encounters with god and often stressing his feelings of unworthiness. I discuss at length the content of the volume in the next chapter, so here a few verses that give the flavor of the work will suffice. First is a brief prefatory verse.[89] "The happiness which destroys the defects of attachment and cruel illusion, and which rests beyond the radiant core of light—my lord, will that happiness come today, tomorrow, or another day? I don't know."[90] The first *Tirumuṟai* begins after this verse with a poem titled "Praise of [Shiva's] Holy Feet." The poem, full of Shaiva theological language, starts with the line, "The greatest wealth is the destiny to enjoy the essence of Shiva, which is full of the pure intelligence of the highest state of being."[91] Given that the editor Velayuda Mudaliyar was a Tamil scholar, lecturer, and intellectual, it may be that he chose to begin with a highly abstract verse in order to foreground the philosophical dimension of Ramalinga's writings.

Most of the poems in the volume, however, are descriptive and devotional, extolling Shiva in various mythological manifestations drawn from Puranic sources. S. P. Annamalai notes that Ramalinga's simple style shares more with works like *Tēvāram* and *Tiruvācakam* than it does with the more technically sophisticated writing of his contemporary Minakshisundaram Pillai.[92] Many verses are highly personal, recounting specific experiences of devotion and interaction with Shiva, lauding particular temples where he worshiped, especially Tiruvotriyur and Chidambaram, and lamenting his moral lapses and unworthiness. For example, in a poem titled "Aruḷiyal Viṉāval" (Examining the Nature of Grace), Ramalinga begins with a verse to Shiva in his form of Masilamani of the temple at Mullaivayil, just west of Chennai. "Oh ocean of divine grace which is sweet like honey! Oh pure nectar, divine nature, oh god who is like the sky, oh Masilamani who lives at Mullaivayil! I lack discernment, dwelling in a fleshy body. Even so, when I came to your holy temple, you did not question my coming, remaining silent. Isn't this the nature of your holy grace?"[93]

Ramalinga frequently recalls his encounters with Shiva throughout his life, beginning when he was a young child. In his poem "Tiruvaruṇmuṟaiyīṭu" (Petition to Divine Grace), Ramalinga writes, "When I was young, without any wisdom at all, playing in the streets, my little legs flapping around, at that period of my life you gave me valuable knowledge and had me sing about you, you who took form in formlessness. Who else enjoys your soothing intimacy?"[94] Ramalinga often speaks of his special relationship with Shiva, claiming that Shiva had elevated him over other devotees. In a verse of his "Piracāta Mālai" (Sanctified Garland), he describes how Shiva singled him out even among other devotees. "Taking on a divine body of radiant beauty, you appeared in your grace before me, your servant. Smiling with grace, you put me in the middle of an assembly of devotees. You gave them all sacred ash, and then turning to me, your face blossoming with compassion, you took a beautiful red flower of light from your alms bag and gave it to me. I don't understand this sign of yours, my guru! Oh master, taking the form of brilliant light, you beautifully performed the dance of enjoyment in the public hall [of Chidambaram] set with jewels, radiant with a robe of a young elephant."[95]

Ramalinga's poetry was clearly influenced by the themes and content of Shaiva bhakti literature, especially the writings of the *nālvar,* the four most important poet-saints of Tamil Shaivism, and he even wrote poems addressed to these four.[96] In the 1867 verses, Ramalinga drew inspiration from the Shaiva literary past for content or genre, not from cosmopolitan or Western influences.[97] The poems are highly conventional, consisting of heart-felt praise to Shiva expressed in familiar idioms; reflections on Ramalinga's own inadequacies, especially when compared to Shiva himself and to other Shaiva saints; and celebrations of the narratives, temples, and geography of Tamil Shaivism. Ramalinga uses a range of meters and forms typical of classical Tamil literature and common in the *Tēvāram,* such as *nēricai, viruttam,* and *patikam.*[98] All poems except those to the *nālvar* focus on the worship of Shiva. We have seen that Ramalinga's letter of November 19, 1865, instructed Irattina Mudaliyar that "you and Selvaraya Mudaliyar may use only those verses which speak of Shiva in my heart."[99] The letter indicates that Irattina Mudaliyar and Selvaraya Mudaliyar had poems that were not specifically about Shiva, poems that Ramalinga did not want to be published. Accordingly, the poems that Ramalinga wrote to Murugan do not appear in the 1867 edition and were only published in 1880 as the fifth *Tirumuṟai.*[100] The exclusive emphasis on Shiva in the 1867 work is a quality that François Gros has noted also for the *Tēvāram:* "The majesty of Shiva dominates the *Tēvāram* and seems not to accommodate anecdote very comfortably. This may be why, in these decidedly Tamil hymns, Murukaṉ has so little place."[101] Whatever the reason for Ramalinga's exclusion of verses to Murugan, the effect was to bring *Tiruvaruṭpā* more in line with the *Tēvāram* hymns. This conventional character of *Tiruvaruṭpā* made the work suited to be compared to other works of the Shaiva canon, and was indeed an essential characteristic of the work that would qualify it to be considered a Shaiva classic.

It would have been difficult to make the case for canonicity of a less conventional work or a work with a message that diverged too much from the teachings of the established Shaiva canon. Accordingly, also absent from the 1867 publication were the radical, confrontational verses that Ramalinga is best known for today, which denounce caste distinctions, orthodox institutions, and Sanskrit works like the Vedas and Shaiva Agamas.[102] These controversial verses only appeared in print in 1885 in the sixth *Tirumuṟai,* published in a third installment of *Tiruvaruṭpā* without the participation of Velayuda Mudaliyar or others who worked on the publication of the first five *Tirumuṟai.*[103] Velayuda Mudaliyar, in his "Tiruvaruṭpā Varalāṟu," indicated that in 1867 he already had in his possession poems that would be included in the sixth *Tirumuṟai,* and he explicitly stated that it was not yet time to publish these.[104] Subsequent to the publication of those polemical verses, Ramalinga's oeuvre has most often been compared to the works of the Tamil siddhas, the decidedly unorthodox, anti-establishment Shaiva poets whose works are not included in the Shaiva canon.[105] In 1867, however, Ramalinga and his followers did not want to publish controversial verses but rather aimed to produce a work that shared the content and message of the canonical Shaiva texts.

CONCLUSION

At the time of *Tiruvaruṭpā*'s publication, print was becoming the most widespread medium for textual transmission in South Asia. Print served a wide variety of religious groups and audiences—elite, popular, orthodox, and heterodox—which used the technology to produce and distribute texts across vast distances and to diverse social groups. However, the publication of *Tiruvaruṭpā* as an expensive volume highlights that the transformative power of print lay not only in being a cheap, efficient medium of reproduction. It carried other meanings for readers and consumers. By the 1860s in South India, print had become the primary medium of canonical publications, and any work that aspired to canonicity needed to appear in print. The printing press, accessible to anyone who had the money to utilize it, provided a tool for religious groups on the margins of established religious centers to make bids for that authority. In doing so, it offered the potential to transform the relationships of authority between established religious institutions and leaders, on the one hand, and those who were articulating new religious visions from the institutional margins, on the other.

If the content and literary style of the first volume of *Tiruvaruṭpā* was largely conventional, its publication was not. In contrast to contemporaneous publications of canonical Shaiva literature, *Tiruvaruṭpā* was produced by a group of individuals working outside traditional centers of Shaiva authority. By publishing the work in the style of classical Shaiva books, they claimed the revelatory authority of new, original verses attributed to a living author. While the content of the text is the work of Ramalinga himself, many of the decisions that shaped the publication as canonical resulted from the cooperation of Ramalinga and his close disciples. These included a skillful Tamil pandit who proved to be a capable editor; a few wealthy men who provided financial backing to the publication; and a group of devoted disciples who worked hard to bring the work to press. Their goal was to produce a text with prestige rivaling that of the Shaiva devotional corpus, a work that would consolidate the legacy of Ramalinga. *Tiruvaruṭpā* came to occupy the center of communities that formed around Ramalinga's teachings, so perhaps it is fitting that the publication was itself a community effort.

Nowhere in his letters did Ramalinga refer to his poems as composing a unified whole. He never set out to write a comprehensive work, and he consistently referred only to individual poems. The longest of the 1867 poems was "Neñcaṟivuṟuttal," which fills just fewer than fifty published pages. The majority of his poems were much shorter, so they were well suited for publication in pamphlet form. However, cheap publications did not carry the authority of a larger volume published to the high standard of Shaiva canonical works. Ramalinga's followers produced the work in a form that would maximize its prestige, opting for an expensive volume made to last, presented as a unified work by a poet-saint. This choice certainly made the work less accessible, since it was beyond the purchasing power of most readers, and it is doubtful that it was on offer in markets and bazaars. Ramalinga and his followers certainly would not have rejected a wide readership, but they were willing to accept a reduced audience in order to present the work as a revered canonical work.

Was Ramalinga's use of print somehow less modern than that of Hindu reformers? It is true that he did not directly engage missionaries or other Europeans through print as did Hindu reformers. His primary world of reference was that of Shaiva literary culture. However, this culture itself was not "traditional" as opposed to "modern," as print, among other things, was helping to shape new notions of Shaiva canonicity. Neither Shaivism nor Ramalinga were fixed in a traditional past. Ramalinga and his followers demonstrated an awareness of the present and the new possibilities that it offered. They employed print as a new technology in a bid to transform established relationships of authority in Shaivism. They deftly exploited new ways of thinking about canon, and it was verse, not prose, that allowed them to advance their claims. If, in the hands of reformers, print was a tool to expand the audience for conservative messages of a fixed canon, Ramalinga employed print in the opposite way, to bring a message of ritual accessibility and equality into the Shaiva canon. The effect was that Ramalinga's egalitarian message acquired an authority that would not have been possible without the availability of print. We cannot oppose a "traditional" Ramalinga to "modern" Hindu reformers, when those "modern" reformers sought authority in elite texts from the past, while Ramalinga viewed the present as a time with the potential to advance new claims to truth, revelation, and authority. Ramalinga's use of print was as transformative, challenging, and "modern" as were reform efforts.

4

Ramalinga's Devotional Poems

Creating a Hagiography

THE MODERNITY OF BHAKTI TRADITION

Ramalinga's 1867 verses can be broadly characterized as works of bhakti, devotion. By calling them bhakti poems, I highlight their devotional character and their place in a long Tamil literary tradition of devotional poetry. Ramalinga situated himself in a lineage of Shaiva bhakti poets, as we will see. Most of his verses directly address Shiva, and much of his 1867 work consists of descriptions of the power, beauty, and benevolence of Shiva. Most, but not all, of the poems are grammatically simple, using a lexicon and images that Ramalinga clearly drew upon from prior Shaiva poet-saints. These poems contain few explicit references to his specific historical context, and they appear to be, at least on a first reading, uncontroversial. They contain none of the radical denunciations of caste, hierarchy, and canon of his poems that were published after his death. Their continuity with prior Shaiva traditions led Kamil Zvelebil to emphasize his links to the past, calling him "the last great and true *bhakti* poet."[1]

In the 1867 poems, Ramalinga presents himself as a "traditional" poet-saint, writing in verse, emphasizing his special relationship to Shiva, and claiming authority as a Shaiva saint and charismatic guru. David Smith has argued that gurus represent "traditional" dimensions of Hinduism. "Nothing better characterizes the gulf between Hinduism and modernity than the guru." Smith acknowledges, however, that the institution of the guru thrives in contemporary India, describing the "dominant position" of gurus "the great innovation in Hinduism in modern times." He considers their contemporary popularity to be a reassertion of traditional Hinduism, in which "gurus are generally maintaining traditional spirituality, but packaging it attractively for the modern world, and also spreading it beyond the shores of India. They are living exponents of the truths of Hinduism."[2] According to Smith's logic, Ramalinga's aspirations to sainthood, and the writings through which he advanced his claim to serve as a leader and guru, were traditional and therefore opposed to modern expressions of Hinduism. Any modern features we find in his persona and teachings are part of a superficial "packaging" that veil the everlasting "truths of Hinduism" in his message.

However, it we simply consign these poems to a literary realm of long-standing Tamil Shaiva bhakti tradition, or consider them to be the writings of a traditional guru, we miss the ways that they contributed to current debates and transformed Shaivism. Indeed, the 1867 publication initiated, perhaps unwittingly, a high-profile, polemical exchange between Ramalinga's followers and Tamil Shaiva reformers based in monasteries. The controversy suggests the salience of these poems in Ramalinga's time, compelling us to examine the reasons for their social impact. I argue here that we do not have to choose between describing these poems as either traditional or modern, nor should we see them as imparting a traditional message in a modern guise. Their historical importance lay precisely in the way that Ramalinga drew on Shaiva literary conventions to advance arguments about the accessibility of ritual, the possibility of revelation, and, perhaps most important, his own leadership claims. By framing these arguments with Tamil Shaiva mythological, theological, ritual, and literary tropes and idioms, he participated in a contemporary Shaiva discursive sphere in which leaders contested distinct formulations of ritual, hierarchy, and canon.

One way to highlight the historical import of his poems is to focus on the public implications of the work, including the potential breadth of its audience and the way the poems supported Ramalinga's leadership claims. These verses narrate personal details that provided the basis of emerging hagiographies about his extraordinary feats. Such firsthand accounts of direct revelation were particularly important to Ramalinga, whose leadership credentials were founded not on ties to established institutions or texts, but on his claims to represent Shiva himself. For Ramalinga, devotion entailed public dimensions as described by Christian Lee Novetzke: "all manifestations of bhakti are performances and, more to the point, public ones, that is, performances that are part of, or help form, publics of reception."[3] I will consider Ramalinga's verses as "performances" that publicly communicate his extraordinary relationship to Shiva. Although he formally addresses most of his poems to Shiva, or to himself, he had an audience in mind when he composed them, passed them on to his followers, and published them. Here I limit my discussion to the poems published in the 1867 volume.[4] Ramalinga and others deliberated carefully over its content, knowing that it would be subject to public scrutiny. This was the only publication of his verses in his lifetime, so it is likely that these poems represent most accurately the image and teachings he wished to publicize.

What was this audience? We have seen that manuscripts of his writings, both Ramalinga's own handwritten originals and copies by his devotees, circulated among his followers for years before 1867. His primary audience, then, consisted of members of his society. The 1867 publication marked an effort to expand this audience. Ramalinga's insistence that the publication should include only poems to Shiva suggests that he sought a broad Shaiva audience that would respond to conventional Tamil Shaiva devotional imagery and tropes. The published verses stress the accessibility of Shiva to all worshipers, regardless of caste or class. Ramalinga celebrates the power of the most simple Shaiva rituals, which are inexpensive and easy to perform, rather than complex temple rituals that demand significant resources and reinforce hierarchy. Most, but not all, of the poems are grammatically simple and employ a lexicon and narratives that Ramalinga drew from his bhakti predecessors. Zvelebil notes that although Ramalinga was capable of producing sophisticated, complex poetry, "most of his poems are simple in language and diction: common, almost colloquial Tamil, is used to express mystic experience, deep philosophical thought, and prayer to God for mercy, forgiveness and grace."[5] Ramalinga chose to write in a style that would be accessible to Shaivas with little education, and here he differed from other Tamil poets of his time who wrote poetry that was technically complex and deliberately opaque.[6] The 1867 publication targeted a broad Shaiva audience that would respond to the message of ritual and personal accessibility of Shiva.

I argue here that Ramalinga's verses were shaped by prior Shaiva devotional literary traditions, but also that they were modern in a number of ways. First, they present autobiographical elements that assert Ramalinga's individual uniqueness among his contemporaries, supporting his leadership claims. Second, Ramalinga viewed Shaiva tradition as flexible and able to accommodate new expressions of revelation and canonicity. Third, he celebrated the power of the most inexpensive, simple, and accessible features of Shaiva ritual. As such, his writings present a subtle critique of the expensive, brahmanic, temple rituals that were instrumental in maintaining caste hierarchies. His writings sought to make Shaivism more accessible, not by expanding the audience of elite messages but by rendering more democratic messages in the idioms and genres of Shaiva devotional literature. He presented all these modern elements through Shaiva models, idioms, and conventions, in a form that addressed the poverty and social inequality around him. His writings were modern not because they incorporated Western messages, but because they redefined Shaivism in ways that addressed the social inequalities of his 1860s South Indian world.

There is, however, some overlap between these modern features of Ramalinga's message and the characteristics of Western modernity, namely, his focus on accessibility, individuality, and the notion that tradition can be consistently transformed and renewed. Timothy Dobe and Brian Hatcher, in their analyses of autobiographical writing among prominent Hindus in colonial India, also noted such overlap, positing a "convergence" between Western modes of autobiography and vernacular forms of literary self-presentation.[7] As Dobe notes, such "convergence" does not need to imply direct, Western influence; prior vernacular literature abounded in autobiographical elements, so that "telling one's unique, personal story" was "*motivated* rather than *constrained* by 'tradition.'"[8] The direct influence of Western autobiography in the case of Ramalinga is doubtful. He did not employ the sort of coherent, comprehensive, narrative structure of Western autobiographical writing. More important, he wrote in verse, not prose, in contrast to the more cosmopolitan authors discussed by Dobe and Hatcher. His use of verse suited the hagiographical character of his self-presentation, as the prestige and mystical potential of verse was contrary to the sort of rationalizing literalism emphasized in prose writing. Verse allowed him to claim canonicity for his writings, and thus sainthood for himself, insofar as Shaiva sainthood was in his time predicated on authorship of revered poetry. His verses would be used in ritual contexts, in ways that they could not have been if he had written in prose. We should therefore view the personal elements of Ramalinga's writing not primarily as a "convergence" with Western sources, but as an extension of bhakti traditions that present the author as a vital aspect of the text. He appears to have expanded on the expression of personal subjectivity in his poems, furthering the evolution of the persona of the Shaiva poet-saint.

In the sections below, I will often cite Ramalinga's verses in their entirety, including formulaic lines in praise of Shiva. This will give the reader a better sense of the tone of his poetry, which would be difficult to communicate with a more truncated presentation of his verses. It also highlights that Ramalinga joined the personal and the divine, constantly reminding the listener/reader of the connection between his personal experiences and the majesty and grace of Shiva. I divide my discussion here into four general foci: the autobiographical; Ramalinga's use of Shaiva literary models and tropes; his conceptualization of textual traditions; and his approach to ritual. These foci are intertwined in many of his poems, but I present them separately for the purpose of analysis.

PRESENTING AN AUTOHAGIOGRAPHY

One of the most notable aspects of Ramalinga's 1867 verses is their highly personal character. This feature is not unique to Ramalinga, and in fact is common to bhakti literature in Tamil and throughout India. Karen Pechilis Prentiss, comparing bhakti works in a variety of regional South Asian languages, states that "One of the most important commonalities is that authors explicitly refer to themselves in their poetry."[9] Norman Cutler describes the transparency of the author as a distinguishing feature of Shaiva and Vaishnava Tamil bhakti literature, and notes that in many of the classical poems, the poet is the subject. Cutler argues that bhakti poetry can be read as providing a historical account of the poet, because the poet describes personal emotions and life experiences, often in very specific detail.[10] In his study of one of Ramalinga's closest Shaiva predecessors, the early eighteenth-century poet Tayumanavar, David Shulman argues that Tayumanavar's works communicate an enhanced subjectivity that was less pronounced in the writings of earlier Shaiva poet-saints. Tayumanavar's writing is highly "autobiographical," presenting the reader with "rich internal dialogues" that express a range of inner states within a notion of selfhood that reflects "a new, almost modern sensibility rooted in a changing anthropology." Shulman situates Tayumanavar "within the evolving ethos of his time, on the edge of the modern era in South India."[11] Ramalinga's emphasis on personal details of his life, his intimate interactions with Shiva, and his ethical struggles continues this tradition of personalization in Shaiva bhakti writing.

If we take seriously the axiom that any bhakti poet assumes an audience for his poems, then we can further suggest that the author presents a strategic representation of himself to his audience through his poetry. Ramalinga's verses, then, give insight into the ways that Ramalinga saw himself and wanted to present himself to his audience. We can view his poems as autobiographical or even autohagiographical, as the personal details that he included would contribute to emerging hagiographies.[12] Ramalinga's self-representation thus served as a tool to draw new followers to his teachings. As I will show, this self-representation, especially his emphasis on his close relationship with Shiva, had important implications for his bid for authority and patronage. His rejection of traditional, institutional power meant that he needed to invest his person, and his experiences, with an authority that would convince his followers of the truth of his teachings.

Hagiographies of Ramalinga frequently contend that his childhood was marked by extraordinary insights and experiences of god.[13] In his verses, Ramalinga indicates that his devotion to Shiva began at a very young age. "Even though I was a young boy, I became your servant. Don't abandon me, oh graceful one, who gave your sweet grace" (3034).[14] He specifies that Shiva "took me as a servant when I was nine years old" (2697). According to Ramalinga, his devotion was reciprocated or even initiated by Shiva.

> When I was young, without a bit of self-knowledge, you graciously took a seat in my heart. Whenever I was confused, you affectionately told me to call you "mother." Sometimes, you made it clear that I should call you "father," and you stayed with me. How should I refer to you? Should I call you my soul? Should I refer to you my friend, my faithful life companion? Should I call you my guru, who with grace removes all my troubles? What should I call you? I'll call you my beloved (3041).

The favor that Shiva showed Ramalinga, and their subsequent intimacy, are features that Ramalinga emphasizes throughout his written corpus. On the one hand, Ramalinga downplays his own talents by locating agency with Shiva. On the other hand, he sets himself apart from other people, because Shiva chose him specifically as a beneficiary of divine grace.

Ramalinga claims that not only was he devoted to Shiva at a young age, but he also began to compose poetry to Shiva, and to Murugan, when he was just a boy. "When I was young, without any wisdom at all, playing in the streets, my little legs flapping around, at that period of my life you gave me valuable knowledge and had me sing about you, you who took form out of formlessness. Who else enjoys your soothing intimacy?" (2218). Ramalinga almost reluctantly acknowledges his poetic abilities but attributes these to Shiva. "When I was young, knowing absolutely nothing about composing poems, you removed my meager knowledge, and gave me a little bit of valuable knowledge, so that even those with understanding of refined poetic composition appreciate my poems. You put lowly me on the path of pure Shiva, which is the pervasive true path. What can I say about your grace?" (3042). By attributing his literary precociousness and talent to Shiva, Ramalinga is able to acknowledge the quality of his poetry without appearing to be arrogant. At the same time, he asserts the divine character of his verses, which, after all, owe their composition to the grace of Shiva himself.

Ramalinga credits Shiva not only with bestowing the ability to compose devotional verses, but with all his learning.[15] "Oh lord! Oh protector who performs the dance of knowledge and bliss in the hall at Chidambaram! You accepted me as your servant, I who had no faith in anything. You entered inside of me, spoke secretly, and made me understand everything without formal study" (2775). This knowledge of the divine that Shiva teaches Ramalinga is not nebulous but specific and concrete. It includes knowledge of the Vedas and classical arts. "I was in darkness, not knowing anything. You made it so that I would obtain a little bit of knowledge. You gave me knowledge, without formal study, of the various classical arts beginning with the recited Vedas. You gave me that understanding, and showed me the true state of grace" (3053). Later hagiographies invariably repeat Ramalinga's claim that he learned directly from Shiva, not through study with a teacher.[16]

Ramalinga presents himself as an undeserving beneficiary of Shiva's grace. He stresses his ignorance as a youth, and his moral and intellectual failings as an adult. His moral shortcomings extend to his lack of control of his lust for women. "Oh bright light that destroys darkness! Oh Shiva guru who sits in the hearts of devotees! My father, I, your servant, abandoned the iron chain called 'woman,' which binds one to domestic life. But as soon as I did that, I became confused, adorning myself with the powerful shackle of desire for prostitutes that sap the strength. Even lowly beasts don't do this! If you put up with the faults of this perverse dog, this would be something new!" (2147). The line about abandoning "the iron chain called 'woman'" is likely a reference to Ramalinga's marriage, which he elsewhere asserts was against his wishes and which hagiographies insist he never consummated.[17] In any case, Ramalinga frequently gives voice to his struggles with lust, sometimes celebrating his victory over his desire (1009). Perhaps predictably, these admissions appear less prominently in hagiographies.[18]

Through his verses, then, Ramalinga presents a detailed self-portrayal of transformative processes of his youth, his acquisition of knowledge, his character, and his struggles with desire. He also mentions very specific events and decisions he made in his life. In these reflections, he invariably refers to Shiva as his most important confidant and companion. Thus, when he contemplates a move from Chennai to his birth area near Chidambaram, he asks Shiva for his advice. "To get rid of my troubles, I don't know if I should remain near Otri, or if I should live at Chidambaram, town of the tiger. Oh Shiva, what should I do? I am an insignificant person of with little of your grace. Why don't you give me your grace, saying 'Come here quickly!'? How can I reach you? Oh, lord of the hall of Otri, which the corrupt cannot approach! Oh lord of the hall of Chidambaram, which everyone praises!" (1083). Ramalinga frames the move in terms of two of Shiva's temples, which are the ones that Ramalinga refers to most often in his verses. Eventually, Ramalinga would choose Chidambaram, moving to Vadalur, just a short distance from his birthplace and twenty-five kilometers from Chidambaram.

On other occasions he refers to less important, mundane events. For example, in one verse Ramalinga recalls an occasion when he forgets to recite Shiva's name before eating. "I'm a lowly degenerate. I forgot the custom of chanting your name, Nilakandam, before having my meal. I stood before you, like iron before gold. Oh beautiful fruit, whose matted hair shines like lightning! Isn't this why you punished me today at Otri, which shines in the world that is surrounded by the vast ocean?" (1050). By including Shiva in minor, everyday events in his life, Ramalinga communicates the closeness and constancy of their relationship.

Perhaps most powerful are those verses in which Ramalinga stresses the intimacy of his relationship with Shiva. He describes specific instances of interaction in ways that suggest physical, not imaginative, encounters. "One night, you came walking, your feet hurting, looking for me, your servant. You opened the door, and happily put one of your flowered feet inside. You beckoned me, saying 'Take this!' When I refused, you firmly disregarded me, and gave it to me in my hand, saying 'Remain here.' In the coming days, I realized the worth of this, and I rejoiced. Oh ruby who dances in the jeweled hall of Chidambaram!" (3066). Shiva's penchant for visiting Ramalinga and giving him things clearly sets him apart from other worshipers and made him the equal of the most celebrated poet-saints of the Shaiva tradition. He describes how Shiva singled him out even among other devotees.

> Taking on a divine body of radiant beauty, you appeared in your grace before me, your servant. Smiling with grace, you put me in the middle of an assembly of devotees. You gave them all sacred ash, and then turning to me, your face blossoming with compassion, you took a beautiful red flower of light from your alms bag and gave it to me. I don't understand this sign of yours, my guru! Oh master, taking the form of brilliant light, you beautifully performed the dance of enjoyment in the public hall [of Chidambaram] set with jewels, radiant with a robe of a young elephant (3162).

While Ramalinga questions the meaning of Shiva's special gift to him, the effect of the verse is to mark Ramalinga's relationship with Shiva as a special one, even when compared to other devotees. References to this special relationship pervade Ramalinga's verses, providing material for emerging hagiographies that would have important implications for his authority as a religious leader.

Ramalinga drew heavily on prior Shaiva idioms, symbols, rituals, and poetic forms in these poems. One might suppose that this immersion in tradition eclipsed any sense of his personal individuality, that is, that his poems were dominated by a mimesis that reproduced traditional Shaiva poetry and precluded any possibility of innovation or expression of unique individuality. Yet such a view reaffirms the persistent and pernicious dichotomy between tradition and modernity, in which it is only with Western modernity that we see the emergence of the modern author. Andrew Bennett characterizes the modern "Romantic conception of authorship" as one that places a "stress on individuality, on uniqueness and originality, on the conscious intention of the autonomous subject."[19] The opposition between an autonomous, modern, Western author and a conventional, traditional, Hindu one is misleading in both directions. That is, there is no such thing as an entirely autonomous subject, and any author, Western, modern, or otherwise, composes in the discursive contexts of specific literary cultures. Moreover, Hindu literary traditions have always valued creativity, improvisation, innovation, and individual expression, as much as they have emphasized conformity to convention.

If Ramalinga's expression of unique individuality aligns with Western modernity's idealization of autonomous subjectivity, it is important to recognize that he announces this unique individuality in the context of divine revelation that had a physicality and sensuousness that stands in contrast to Western sensibilities of modernity. However, I consider Ramalinga's emphasis on revelation to be itself modern, as it is through his claims to revelation that he successfully advanced his public bid for authority. His rejection of, and rejection by, powerful Shaiva institutions meant that he needed to build his authority on his personal experiences, which he does through these writings. This basis of authority is particularly important given the unorthodox character of some of his teachings, such as his radical ideology of ritual gifting of food to the poor. Thus, Ramalinga's personal revelations would come to serve his leadership aspirations in his own life, and his legacy and teachings after his death. His verses were not survivals from a traditional past, but they were forceful statements that wielded the potential to transform current relationships of authority and ideologies of social organization.

RAMALINGA'S USE OF BHAKTI TROPES

If Ramalinga advanced his leadership claims by presenting elements of autohagiography, he also asserted his place among revered Shaiva saints by modeling his poems on revered devotional works. Ramalinga drew from classical bhakti literature for the narratives, idioms, symbols, and models in which he described Shiva, himself as poet, his relationship with Shiva, and a sectarianism that demanded exclusive devotion to Shaiva gods. By juxtaposing personal experience with traditional formulae, Ramalinga's verses anchor his biography in Shaiva literary traditions. Despite his position outside the Shaiva halls of power, Ramalinga presents himself as a Shaiva saint, articulating a vision of Shaivism that emphasizes direct experience rather than Shaiva institutions and their attendant hierarchies.

Ramalinga draws on the rich narrative tradition of Tamil Shaivism in his lavish descriptions of Shiva and his feats. In many instances, these references are to pan-Indian Puranic narratives. "You took a special form, when Brahma and Vishnu looked high and low for you. Your matted locks are crowded with the [Ganga] river, *kondrai* flowers, snakes and the crescent moon. You have countless names and abodes. We'll light holy lamps at the temple where you live, supreme lord visible at excellent Otri" (895). Here Ramalinga cites a well-known story in which Shiva takes the form of a pillar of fire, and Vishnu and Brahma unsuccessfully search for the ends of the pillar. Ramalinga frequently evokes this sort of Puranic imagery. "He has three eyes and a dark throat; he is lord of the Ganges; he is part woman" (888). Or, "He wears an earring; he wears a tiger skin; he rides a bull that sleeps on the ocean; he has a battle-ax and a deer; he carries the skull of the head of Brahma; he is the one of Otriyur; he is of the famed white forest; he has an eye in his forehead; he is my god of grace!" (824). Any Shaiva, Tamil or otherwise, would recognize Shiva with a tiger skin or carrying Brahma's skull. Ramalinga likely learned these narratives through Tamil, not Sanskrit, literature, as his knowledge of pan-Indian Sanskrit works was limited and the narratives he uses are commonly recounted in Tamil Shaiva literature.[20]

Ramalinga juxtaposes these pan-Indian Puranic elements to references that are unique to Tamil Shaivism, situating Shiva at the important temple at Otri and in the white forest of Venkatu. This technique of linking local and pan-Indian Shaiva myths is one that was commonly used by the authors of the *Tēvāram*. Indira Peterson notes that "the typical *Tēvāram* verse juxtaposes and links—through syntax and implication, as well as explicit statement—the cosmic deeds and forms of Śiva with his strictly local persona and acts." Another common "blending technique" used by the poets of the *Tēvāram* is to link those cosmic and local acts of Shiva with a specific devotee.[21] Ramalinga, similarly, lists the accolades of Shiva in a variety of scales: as a pan-Indian, universal god; as a local, Tamil god; and as a personal god, the god who bestows his grace on Ramalinga. The power of these verses lay in the wonder expressed by Ramalinga that such a widely celebrated god could also be his personal god. These linkages allow Ramalinga to ground his distinctive experiences in well-established Shaiva literary traditions.

It is with reference to narratives, places, and idioms unique to Tamil traditions that Ramalinga's knowledge is most impressive and detailed. The most important sources for his descriptions of Shiva were works of the Shaiva devotional canon, most importantly the *Tēvāram,* the *Tiruvācakam,* and the *Periya Purāṇam.* He was also familiar with important Tamil temple Puranas, *talapurāṇam,* like the *Tiruviḷaiyāṭal Purāṇam* of the Minakshi temple in Madurai. In his long, 417-verse poem "Viṇṇappak kaliveṇpā" (A Petition in Kalivenpa Meter), Ramalinga recounts a number of Shiva's exploits, many of which are unique to Tamil Shaivism. "You were unable to bear the suffering of the piglets, who couldn't suckle from their dead mother, so you took form as their mother and gave them breast milk. You became a servant and sold firewood for the sake of the bard who had given word to the Pandyan king to take part in a musical competition" (1962.376–377). Ramalinga here refers to two stories from the *Tiruviḷaiyāṭal Purāṇam.* In the first, Shiva suckles pigs whose mother is killed by the Pandyan king in a hunt. In the second, the Pandyan king asks a local bard, Panapattiran, to participate in a competition with a skilled singer from the North. Panapattiran, doubting his skill, prays to Shiva. Shiva takes form as a humble seller of firewood and sings beautifully in the earshot of the foreign singer, who asks him who he is. Shiva says he is the student of Panapattiran, and the foreign singer, convinced of the superior skill of his opponent, flees the Pandyan country.[22]

Ramalinga also depicts images of Shiva that are specific to Tamil Shaivism. "I think joyfully about that eternal, beautiful vision of him seated with the woman who bestows grace on devotees, and with the boy holding a spear. Why doesn't he give me any grace? He is the accomplished lord, the lord of Tillai, the divine lord, Shiva. He is the crazy god, Tyaga Peruman of Otri, the beggar god" (776). Here Ramalinga describes Shiva at the Chennai temple of Otri accompanied by "the boy with the spear," a reference to Murugan, the much revered Tamil form of Shiva's son. Ramalinga frequently addresses Shiva in specific manifestations in temples at Otri and especially Chidambaram. He praises Shiva as "my master, who performs the dance of bliss in the flawless, jeweled hall" (3044), and as the "profound truth, who with joy performs the dance in the hall, which is the inner heart of the True devotees" (3045). Ramalinga draws on bhakti literature in describing Shiva in his form as Nataraja, the lord of the dance, and the "hall" here, as every educated Tamil Shaiva would know, is the sanctum at Chidambaram. By situating Shiva at these temples, he accentuates the Tamil character of Shiva. His focus on Tamil idioms and places points to an audience limited to Tamil speakers, especially those with some knowledge of Tamil Shaiva tradition. This is one reason that Ramalinga's popularity has never extended beyond Tamil-speaking communities.

At times, Ramalinga employs these formulaic references to add significance to his autohagiographical recollections. Here, too, he favors Tamil tropes, such as references to Shiva's attendance at the poet-saint Sundarar's marriage. "You went to the wedding of Sundarar, who wore a garland on his shoulders. You had an argument there. If you're happy to call me your servant, you wouldn't need to show any document. If you ask me to do not one task, but many, I will do that with pleasure, with no hesitation" (1182). Here Ramalinga describes a story, recounted in the *Periya Purāṇam,* in which Shiva takes the guise of an ascetic and appears at Sundarar's wedding. He disrupts the proceedings, announcing in the middle of the ceremony that he, in fact, owns Sundarar. When questioned, he produces a document to prove his case.[23] In another poem, Ramalinga notes that Shiva did not come to his wedding as he did that of Sundarar, but that if he had, Ramalinga would happily leave his contracted marriage and wed Shiva (2019). Ramalinga's playful references contrast Sundarar's reluctance to acquiesce to Shiva with his own willingness to be Shiva's servant. Ramalinga imaginatively inserts himself into the narrative landscape of Tamil Shaivism, giving the personal details of his biography a Shaiva character.

Ramalinga also employs a variety of bhakti tropes in describing his relationship with Shiva. He downplays the effectiveness of asceticism, asserting that the deepest understanding of Shiva only comes through devotion and direct interaction (e.g., 2125). He writes that his heart "melts" when thinking of Shiva, using a term, *uruku,* that is one of the most frequent descriptors of the emotional effects of bhakti. He often focuses on Shiva's feet, in part a symptom of his projected unworthiness. "My hard heart melted (*uruku*) when I saw the holy feet of Tyaga Peruman, Lord Shiva, who once gave the golden cymbals, a pearl palanquin, and an umbrella to the benevolent one of the town Kali. How do I describe that vision?" (1369). He emphasizes his unworthiness with respect to Shiva, calling himself a dog, the lowest of the low, another trope of Shaiva bhakti poets. "I have a rubbish bin of a mind, a magnet for deceitful acts. I am the cruelest of all people" (1139).[24] He thereby highlights Shiva's grace in accepting such a degenerate devotee and makes himself appear more human, providing an accessible role model for his audience. Ramalinga builds on his personal biography through these common bhakti tropes. In doing so, he gives a strong, Shaiva character to the unique, individual elements of his biography that we saw in the previous section. In following prior poet-saints in describing himself, Ramalinga makes a case for his own sainthood. This also suggests the difficulty of disentangling the personal from the formulaic, that is, what was distinctive in Ramalinga's experiences and what he drew from Shaiva literary tradition.

Ramalinga often portrays Shiva's reciprocation of his devotion in terms of specific relationships, which again follow prior bhakti models. Most frequently, he characterizes his relationship with Shiva using the language of kinship. Thus, Shiva often calls Ramalinga "son," and Ramalinga calls Shiva "father" or less frequently "mother." In referring to Shiva as a father to his devotees, Ramalinga emphasizes specific aspects of Shiva's character, especially his compassion and mercy. "Those who are dear to you, they think of their lives, that are filled with your compassion, and they praise you, 'Our father! Our father! Our father!'" (601). Shiva, like a father, is a protector of his devotees, providing them a place of sanctuary. "My mind, let's seek refuge in the feet of our father" (784). As a father and a mother, Shiva also provides for his devotees. "Father, when your servants beg for food, you feed them like a mother" (1048). Ramalinga stresses their reciprocal duties as father and son. "Oh father of Otri, it is your duty to show me the path to salvation, and my duty to serve you" (915). He appeals to Shiva not to abandon him, addressing him as "father," reminding him that he "enslaved" Ramalinga at a young age, and lauding Shiva's "enormous compassion" (2698). Their relationship as father-son is in part predicated on their association since Ramalinga was very young. "When I was young . . . you made it clear that I should call you 'father,' and you stayed with me" (3041). Their relationship is also one of love and pleasure. "In this world of attachments, there are thousands of mothers who have love for their children, but are any equal to you in your love? There are countless fathers, who take pleasure in their children, but do any equal you, oh god?" (1962.386–388). In conceiving of his relationship with Shiva in kinship terms, Ramalinga emphasizes their close connection, while maintaining the sense of hierarchy between them.

Perhaps most strikingly, some of Ramalinga's poems include descriptions of Shiva as Ramalinga's lover. In these erotic poems, Shiva makes sexual advances toward Ramalinga, and visions of Shiva stimulate Ramalinga's desire. In the following verse, Ramalinga writes as a woman speaking to a friend. "I went with the other towns-people to the procession of Tyagaperuman of Otri, fertile and beautiful. On seeing him, my heart was filled with delight. My breasts, constrained by cloth, grew to the size of mountains, and the bangles on my arm loosened. Oh friend with beautiful hair, what is this? I stood there, nothing but desire!" (1493).[25] Ramalinga speaks of his early "marriage" to Shiva. "Nataraja, who abides in the hearts of true devotees, came to me with desire when I was young and ignorant. He put a garland on me, marrying me" (3017). Elsewhere, Ramalinga presents Shiva as a sexual aggressor, approaching him in inappropriate ways. "The thief stood here, with pleasure in his eyes. He said that he was from Otri. With his mouth that sings melodies, he said, 'Give me alms.' I came and gave it to him. Then he said, 'Women give something other than this.' I asked, 'What offering are you talking about?' He replied, 'The sort of offering that you have in your mind.' Oh, my friend, what is this?" (1779). Zvelebil points out that such erotic poems are common in Tamil bhakti literature, with the poet, whether male or female, usually taking on the persona of the female counterpart of Shiva.[26] It is likely that Ramalinga here follows Manikkavacakar, who frames devotion to Shiva in terms of an erotic, even sexual, relationship.[27]

Another important element of Ramalinga's bhakti is a sectarianism that demands exclusive loyalty to Shiva over non-Shaiva Hindu gods, especially Vishnu and Brahma. "You should in your grace accept this simple man, whether I live or die. My tongue won't stir to sing of anything other than your feet, which are firmly planted in the hall of Chidambaram, even if Vishnu, Brahma, and other gods threaten to hang themselves. This is the truth. If you think of finding evidence for this, why not consider your two feet, which are a refuge fixed inside of me?" (1093). These assertions of the superiority of Shiva are also statements about sectarian communities that organize themselves around specific gods. "Oh father who is the heaven of true wisdom. Here is a request to you: on this earth, there are many people committed to sects who worship a few minor gods. Please make sure that I don't join them!" (2066). Elsewhere he specifies more clearly what these opposing sects may be. "Oh my mind, tremble, tremble if you see lustful people; argumentative Jains; poor beggars; male slaves; those with a desire for Vaishnavism; or those with jaded tongues. They gather around the eternal one, the faultless pure one, the dancer of Chidambaram, the unique lord, him of pure truth, he of wise bliss that blossoms at Otri, but they don't praise him" (907). Ramalinga's assertions of the predominance of Shiva over other gods, and Shaivas over other sects, is consistent with the Puranic and Shaiva devotional literature from which he draws. His rejection of "minor gods" would not include Shaiva gods like Murugan or Shiva's consort Devi, since Ramalinga wrote many poems to them both. However, by omitting his poems to Murugan from the 1867 publication, Ramalinga ensured an exclusive focus on Shiva, which might be linked, in part, to his caste. As Indira Peterson points out, non-brahman *vellalars* like Ramalinga have been Shaivism's "core constituency and leadership" from its inception. Other non-brahman Tamil castes have tended to worship local deities.[28]

Accordingly, Ramalinga expresses his desire to associate only with true devotees of Shiva. "Oh my elder brother, don't give me over to those ignorant of him of three eyes! It isn't worthy of your grace. Please place me in the crowd of your servants, who seek you out, telling them, 'This is my devotee'"(2065). Who are these devotees? They are clearly those devotees to Shiva, and can be recognized by their adherence to Shaiva ritual practices. In a poem in praise of Shiva's consort Uma, Ramalinga writes, "I want to lead a truly rich life, which consists of praising the feet of the wise who have knowledge of Shiva. They have obtained unique splendor. They put on sacred ash; they wear radiant *rudraksha* beads; they stand fast on the noble Shaiva path; they hold dear the meaning of the flawless five letters, which embody you; they do *puja* to your feet. Oh ambrosia, please quickly grant me this wish!" (2600).

Throughout the 1867 verses, Ramalinga celebrated a conventional Shaiva path, consistent with certain ritual practices of established Shaivism. There are only hints of the tantric-leaning, death-defying, anti-caste, anti-establishment siddha poet who was to appear with the publication of the sixth *Tirumuṟai* in 1885. For example, Ramalinga praises Shiva as the one who "doesn't recognize caste or lineage" (2985), and he praises both Shiva and Uma for "removing the bondage created by caste in this world" (1972). However, this is hardly a statement that urges his audience to abandon caste sensibilities. Also largely absent in these verses are his later frequent claims, following tantric and siddha traditions, that he had attained extraordinary powers and immortality. In one rare exception, he writes that Shiva "showed me the state of deathlessness; you showed me the innermost state; you showed me the place where the mind, which is like the blowing wind, dissolves away." It is likely that here Ramalinga refers to a figurative sense of deathlessness rather than a bodily one, as the other states that Shiva shows him are mental or otherwise non-physical. Moreover, this is no affirmation of siddha traditions, because in the preceding line, Ramalinga writes "you showed me the unique deviousness of the self-satisfied siddhas" (3038). We can safely conclude, then, that the 1867 verses were poems that adhered closely to the conventions of classical Shaiva bhakti, devoid of the tantric and siddha flavor that characterized Ramalinga's poems published after his death.

Ramalinga accomplished several things by following these conventions. First, he minimized the potential that he would be viewed as a radical or rebellious figure. By withholding his polemical poems, he presented himself as a figure who conformed to Shaiva devotional traditions. Second, his poems would appeal to an educated Shaiva audience who would be familiar with the narratives and conventions of canonical devotional literature. As an emerging Shaiva leader, it was crucial that his poems have the aesthetic power to elicit responses of devotion among his readers. Third, by depicting himself and his experiences through models of the Tamil Shaiva poet-saints, he placed himself in the lineage of revered saints. This claim to sainthood was accepted by many, enabling him to expand his devoted community of followers. His verses, and fame, spread beyond this community.

Even though Ramalinga employed specific formulae in his poems, this does not mean that he did not experience the emotions he describes, or that did he did not imagine his relationship with Shiva as one of kin or as erotic. I think it would be a mistake to view his poems solely, or even primarily, as unreflective imitations of prior Shaiva models or as cynical vehicles for his leadership aspirations. Indeed, Ramalinga was immersed from childhood in Shaiva traditions, which shaped his individual experiences, perceptions of the world, and emotional responses in formative ways. We cannot definitively separate the personal from the formulaic in Ramalinga's poetry. He uses bhakti tropes and models not simply to give his individual experiences a Shaiva flavor, because the Tamil Shaiva tradition provided Ramalinga the basic building blocks through which he experienced emotions, relationships, inspiration, and responses. In this sense, his tradition was not characterized by the momentum of the past, but it was a fluid ideology that continued to shape experiences and creativity in the present.

THE CREATIVITY OF SHAIVA TRADITION

Through the nineteenth century, religious and administrative leaders contested the bases of authority and the contents of canons. Hindu reform leaders located revelation and authority in past texts, emphasizing the fixed character of canon and expressing skepticism at the possibility of new revelation. Ramalinga, on the other hand, viewed tradition as flexible and open to additions, publishing his volume of poems as a new contribution to the Shaiva canon. It will be worthwhile here to expand on Ramalinga's conception of tradition, sainthood, and textual authority, which differed significantly from the formulations of more cosmopolitan Hindu leaders of his day. For Ramalinga, the texts and authors of the Tamil Shaiva canon were not fixed in a traditional past, but they were living presences that spoke to him and inspired his teachings and innovations.

Ramalinga's sense of tradition was dominated by Tamil Shaivism. He had limited knowledge of Sanskrit traditions that were not filtered through Tamil works. His writings display no detailed understanding of the content of the Vedas and Agamas, and he considers the Vedas to be Shaiva works. "Wise people . . . accept the true conclusions of the eternal Vedas and Agamas, which speak endlessly of Shiva, the god who, shining as part woman, sits alongside Parvati at Chidambaram" (2608). "What is the conclusion of the Vedas and Agamas? You made me realize that it is your dance in the hall of Chidambaram" (3050). Shiva is the "deepest meaning at the end of the Vedas" (598); the "hero of the Vedas, which teach the unique truth" (948); the "bright lamp that shines at the apex of the Vedas and Agamas" (3029); the "essence of the famed Vedas, which are recited by great people in the flowered temple of holy Otri" (1962.259).

Despite these associations between Shiva and the Vedas, Ramalinga often suggests the limits of Vedic texts, foreshadowing the critiques of orthodox works that he would articulate much more forcefully in poems of the sixth *Tirumuṟai*. He praises Shiva as "the profound meaning that grows beyond even the full significance of the flawless Vedas" (2105). "His holy feet are beyond the understanding of the Vedas" (2740). He extols Shiva by asserting Shiva's superiority to the Vedas: "Oh divine brilliant light, you spread the light of wisdom far and wide, to all places that even the Vedas can't reach" (2115); "Our lord, who even the great four Vedas find difficult to fathom" (1267); "The Vedas know nothing about your nature" (860). In a few verses he advances a more critical position. "Doctors, *yogis, siddhas, munis,* and other celestial beings, they searched for you. They went away, one by one, their wills destroyed, lamenting, 'we examined the Vedas, and other works, but didn't find anything.' They grieve there, Oh you who occupy a deceptive, inscrutable space! Oh god whose space is bliss!" (2130). When Ramalinga laments his ignorance, Shiva comforts him with the words, "That which was spoken long ago by all the great Vedas, that is only speech. Perhaps it is deceptive speech?" (579). When Ramalinga questions Vedic knowledge, he criticizes elite traditions of Sanskrit learning, thus extending the possibility of Shiva's grace to the vast majority of devotees who are unfamiliar with Sanskrit works. He offers these worshipers glimpses of Shiva by other means, including Ramalinga's own poems.

In Ramalinga's estimation, the most useful texts in Shaiva tradition are the writings of the Shaiva poet-saints. The 1867 publication includes a fascinating group of poems dedicated to the *nālvar,* the four great Shaiva poet-saints of the *Tēvāram* and *Tiruvācakam:* Sambandar, Appar, Sundarar, and Manikkavacakar.[29] These poems are the only ones in the volume that do not address Shiva, and they appear at the end of the work.[30] Ramalinga calls the four poems *aruṇmālai,* "garlands of grace."[31]

It is in these poems that Ramalinga reflects most deliberately on Tamil textual traditions. He contrasts the *nālvar*'s poems to the Vedas. He sings to Sundarar that "comparing the best of the Northern [Sanskrit] works to your works is more absurd than comparing the smallest particle to the golden mountain beyond measure" (3249). Ramalinga consistently emphasizes that the *nālvar*'s works are effective vehicles for experiencing Shiva, while "the works starting with the Vedas, even though they are recited endlessly, can't come close to seeing the flowers that are Shiva's feet" (3250). He praises Sambandar for giving him deep insight, for granting him the "experience of grace which is beyond words" (3229). Sambandar uses "the holy path of Tamil" to dismiss the misconceptions of others, while a single word of Manikkavacakar's *Tiruvācakam* unites Ramalinga with his master, Shiva (3234, 3264). The limitations of Sanskrit works are not generalizable to texts per se, because Tamil Shaiva bhakti texts present the fullness of Shiva to their audience. Ramalinga even calls Sundarar's verses "aruḷ-pāṭṭu," songs of grace, a synonymous term to the eventual title of Ramalinga's collection, "Tiru-aruḷ-pā," poems of divine grace (3254).[32] Ramalinga repeatedly refers to the actions of these saints and of Shiva as "full of grace" or "bestowing grace." By emphasizing the character of grace as the most significant aspect of the poems of the *nālvar,* and by calling his own works "Poems of Divine Grace," Ramalinga definitively places his poems alongside those of the *nālvar.*

Ramalinga's Tamil-centrism is consistent with his caste tradition. Peterson points out that from the time of the *Tēvāram,* the literary and ritual practices of *vellalar* Shaivas have been grounded in Tamil devotional and philosophical works.[33] This is in contrast to Smarta brahman Shaiva traditions, which much more actively incorporate Sanskrit traditions, especially those of the Agamas. Ramalinga views himself as continuing the line of the *nālvar,* calling Sambandar his "caṟkuru" or true guru (3227, 3228), and speaking of the saint as being near to him (3228). He gives credit to Sambandar for leading him to the "path of grace." "When I was a young child, without any knowledge of the world, you came inside of me, and raised me to the path of grace. When I frequently and inappropriately went astray, you put me back on track. Later, you graced me with unerring adherence" (3226). Ramalinga recalls a time when, after he unsuccessfully sought a vision of Shiva, Sambandar appeared and gave him a vision of Shiva's hair and feet inside of Sambandar himself (3232). Ramalinga also credits Sambandar with Ramalinga's own spiritual talent: "in one day you bestowed on me all of the skills which are hard to come by, even with great effort over the course of eons" (3235). While Ramalinga at times asserts his unworthiness compared to the "lineage of devotees" (3196), elsewhere in the 1867 publication he includes himself in this lineage. "I am your [Shiva's] devotee, in the line of devotees born on this earth. You know in your mind that this is true, so without fail give your grace to me, oh king of Otriyur!" (1068). Consistent with calling his poems "Tiruvaruṭpā," songs of grace, Ramalinga places himself in the line of revered Shaiva devotees, a lineage which begins with the *nālvar* themselves.

Ramalinga demonstrates his knowledge of the *Tēvāram* by directly citing lines from the work in his own verses. In one, he quotes lines from Appar, "you placed the nine apertures in the one [body]" (3241, *Tēvāram* 6.99.1),[34] and from Sundarar, "I reflected reverently and deeply on the meaning of the excellent words you spoke before: 'You are the seven notes, the benefits derived from music, sweet nectar, and my friend'" (3251, *Tēvāram* 7.51.10). Ramalinga includes hagiographical details of these saints, indicating that he was also familiar with the *Periya Purāṇam,* the medieval work by Cekkilar on the sixty-three *nāyaṉmār* Shaiva saints. He cites Cekkilar's accounts of the miraculous feats performed by the *nālvar,* such as an episode in which Sambandar restores a young girl named Pumpavai to life from her cremated bones (3234).[35] In a verse to Sundarar, he refers to a story in which Sundarar places gold in a river and then retrieves the gold from a nearby temple tank after Shiva has miraculously conveyed it (3248). Ramalinga follows Cekkilar in praising the superhuman acts of the *nāyaṉmār,* which serve to underline their close relationship with Shiva and justify their place at the apex of Shaiva saintly pantheon. The celebration of the miracles of the *nālvar* may have had a self-referential quality: as we have seen, Ramalinga's own poems provided the seeds for a hagiography that linked him with miraculous abilities and events.

Ramalinga also follows Cekkilar in formulating exclusive and at times aggressive Shaiva sectarianism. He praises Sambandar as "the light who took birth in order to destroy the darkness of Jainism" (3233). He lauds Tirunavukkaracu as "the Shaiva path itself, which was purified after you overcame, with the power of holy grace, all the deception of the Jains, who are devoid of truth" (3238). He praises Sundarar, who "gathered together those who follow the path of despair, which eschews wearing the sacred ash, and threw them into the mud" (3248). Perhaps most aggressively, he celebrates Sambandar as one "who impaled on the stake the deluded, quarrelling Jains" (1673). Both the *Tēvāram* and the *Periya Purāṇam* advocate persecution of non-Shaiva traditions, and Ramalinga's reaffirmation of these views complicates his ecumenical reputation. The actual presence of Jains in the areas where Ramalinga lived would have been unusual, which indicates that he modeled his sectarianism on these canonical bhakti works.

How did Ramalinga conceptualize the process of transmission and reception of these Shaiva canonical works? In one verse, he makes it clear that he is literally reading the verses of these poets. Addressing Sundarar, he asks the saint to take note that "I read and study (*paṭi*) your holy songs daily, completely forgetting myself when I do." This is not silent reading but reading with the tongue, that is, aloud. He then expands the act of reading to include his entire body: "Is it only the tongue which reads? My flesh reads, my heart reads, my life (*uyir*) reads, and the life of my life reads" (3253). For Ramalinga, this is a participatory, devotional act.

Ramalinga approaches these Shaiva texts not as written documents to be read in isolation. He writes of his encounter with Shaiva literary traditions as oral, or even as visual. He speaks of the *nālvar* as present to him on many occasions. Sambandar appears before him and looks at him compassionately (3232), while Tirunavukkaracu is "in my thoughts, in my eyes" (3240). He addresses them in vocative forms that contribute to the sense of their presence. He also acknowledges their literary skills. He calls Tirunavukkaracu the "god who is the king of words," and he praises Sundarar for "stringing together garlands of words" (3246, 3247). For Ramalinga, the words of these saints are usually communicated orally, "sung" by the saints themselves, and recited and heard by devotees afterward. The "great Tamil Veda flowered from the holy mouth" of Manikkavacakar (3257). Ramalinga ponders the poetry that Manikkavacakar "spoke" (3262), and he becomes absorbed, "singing" Manikkavacakar's compositions (3263). Even the "lowest sorts of birds and most vicious beasts" who overhear *Tiruvācakam* develop a longing for truth (3266). This emphasis on the orality of literature is a long-standing characteristic of Tamil literary imaginings. Tirunavukkaracu, after all, means "king," *aracu*, of the tongue (*nā*), and the *Tēvāram* and *Tiruvācakam* continue to be sung in temples today. Ramalinga spoke of his own composition of poems as a process of "singing" rather than writing. By emphasizing the orality of the *nālvar*'s poems, Ramalinga highlights their living presence.

For Ramalinga, then, the works of the *nālvar* were the most authoritative of all texts because they have the following characteristics: (1) they were meant to be recited and heard; (2) they were composed by poet-saints who had direct experience of Shiva; (3) they were composed by poets who were connected with miraculous events, which testify to Shiva's grace; (4) they have the ability to impart divine grace, transporting the listener to a state of experiencing Shiva; (5) they are not works of hoary tradition but have a living presence; and (6) they are in Tamil, accessible and spoken, rather than in the more obscure, and elite, Sanskrit. These features constitute the bases for Ramalinga's sense of textual authority. Notably absent is any notion of ancient tradition or reference to institutional backing and promotion. The living quality of these works indicates that for Ramalinga, canon was not a closed category but could be expanded to include new works that share these features. Ramalinga's verses appear to satisfy all of these criteria, and his implicit agreement to call the collection of his verses *Tiruvaruṭpā* asserts that his works should be placed alongside those of the *nālvar.*

As we will see in the next chapter, Ramalinga's sense of tradition differed from that of cosmopolitan leaders. Hindu reformers increasingly imbibed Western, historicist sensibilities that distinguished the time of tradition from the modern present, and that located revelation and its authority in the traditional past. For

Ramalinga, Shaiva tradition was not of the past but of the present, speaking to him and inspiring him. He interacted with his tradition not as a historian viewing a past marked by radical difference, but as a interlocutor and participant. Tradition, for Ramalinga, was modern in the sense of being a vital force in the present.

SIMPLIFYING SHAIVA RITUAL

We have seen that Ramalinga's food-giving ideology departed significantly from established Shaiva ritual practices of *dāna*. He also expressed his dissatisfaction with Shaiva temple-based ritual by building a temple that served as a site for new worship practices. His 1867 verses do not reject Shaiva rituals but advocate adherence to the most simple practices, namely, the wearing of sacred ash and the chanting of the five-syllable mantra, "civāya nama" (praise to Shiva). These are the most accessible of Shaiva rituals and also the least hierarchical, unlike the more complex agamic ritual practices that dictate temple worship according to caste hierarchies. Ramalinga's emphasis on inexpensive, simple, and accessible ritual practices suggests that his intended audience was broad and cut across caste boundaries. He also extolled the benefits of singing verses in praise of Shiva, and his own poems were being sung by devotees in Shaiva temples.

The wearing of sacred ash, *tirunīṟu,* marks the devotee's body with a powerful symbol of Shaiva identity. Unlike more expensive, complex worship practices that require a ritual specialist, applying sacred ash is a simple gesture that costs nothing. For Ramalinga, it was a practice that was within the grasp of any devotee, and so it suited his bid to speak to a broad audience that was not limited by caste or class. Despite this relative simplicity, Ramalinga asserts the power of the gesture and its important consequences. He composed a poem called "Civa Puṇṇiya Tēṟṟam" (The Certainty of Shiva's Virtue), which praises the virtues of wearing the sacred ash and warns of the dangers to those who eschew it. "Oh, eyes, turn away from looking, even in a dream, at the wretched people who don't wear god's ash. Instead, look with love at the devotees who wear the holy ash, which removes all blemishes of the heart. Then we can approach the lord of Otriyur" (997). Ramalinga asserts that the ash is an important marker of moral character and of sectarian identity. "Oh, my body! If those who do not wear the holy ash, which gives liberation, were to touch you with their hands, tremble with anger as if they pierced you with thorns. If those devotees who wear the holy ash, which fosters devotion, were to jump on you and kick you with their feet, you should cherish that and rejoice. Look at this as wisdom" (1003). Ramalinga calls those who do not wear the sacred ash "degraded" (998), "small" (999), "demons" (1000), "dogs" (1001), and "fools" (1005). These verses are highly prescriptive, advising a human audience to maintain Shaiva ritual behavior and sectarian boundaries. Ramalinga formally addresses these verses to various parts of himself—his eyes (997), nose

(1001), tongue (1002), body (1003), feet (1005), et cetera—but it is clear that he is speaking to an audience of Shaiva worshipers.[36]

The other simple Shaiva ritual convention that Ramalinga urged his devotees to follow was the recitation of "civāya nama," praise of Shiva, known as the *pañcāṭcaram,* or the five-letter mantra. In a letter sent on Aug 13, 1860, Ramalinga reminds Irattina Mudaliyar to "always keep Shiva and the five letters in mind."[37] In another letter to Mudaliyar, he writes, "meditating without pause on our Shiva's feet and on the five letters, is the only important thing."[38] In another he advises that "meditation on the five syllables is the most important way to attain [Shiva's grace]." He gives evidence in support of this, citing his own verse that would appear in the 1867 publication: "If one asks what is the good deed that I have done, it is attaining the fleshy tongue that recites 'praise to Shiva.'" He tells Mudaliyar that "if you understand this and meditate, everything will become clear."[39] Ramalinga conceives of the five letters as sounds to recite aloud, but also as a mantra that serves to focus the mind on Shiva.

Ramalinga's verses promise that with the recitation of the five letters, the devotee will receive not only Shiva's grace but a range of associated benefits. "The words 'civāya nam(a)' will confer the ability to sing sweetly; they will gladly dispense milk and rice; they will provide the company of sweet devotees; they will instill good character. Don't fear, my heart, which delights in dance. You have observed my oath to wear the holy ash and chant these words, which give a sweet bounty that is rare to find" (834). Ramalinga details a long list of benefits that come with chanting "civāya nama." These words "destroy dark delusion; reveal the path that conquers death; and extinguish the desire for foolish women, who bewitch with great lust" (835). They "eradicate fierce karma at the root, and reveal the stainless path of liberation, through which one achieves the place of true knowledge" (836); they "create the great medicine that destroys disease" (840). The recitation of the five syllables, while wearing the holy ash, confers a range of worldly, ethical, and soteriological benefits. In most of these verses, Ramalinga addresses his heart or mind, or he leaves the addressee obscured, indicating a more deliberate cognizance of a human audience of followers and potential recruits. Ramalinga urges this audience to adhere to these simple ritual practices, and he entices them with somewhat grand promises of the effects of those practices.

The ritual implications of Ramalinga's verses were not limited to their content. His poems were ritually performed in temple and other contexts, placing him in a long-standing Shaiva tradition. The *Tēvāram* and *Periya Purāṇam* are replete with episodes in which the *nālvar* sing extemporaneous verses of praise to Shiva at specific temples. Cutler argues that the Tamil bhakti poet-saints, both Shaiva and Vaishnava, played a vital role in the emergence of temple-centered worship practices. He suggests that the initial process of canonization of the *Tēvāram* works in the Chola court might be linked to their recitation in the Brihadesvarar temple in Thanjavur as early as the tenth century C.E.[40] As Peterson and others have noted, the recitation of the *Tēvāram* poems remains an important ritual element in Shaiva temples and festivals.[41]

Ramalinga's poems in the 1867 edition describe Shiva at two temples, Tiruvotriyur and Chidambaram, which Ramalinga appears to have frequently visited. His poems describe Shiva especially vividly in his dance posture at Chidambaram. These rich descriptions perpetuate a literary tradition, but they do more than this. The images that he lovingly paints of Shiva in residence at Chidambaram or Tiruvotriyur portray and evoke a ritual context that he and his followers participated in, actively encouraging temple worship. "My mind, come with me to the beautiful Otri temple. There, chant 'Om Shiva, Murugan, Shiva, Om, Om to Shiva,' so that you will be able join with the devotees who are praised in poems, and cross forever the ocean of birth" (801). Ramalinga's criticism of the elite, exclusionary ritual practices at temples did not extend to simple worship to temple deities, a practice for which he held great reverence. He sings to Shiva that "all your devotees sweetly sing of the glory of your grace. They worship you, seeing your beauty" (601). The public recitation of poems to Shiva is transformative to both the singer and listeners, extending the ritual benefits of recitation to devotees without the training to learn and recite poems. "If we reach a state of devotion, and stand close and listen to those who sing his praises in poems, all our karma will leave us" (1965.234–235). Although Ramalinga does not explicitly suggest that devotees sing his own poems in public, ritual contexts, it seems clear that he composed his verses to be recited. This would be consistent with his conception of poetic composition as an act of singing, not writing. He described his songs as vehicles for his personal experience of Shiva. "I, an insignificant person, have received a great boon, singing of you alone. I have attained a state of grace!" (3170) Ramalinga certainly viewed his poems as worthy for public recitation, noting that they are full of "sweet, honey-like words" and that "even eminent people of true wisdom" delight in his verses (1975, 3055). Perhaps most important, Ramalinga's songs please Shiva, who "hears me sing and rejoices" (1965.186).

Ramalinga's 1867 edition did not specify a particular musical mode for his verses. This is in contrast to the *Tēvāram* poems, though it is clear that the musical modes that are today connected to those poems were not established by their authors.[42] Ramalinga employed a variety of metrical forms used by the *nālvar*, including *viruttam* (especially *āciriya viruttam*, but also *kali viruttam* and *canta viruttam*), *tuṟai* (*kaṭṭaḷai kalittuṟai*, *kalinilaittuṟai*), *nēricai veṇpā*, *koccakak kalippā*, and *kaṭṭaḷai kalittuṟai*.[43] Given the prevalence in Shiva temples and other ritual contexts of the recitation of canonical Shaiva literature with these same meters, it would not have been difficult for worshipers to render Ramalinga's poems in song for ritual recitation.

Indeed, they do just this today. In 2010, I visited his temple and almshouse in Vadalur, and observed that his verses were sung at the almshouse prior to the distribution of food to the poor and then at the neighboring temple that he established in 1871. It is unclear precisely how far back these practices go, but it seems that in his own day, his poems were being sung by devotees at temples. In his "History of *Tiruvaruṭpā*," Toluvur Velayuda Mudaliyar writes about the verses published in 1867. "There were just a few people who knew them, but in time, some ignorant people came to know of them. There was a learned man of the name Muttusami, a man of abundant grace. He displayed his devotion, singing aloud [Ramalinga's] verses in the divine presence of Shiva at holy Otri. His devotion was full of the grace that produces tender affection. A few people, of true devotion, spoke about their desire to know Ramalinga's flawless songs of grace (aruṭpā)."[44] Muttusami was singing Ramalinga's verses in praise of Shiva at Otri, and this was overheard by others, who also wanted to know these songs, perhaps for their own recitation. Arumuga Navalar would later, in his 1869 polemic, write that Ramalinga's verses were being sung in temples at the expense of *Tēvāram* verses.

In reciting Ramalinga's poems, devotees would take on his persona, effectively identifying with him in their reverence of Shiva. Cutler notes that bhakti poems present an "occasion for a ritualized reenactment of the events and emotions portrayed in the poem. During the ritual recitation of a bhakti poem, the identity of the reciter temporarily merges with that of the poet-narrator, and the devotee listening to the recitation becomes a direct observer of the poet/reciter's experience. Ultimately, through the reciter, the devotee identifies with the poet, and, in this way, the devotee becomes an immediate participant in the poetic reenactment."[45] Ramalinga's poems effectively join an audience, the reciters of his poems, and Ramalinga himself in relationships of identification. They can do this in part because they are in Tamil, rather than in Sanskrit or Telugu, which are prevalent in more elite ritual and musical contexts.[46] Ramalinga's verses, in a literary form but relatively accessible, could be savored by many Tamil worshipers who had some exposure to Shaiva literature. In this way, Ramalinga's verses function very much like the *Tēvāram* in bringing together "mantra and *stotra* [praise poems], classical and popular song, and ceremonial and personal scripture."[47] The literary qualities of his work give his poems prestige and make them suitable to praise Shiva, yet they are accessible enough to "melt the hearts" of devotees.

It may be, then, that the publication of Ramalinga's verses in 1867 was at least in part an attempt to bring his poems to devotees for their recitation in worship of Shiva. Like other Shaiva bhakti works, the poems were not composed and then published for silent, individual reflection, but for private and public recitation and consumption. Although Ramalinga would later gain a reputation as a radical thinker who rejected conventional rituals, in these 1867 verses he sought to make a new contribution to Shaiva ritual. He emphasized the most accessible elements of Shaiva ritual, in conformity with his project to foster a broad Shaiva community. If this seems like an innocuous project, the attacks on Ramalinga that ensued highlight that his publication and message presented a fierce challenge to established Tamil Shaivism.

CONCLUSION

Ramalinga's poems link him with his audience in veneration of Shiva. He made liberal use of bhakti literary tropes that would resonate with devotees familiar with Shaiva canonical literature. He viewed past tradition not as a ossified source of authority, but as a flexible and living tradition. He embraced Shaiva rituals that were simple and accessible. Deploying his poetic skills and his knowledge of Tamil devotional literature, Ramalinga re-presented the world of the *nālvar.* It seems that he did this effectively, since devotees began to recite his verses at Shaiva temples alongside the works of the *nālvar.*

To mobilize this audience and build a community of worshippers, however, it was not enough that Ramalinga merely follow traditional tropes and models. He had to create a new work, and a new vision, that would capture imaginations and hearts. His 1867 verses announced a new revelation, even if it was one that conformed in many ways to conventional Tamil Shaiva models. This was a "respectable" revelation, which did not advance the polemical critiques of Shaivism that would appear in the poems of the sixth *Tirumuṟai.* The modernity of this revelation lay in its power to transform Ramalinga's world in novel ways. This expression of revelation asserted the salience of accessible ritual and literary elements with almost no reference to elite or brahmanical practices. These verses advanced a Shaivism that was not defined by caste hierarchy or established institutional authority. For Ramalinga, this new vision was not so much a modern departure from tradition as it was a development of tradition, since he saw tradition as a living source of inspiration that continued to shape present-day experiences of the human and divine worlds.

Perhaps most importantly, the "newness" of his vision was located in the person of Ramalinga himself. Shaiva bhakti literature provided an effective model not only for the articulation of his love for Shiva, but also for his leadership aspirations. The strongly personal character of his verses, and their many autohagiographical details, contributed to an emerging legend which continues to this day. Ramalinga's poems, for those whom they moved, served as testimony that a saint-poet lived who was the equal of the revered saints of canonical lore. As autohagiography, the 1867 poems made a significant impact in the Tamil Shaiva world. Ramalinga was a leader whose star was on the rise. He had a number of capable followers who worked to propagate his teachings and spread his fame. His close followers could participate in Ramalinga's sainthood in their daily interactions with him. The publication of his verses extended this experience to a wider audience, who could join in Ramalinga's devotion through the recitation of his verses. Ramalinga's claim to sainthood, and the soteriological potential of his poems, proved to be a powerful draw.

The transformative power of Ramalinga's work becomes most clear when we view it within two contexts: long-standing Shaiva tradition, and Ramalinga's specific present. These are not opposed contexts, nor do they coexist in a state of tension. Ramalinga's volume was published in February 1867, just three months prior to the opening of the almshouse, which presented a much more explicit and critical challenge to establish Shaiva ritual ideology. In the context of this more radical challenge, and in light of Ramalinga's growing reputation as a leader and saint, the 1867 poems presented the public with another element of his movement, a corpus of poems that invited comparisons with canonical literature. Ramalinga was building an innovative institutional and ideological complex that could serve as an alternative to the institution of the mathas. Part of the power of this challenge lay precisely in Ramalinga's employment of aspects of tradition, which continued to exert authority. For Ramalinga and his followers, Shiva was alive and well, not just in past texts, and all true devotees could experience his presence. Ramalinga was not out of tune with his times, nor was he a Shaiva fossil who refused to modernize. Indeed, his dedicated following in his day suggests that his message resonated strongly with Tamil Shaivas, and his continued popularity to this day highlights that tradition contains within itself the power to innovate and modernize.

5

The Polemics of Conflicting Modernities

The conventional character of Ramalinga's 1867 publication did not mean that it was uncontroversial. Indeed, Ramalinga's claim that he belonged in the lineage of revered Shaiva poet-saints, and that his poems constituted a new addition to Shaiva canon, were antithetical to new considerations of religious authority that were coming to define reform Hinduism. Cosmopolitan leaders viewed canon as closed and complete, and they rejected new bids for inclusion. Ramalinga's claim that his poems announced a new revelation challenged this view and led to an acrimonious dispute over Shaiva canon and authority. A close analysis of this conflict gives us insight not only into Tamil Shaiva debates but also into contrasting styles of religious leadership and practice that characterized transformations of religion in colonial India.

The tensions between Ramalinga's vision of Shaivism and that of emerging reform positions, which were allied with established Shaiva institutions, came to a head in the years following the publication of *Tiruvaruṭpā*. In 1869, the Tamil Shaiva leader Arumuga Navalar published a critical response to Ramalinga's volume. A heated dispute followed that lasted for decades. In his polemic, Navalar punned that Ramalinga's verses were "maruṭpā," verses that confused and deluded, not "aruṭpā," verses of divine grace. Their conflict was not just one between two very prominent, and very different, Shaiva leaders. It also highlights the chasm between two influential and contrasting visions of Tamil Shaivism that were characteristic of broader redefinitions of religious tradition and authority in South Asia. This dispute gives a fascinating glimpse into the tensions between, on the one hand, new criteria of authority developed in colonial contexts and, on the other, notions of authority that were more closely grounded in precolonial traditions.

While scholarly work on Ramalinga has been fairly thin, there have been many excellent studies of Navalar in the past three decades, in both English and Tamil.[1] As with Hindu reform leaders more generally, the scholarly interest in Navalar results from his engagement with Western discourses and agendas. He was a cosmopolitan figure who learned from, and then opposed, missionaries, and he drew on Western ideas and models in his efforts to reframe Shaivism. It is Navalar, therefore, who has been called "the father of the Tamil renaissance"[2] and "the leading activist in Saivism . . . until his death in 1879."[3] R. Balachandran asserts that "Navalar was responsible for the modernization of Saivism in Tamilnadu."[4] I argue here that Ramalinga has as much a claim to these titles and achievements as Navalar. Indeed, Ramalinga would inspire perhaps the greatest intellectual leader in Tamil Shaivism in the twentieth century, Maraimalai Adigal.[5] Ramalinga came to serve as an influential figure for Tamil nationalists in the twentieth century. He is well known among Indian Tamils today, his popularity cutting across caste and class, while Navalar is little known except among scholars. Even if Ramalinga was on the margins of colonial cosmopolitanism, he was not marginal to the thousands of Tamils who followed him in his lifetime and after, nor should he be simply a footnote in studies of the emergence of modern Hinduism. My goal in this chapter is to consider together the two contrasting visions of Shaivism advocated by Ramalinga and Navalar, in order to clarify the crucial differences between them. The fact that both figures played pivotal roles in the transformations of Tamil Shaivism from their time to today suggests that genealogies of the emergence of modern Hinduism need to take greater account of both of their projects, as well as the innovations of other Hindu leaders working on the margins of colonial cosmopolitanism.

REVISING TRADITION IN COLONIAL INDIA

As we have seen in prior chapters, Ramalinga developed his vision of Shaivism through creative engagement with Shaiva devotional and siddha traditions. This contrasts with cosmopolitan reformers who drew on Western models and ideas in developing new notions of Hindu tradition. David Washbrook notes that "Indian 'tradition' had been re-defined and structured into society under colonial rule, apparently to a far greater extent than 'modernity' ever had been."[6] While economic relationships, social status, property, and other forms of power were marked by competition and fluidity in precolonial India, the colonial state sought to stabilize or "fix" these variables through new regimes of taxation, property ownership, law, and polities. Legal authority shifted from one of "dynamic and contestatory processes . . . to the static principles of ancient precedent, hereditary succession and caste hierarchy."[7]

The bases of authority themselves shifted in colonial contexts, where written sources took precedence over oral ones. According to Washbrook, local elites, especially brahmans, sought to redefine tradition in ways that served their economic and social interests. They adhered to a new "rhetoric of right" that conferred authority on the basis of antiquity and textual documentation. This redefinition was characterized by stricter conformity to brahmanical norms, greater social stratification, greater authority of texts, and a notion that tradition is permanent and unchanging. What emerged was a "neo-colonial constructed 'tradition' of . . . Anglo-Brahminised 'Hinduism,'" within which claims for tradition were framed as existing in a static state from "time immemorial."[8] Likewise, elements of past tradition that did not conform to these criteria were increasingly marginal to central considerations of power. Washbrook reads these efforts as acts of resistance, in which Indian elites made claims to social and economic power, often at the expense of the colonial state. Of course, at the same time these were also acts of oppression, in which elite Indians consolidated their wealth and status at the expense of those who did not enjoy the privilege of a textual corpus stacked in the favor of upper castes.

The process of this redefinition of tradition was diffuse and entailed a variety of sites of contestation. Lata Mani has shown how debates about *sati* in the early decades of the nineteenth century occupied a range of actors, including reformers, conservative Hindus, and colonial administrators.[9] Despite their varied positions, they largely agreed that any argument in favor of, or opposed to, the banning of *sati* needed to be made on the basis of scriptural evidence. In cosmopolitan settings, these debates enhanced the status of brahmanical texts at the expense of everyday, customary practices. Rammohan Roy argued that "original" texts should guide the debate on *sati,* as ancient scripture could serve as "the only safe rule to guard against endless corruptions, absurdities, and human caprices."[10] For Roy, Dayananda Saraswati, and other cosmopolitan reformers, Hindu traditions had been compromised by centuries of revision and interpolation, and so they advocated textual fundamentalism in seeking an authentic, unified Hindu tradition.[11] Mani notes that this emphasis on textual authority was not, however, a return to earlier notions of tradition but was "a modern discourse on tradition . . . one in which both 'tradition' and 'modernity' as we know them are contemporaneously produced."[12] As Robert Yelle notes, it was also a Protestant discourse, one that took shape in the Reformation in opposition to Catholic ritual and idolatry.[13]

Law played a particularly important role in the emergence of these new notions of tradition. These legal contexts highlight the role of the colonial state in reconfigurations of Hindu tradition, usually in line with brahmanical ideals. Rosane Rocher notes that the bias toward textual authority was inscribed in Anglo-Hindu law at its conception. This judgment of canon as the sole authority was consistent with Protestant conceptions of *sola scriptura,* and it also reflected European views that Indian civilization had decayed from a prior golden age.[14] Davis and Lubin note that another of the effects of the imposition of colonial law was the redefinition of Hinduism as a unified tradition. "Aided by Indian social reform movements, colonial law helped to create a homogenous, unitary conception of Hinduism within which internal differences were hard to recognize."[15] Practices that did not conform to high-caste ideals, such as hook-swinging rituals in South India, were consigned to the realm of custom, rather than religion, with its lower level of legal authority.[16] This imperative to articulate a unified Hinduism can be traced to the beginnings of Anglo-Hindu law, which strove for "consistency" and "uniformity."[17]

These new notions of tradition took hold in cosmopolitan contexts. In the courts, the colonial state determined the criteria by which claims could be legitimated. Nicholas Dirks notes that European administrators and Orientalist scholars sought to build an archive of knowledge about Indian castes and customs, which also contributed to these processes of traditionalization. "Regulation and knowledge thus collaborated in the fixing of tradition, by which I mean both the stabilizing and the repairing of a canonic sense of what had always been done."[18] Christian leaders also played a vital role in this process, formulating a unified Hinduism based in brahmanical texts.[19] Indigenous actors were crucial in advancing these processes. Indian litigants exploited the biases of Anglo-Hindu law to secure property claims.[20] Pandits played a crucial role in providing evidence for courts, and they also were vital to the development of Orientalist knowledge.[21] Donald Davis and Timothy Lubin suggest "that modern Hinduism emerged through the force of government legal power and educated Hindu opinion operating in tandem to 'reform' Hindu institutions and practices."[22] They are certainly right to point to the Indian engagement with European institutions and ideals as central to this cosmopolitan redefinition of tradition, even if we can question their equation of this process with the emergence of modern Hinduism.

Mani highlights that one of the most important effects of this cosmpolitanization of tradition was to marginalize certain forms of authority, including orality and customary practices. However, outside cosmopolitan contexts, one might expect that these new formulations of tradition faced stronger contestation by views drawn from premodern conceptions or by novel expressions. Indeed, Ramalinga and Navalar disagreed not only about the content of tradition, but also about the very form tradition should take and its bases of authority. Navalar largely adhered to emerging cosmopolitan views that were coming to dominate reform Hinduism throughout India. Ramalinga, on the other hand, drew from prior Shaiva conceptions in describing tradition as flexible and living. His emphasis on orality over written text, presumption to make a new contribution to the Shaiva canon, and announcement of a new revelation all ran counter to new definitions of tradition as textual, static, and brahmanical.

Print served to advance both of these contrasting positions. Navalar and other reform leaders used print to expand the accessibility and influence of canonical works, while, as we have seen, Ramalinga used print to stake a claim for the canonical status of his own writings. Thus, it is difficult to argue that print better served established power or marginal voices. What is indisputable, though, is that print facilitated conflict between contrasting positions. It was, after all, the *printing* of the 1867 volume that sparked the conflict between Ramalinga and Navalar. The role of print in exacerbating conflict was not limited to colonial South Asia but was also apparent in early modern Christendom. As Elizabeth Eisenstein writes, "Heralded on all sides as a 'peaceful art,' Gutenberg's invention probably contributed more to destroying Christian concord and inflaming religious warfare than any of the so-called arts of war ever did."[23]

In nineteenth-century India, print facilitated the participation of new constituencies in public debate, and the capacity of print technology to propagate messages quickly and relatively cheaply made it an ideal medium for polemical exchange. It was in part due to print that critique was one of the primary modes of religious expression at the time, with religious leaders and groups engaging in often virulent debates and even litigation.[24] In Tamil, the acrimonious exchange between the parties of Ramalinga and Navalar was just one instance of wider polemics, as rapid religious, social, and technological changes led to hostilities over ritual, authority, and community. A. R. Venkatachalapathy notes that Tamil *kaṇṭanam* or polemical literature records debates between Hindus and Christian missionaries, and also between Hindu sects, primarily Vaishnava and Shaiva, with Navalar being the most prolific contributor.[25] This literature provides rich material for analysis, documenting important conflicts about community, authority, ritual, canon, and caste.

The chasm between the Ramalinga and Navalar factions encapsulates many of the tensions between two important contrasting formulations of traditions, marking a crucial divide in South Indian Hinduism over the terms of Shaiva community, leadership, and authority. After outlining some of Navalar's broader projects, I will look closely at his critique of Ramalinga's verses in order to highlight how his vision of Shaivism differed in fundamental ways from that of Ramalinga. Then, I will turn to a written response published by one of Ramalinga's followers. Their polemics illustrate the contrast between new forms of authority in colonial India and other, non-elite, less cosmopolitan considerations of religious power. As we will see, their positions are not easily described according to templates of reform versus orthodox, or modern versus traditional. My analysis demonstrates that tradition, like modernity, is a contested category that is ever-changing, and that both Ramalinga and Navalar articulated visions of Shaivism that were relevant to their world. More broadly, then, I question the equation of cosmopolitan reform Hinduism with modern Hinduism.

NAVALAR'S COSMOPOLITAN FORMULATION OF SHAIVA TRADITION

Arumuga Navalar (1822–1879) was born as Arumugam Pillai in Jaffna, Sri Lanka, an important center of Tamil Shaivism that also had an influential missionary presence in the nineteenth century. He was born into a Karkatta *vellalar* family, a dominant landowning caste. He had a traditional Tamil education, and at the age of thirteen he was sent to the Wesleyan Mission School in Jaffna for English schooling. He eventually worked with the missionary Peter Percival in Jaffna, helping to translate the Bible into Tamil.[26] He drew on these linguistic and cultural worlds—Tamil, English, Shaiva, and Christian—in developing his style of Shaiva revivalism and transforming Tamil modes of communication. Navalar's educational and professional history was thus thoroughly cosmopolitan, similar to reform figures in other regions of India. His recasting of Shaiva tradition shared much with the emerging cosmopolitan views of tradition discussed above. That is, he sought to reformulate a Shaiva tradition that was centered on texts, highly systematized, and elite in its authority and practices.

Through his translation work in the mission, Navalar came to regard texts as paramount in shaping a new and enduring religious community that could resist the proselytizing efforts of Christian missionaries. He asserted that divine grace could only be found in a closed corpus of texts, a view that led him to protest Ramalinga's claim of a new revelation. For Navalar, the touchstone for authority was always the past, not the present, and he rejected contemporary Hindu practices that did not have scriptural precedence. He worked to systematize Shaiva theology and ritual on the basis of canonical texts, most importantly, the Sanskrit Agamas and works of the Tamil Shaiva *Tirumuṟai*. Navalar's goal to establish a unified Shaivism was perhaps best exemplified in his campaign to standardize temple rituals, which often brought him into conflict with temple priests.[27] This was an elite project, since Navalar gave particular importance to the liturgical prescriptions of the Agamas, works that emphasize ritual hierarchies based on caste. His formulation required scholarly and priestly leaders to perform rituals and communicate ethics, theologies, and practices to a community of Shaivas. He received significant support from the powerful Tiruvavadudurai monastery in Tamil Nadu, which provided economic patronage and an institutional home, and which conferred on him the title of "Navalar," "he of the mighty tongue." Navalar's Shaivism was based on caste, scripture, hierarchy, and powerful institutions.

Although Navalar's message was elite, he sought to reach a broad audience of educated Shaivas, employing print to spread his hierarchical vision of Shaiva community and authority.[28] He engaged in multifaceted scholarly and publishing enterprises, writing prose renditions of canonical works, editing and printing classical Shaiva texts, developing school readers, and writing polemical literature. He focused his attacks on Protestant missionaries, but he was also critical of Shaiva institutions and leaders who did not conform to his view of Shaivism.[29] In his eager employment of print, Navalar was likely influenced by his work with Percival on a Tamil Bible translation and publication, and also by anti-missionary Hindu societies in Madras. These Hindu societies effectively used print to propagate their messages after the press in India was deregulated in 1835, allowing Indians to run their own presses.[30] On a trip to India in July 1849, Navalar bought a printing press in Chennai and brought it back to Jaffna, setting up the "Preservation of Knowledge Press."[31] He installed the press at his "School of Shaiva Splendor," which would challenge the missionary schools that dominated Jaffna education at the time.[32]

Among the earliest publications of Navalar's press was his 1852 prose rendition of the Tamil Shaiva classic *Periya Purāṇam*.[33] He intended that the work be broadly read among Shaivas, writing on the title page that "This book has been rendered in prose form by Nallur Arumuga Navalar, so it is readily accessible to all Shaivas, learned and otherwise."[34] Despite this goal to reach a broad audience, he was not advocating a sort of *solus Christus* or rejection of sacerdotalism. Rather, he insisted that all Shaivas should seek out an experienced preceptor and undergo initiation.[35] Navalar chose the *Periya Purāṇam* for his prose rendition because it upholds hierarchical principles while extending Shaiva community to a range of caste communities.[36] He considered it to be one of five works essential for Shaivas to understand, along with the *Tēvāram, Tiruvācakam, Tiruvicaippā,* and *Tiruppallāṇṭu*. These five works constitute the bulk of the Shaiva devotional canon, the *Tirumuṟai*. Navalar calls these works "aruṭpā," verses of divine grace, the term that Toluvur Velayuda Mudaliyar would later give to Ramalinga's verses. Navalar notes that these works are called "aruṭpā" because they were composed with the grace of Shiva, and because they could be used liturgically, recited in a variety of temple rituals.[37] For Navalar, the designation of a work as "Tiruvaruṭpā" stakes a claim for that work's canonical and ritual status.

Navalar's emphasis on textual authority, and his publishing efforts that made canonical works more widely accessible, shares much with the projects of other cosmopolitan reformers. As we have seen, Rammohan Roy and Dayananda Saraswati similarly redefined Hindu traditions on Vedic works, and they published commentaries and translations of these works in order to render canonical work in accessible language. These reformers took liberties in their translations and renditions. Dermot Killingley notes that Rammohan Roy claimed to follow Shankara's Vedantic reading of the texts, but he often diverged in his translations and interpretations from his claimed sources.[38] Navalar's rendition of the *Periya Purāṇam* was not always faithful to Cekkilar's original, as he made important deviations from the text to suit his agenda.[39] For these figures, past texts provided content for their contemporary reformulations of Hindu traditions, and they were also symbols of authority that reformers filled with new meanings and messages.

While much in Navalar's view of Shaiva tradition corresponds to broader cosmopolitan models of tradition, he also departed from these pan-Indian sensibilities in significant ways. By stressing the authority of the Sanskrit Agamas but also Tamil canonical traditions, his elitism was one that conferred power on high-caste, non-brahman, *vellalar* traditions like his own, as well as on brahmanical traditions. He highlighted the importance of non-brahman ritual roles, such as the singing of the *Tēvāram* verses in temple rituals, while upholding the primacy of Sanskrit in ritual practices. Moreover, he maintained close links with powerful non-brahman monasteries, which were influential in Shaiva scholarly traditions, and emphasized their institutional importance to Shaivism. As a non-brahman Tamil scholar, he did not hesitate to criticize brahmans whose ritual practices did not adhere to the Agamas, bringing him into frequent conflict with temple priests.[40] At the same time, he maintained a general commitment to the dictates of *varnashrama,* caste duties, by limiting authority to upper castes; maintaining that dalits should be excluded from temple worship; and advising that if dalits wish to undergo Shaiva initiation, they must seek out a preceptor specific to dalit communities.[41]

Navalar's insistence on the centrality of ritual practice also departed from other Hindu reform ideologies. He did not seek to rationalize Hinduism along the lines of a Vedantic view of philosophical monism. Gauri Viswanathan notes that many cosmopolitan Hindu leaders in the nineteenth century worked to distance themselves from Hindu iconographic traditions as a result of colonial and missionary critiques of Hindu "idolatry." These leaders turned to Vedanta as a rational, monotheistic Hindu philosophy, which displayed an intellectualism that was even superior to that of Christianity.[42] For Navalar, ritual continued to be central to Shaivism. He did, however, seek to transform temple ritual, attacking practices that might be characterized as "folk," such as the worship of minor deities or the performance of animal sacrifice.[43]

One further crucial departure from pan-Indian cosmopolitan sensibilities was his promotion of Tamil Shaivism rather than a broader Hindu community. He did seek to unify and systematize his tradition, but only Shaivism, and only among Tamils. This is, I think, in part due to his personal status as a *vellalar* whose claim to expertise was founded on his mastery of Tamil. The entirety of his publishing work focused on texts in Tamil, consistent with his education and upbringing in a *vellalar* family. Those Hindu leaders who formulated a unified Hinduism based their efforts on Sanskrit works that they claimed were the basis of all expressions of Hinduism. Navalar's knowledge of Vedic works appears to have been minimal, and it would have been difficult to formulate a broad, pan-South Asian Hindu community on the basis of Tamil texts. Furthermore, there are no important non-sectarian Hindu works in Tamil, so he was limited to a sectarian formulation. The audience he addressed, and the community he redefined, was a Tamil Shaiva one.

Navalar reformulated Shaiva tradition in a way that grounded its authority in Sanskrit and Tamil canonical works in an attempt to systematize its ritual practices and principles. He pursued this redefinition in a period of conflict and contestation. His new articulation of Shaiva community was born out of his opposition to Christian missionaries. This led to frequent polemics, and like some other cosmopolitan leaders, Navalar displayed throughout his life a love for controversy. He presented himself as a champion of native religion against the proselytizing efforts of foreign missionaries. Moreover, as a figure of the Shaiva establishment, he tried to marginalize and at times eliminate Shaiva texts and practices that he deemed to be contrary to textual orthodoxy. In particular, he attacked practices, ideologies, and claims to authority that did not adhere to Agamic strictures.[44] In the late 1860s, he turned his attacks to Ramalinga, whose canonical claims and assertions of an accessible Shaivism challenged Navalar's vision of a hierarchical community subject to the authority of established texts and leaders.

NAVALAR'S CRITIQUE OF RAMALINGA

The debate between these two camps, one loyal to Navalar and the other to Ramalinga, began soon after the publication of *Tiruvaruṭpā* and continued into the 1980s.[45] Ramalinga's followers made their case by assuming that Shaiva tradition was alive, flexible, and able to accommodate new revelations and scriptures. Navalar and his followers advanced a position that paralleled emerging cosmopolitan notions of tradition that I described above, namely, the closed character of canon, a bias toward textual authority, and the impossibility of a new revelation. They attacked Ramalinga's character and scholarly accomplishments, questioned his authority, and ridiculed the quality of his writings. Here I will discuss Navalar's critique, and in the next section I will detail the response of one of Ramalinga's followers.

The most important contribution to the conflict from the Navalar camp was by Navalar himself, a twenty-page pamphlet entitled "Pōliyaruṭpā Maṟuppu," or "Critique of the Pseudo-Divine Verses." Navalar published his critique in 1869 under the name Mavandur Tyagesa Mudaliyar.[46] As Venkatachalapathy points out, it was not unusual for authors to publish polemical tracts under false names.[47] There is common agreement that the author of the work was, in fact, Navalar.[48] The tone and content clearly point to Navalar's authorship, and the tract itself ends with the summary of a letter in Navalar's possession. It appears that Navalar gave lectures attacking Ramalinga and *Tiruvaruṭpā* at least a year before publishing his critique. One of Ramalinga's followers, Shanmugam Pillai, had already published a response to Navalar's criticisms in January–February 1868. In this response, which I will analyze later, Pillai gives a summary of a lecture by Navalar that includes many of the criticisms that Navalar would publish in 1869.[49] Although Navalar's critique was published two years after *Tiruvaruṭpā*'s publication, his public opposition to Ramalinga's work began at least a year earlier.

Navalar begins his critique with a list of five works that he describes as "aruṭpā." These are the *Tēvāram, Tiruvācakam, Tiruvicaippā, Tiruppallāṇṭu,* and the *Periya Purāṇam,* the same five that he named in his preface to *Periya Purāṇam.* Because they are regarded as "aruṭpā," they are qualified to serve as liturgical texts for a variety of Shaiva rituals. Navalar cites the text *Tirukkōvaiyār Uṇmai* as the authority for this view.[50] This is a work that advances an allegorical interpretation of the devotional and often erotic verses of *Tirukkōvaiyār.* The *Tirukkōvaiyār Uṇmai* has been important to monastic scholars, with the Tiruvavadudurai monastery publishing C. Dandapani Tecikar's 1965 commentary on the work.[51] Navalar cites additional Shaiva doctrinal texts, both Tamil and Sanskrit, that testify that these five works present the words of Shiva, because the authors of these texts, the *nāyaṉmār*, transcended ordinary perception and achieved knowledge of Shiva. He notes that "texts mentioned in the *Civarakaciyam*" confirm that the words of the *nāyaṉmār* are *aruṭpā*, and that their poems display the most affection toward Shiva of any of the Vedas. He refers to "*Tattuva Pirakācam*, etc.," as texts that outline the proper worship of Shiva and the *nāyaṉmār*. He also asserts that the recitation of these five texts has been a part of temple ritual from ancient times.[52] These five works cover much, but not all, of the *Tirumuṟai*, the Shaiva devotional canon. His list omits *Tirukkōvaiyār* itself, *Tirumantiram*, and the various works of the eleventh section of the *Tirumuṟai*. In highlighting that only certain works of the Shaiva canon are deserving of the name "aruṭpā," Navalar asserts a view that departs from more inclusive canonical understandings of Tamil Shaiva tradition.

According to Navalar, canonical status must be adjudicated on the basis of doctrinal authority and ancient usage, not on present-day assessment of the literary or soteriological qualities of a text. The claim of any work to be *aruṭpā* therefore requires the authorization of past tradition. For Navalar, this tradition consists of learned works that wield authority in Shaiva scholastic traditions. In citing doctrinal evidence for his position, Navalar suggests that the category of *aruṭpā* is closed and that only these five works qualify. For Navalar, Shaiva authority is scriptural, established in monasteries, and realized in long-standing practices that date to ancient times. His insistence on a limited canon of established texts was consistent with broader processes of cultural and religious debate in nineteenth-century South Asia.

Navalar then turns his attention to Ramalinga, presenting a contrast between this hallowed, ancient, scholarly Shaiva tradition, and Ramalinga's verses. "Currently someone named Ramalinga Pillai of Karunguli has composed a few poems so that the general population ('*ulakattār*,' or 'people of the world') will worship him, believing that he has realized Shiva. He calls himself 'the generous one with the splendor of holy grace,' and he calls his verses *Tiruvaruṭpā*. He has had one of his students compose a mythological account (*purāṇam*) about him called '*Tiruvaruṭpā Varalāṟu*,' which he added to the end of the work, published it, and is selling it."[53] Navalar worries that Ramalinga's influence threatens the recitation of the five established *aruṭpā* works in temples. "A few ignorant people consider Ramalinga Pillai equal to the Shaiva saints, and consider his verses equal to the *Tēvāram* and *Tiruvācakam*. They recite his verses when performing *puja* [worship rituals] and Shiva *darshan* [viewing the deity]. A few times in Chennai, at a few temple festivals, they have stopped reciting *Tēvāram*, etc., and instead recite Ramalinga Pillai's verses."[54] He portrays Ramalinga as a demagogue with followers who are complicit in perpetuating a perception of Ramalinga's divinity.

Navalar was right to suggest that Ramalinga presented himself as a Shaiva saint, as I have shown earlier. Navalar also stresses that Ramalinga and his followers are "selling" his work, implying that they seek to enrich themselves. Most troubling for Navalar, though, was the singing of Ramalinga's verses in Shaiva temples. The ritual recitation of Ramalinga's verses appears to have been widespread. A few years later, in 1875, in his long-standing dispute with temple priests and managers of the Kandasami temple in Jaffna, Navalar notes that even in northern Sri Lanka priests were using Ramalinga's verses.[55] This ritual use of new verses by someone claiming to be a saint, at the expense of established works authorized by long-standing traditions of exposition and legend, presented a clear challenge to Navalar's notion of canonical authority based in revered scripture, established doctrine, and ancient usage.

Navalar's response testifies to the growing popularity of Ramalinga's teachings and writings. It also highlights the emerging power of print. While Ramalinga's verses were being sung at temples even before 1867, the publication of *Tiruvaruṭpā* had the potential to further extend their influence. This is why it was the *publication* of the work that compelled Navalar's response. Navalar worried about Ramalinga's influence on the "ulakattār," the "people of the world." It is this broader Shaiva public that Navalar addressed in his own publications, so Ramalinga's book posed a direct challenge to Navalar's efforts. Navalar's primary concern was the ritual use of Ramalinga's verses, not that Shaivas would read them in quiet reflection. In Shaivism at this time, it appears that print did not replace orality but facilitated it through spreading content for ritual recitation.[56] With the publication of *Tiruvaruṭpā,* print helped to expand the content of Shaiva ritual. This was directly opposed to Navalar's publication project, which sought to systematize Shaiva ritual by limiting its basis to specific scriptures. These two important Shaiva leaders used print for contesting ends, highlighting the power of print to serve positions of established authority as well as critiques of that power.

Perhaps the greatest challenge that Ramalinga posed to Navalar was the potential to win over Shaivas to his vision. Navalar declares his concern for Shaivas, addressing his tract to "people of the world." He calls those who have begun to follow Ramalinga, and who have begun to sing his verses in temples, "ignorant," "simple people," and "fools." "These simple people have become confused and corrupted because Ramalinga and his students go around saying that he knows alchemy and performs lots of miracles, and his poems state that he has received divine grace." Navalar states that he has written this polemical tract to expose Ramalinga's deception of "those simple people" out of "sympathy" for them.[57] Navalar's concern for those who have chosen to follow Ramalinga suggests some overlap in the audiences that these two Shaiva leaders sought to address. Indeed, Navalar hoped that his publications would reach both literate and illiterate audiences, suggesting in the preface to his prose *Periya Purāṇam* that literate Shaivas read the work aloud to illiterate listeners.[58] Devadarshan Ambalavanar notes that Navalar addressed a collective audience of Shaivas, often using the term "caṉaṅkaḷ," "people," rather than specific groups such as priests, teachers, or scholars. However, this Shaiva public did not extend to dalit castes, nor perhaps even to low-caste shudras.[59] Dagmar Hellmann-Rajanayagam points out that Navalar's primary audience consisted of "satsudras," that is, upper-caste *vellalar*s like himself.[60] Ramalinga's audience would likely have been broader than Navalar's, including lower-caste Shaivas who would have been attracted by Ramalinga's stress on accessibility and rejection of elite ritual practices. This may explain why Navalar took such a patronizing attitude toward those people who were attracted to Ramalinga because of his miracle-working fame.

Navalar proceeds by presenting specific verses from *Tiruvaruṭpā,* focusing on passages in which Ramalinga claims that he performed extraordinary acts or had direct experience of Shiva. Navalar cites a verse in which Ramalinga declares that Shiva "entered inside of me, spoke secretly, and made me understand everything without formal study."[61] He points out that Ramalinga's education is in fact well known, and he questions the extent of Ramalinga's knowledge. "When saying that 'I knew everything without formal study,' does that mean all languages? Or only two, Sanskrit and Tamil? Or only one, Tamil? Is that all texts in Tamil? Is it all texts in the fields of grammar, literature, and philosophy? If that's the case, what is the explanation for all the errors in his published books?"[62] Navalar ridicules Ramalinga by literally reading Ramalinga's vague claim that Shiva helped him to realize "everything."[63] Most importantly for Navalar, Ramalinga lacks the formal training of the sort modeled at Shaiva monasteries. This critique of Ramalinga's scholastic credentials is one that Navalar repeats several times in his tract.

Although *Tiruvaruṭpā* is not a scholarly text, Ramalinga did produce two works in which he engaged in scholastic activities. These were a commentary published in 1851 on the doctrinal work *Oḻivil Oṭukkam* and a contribution to a debate about the proper use of the term for the northern Tamil region, "*Toṇṭaimaṇṭalam,*" published as *Toṇṭamaṇṭala Catakam* in 1855. Navalar ridicules Ramalinga's claim to have "realized everything" by pointing to his scholarly failings in the 1851 commentary on *Oḻivil Oṭukkam.* He criticizes Ramalinga's ignorance of a "basic doctrine that any educated person would know," noting that Ramalinga mistakenly includes Brahma, et cetera, in the intermediate class of beings. He lists grammatical mistakes that he found in the work and jokes that finding errors in Ramalinga's commentary is as easy as finding grains of sand on a beach. He contrasts Ramalinga to the seventeenth-century Shaiva poet Kumarakuruparar, who was dumb until he received the grace of Murugan when he was five years old. Despite lacking formal education, Kumarakuruparar composed a poem in praise of Murugan which was free of grammatical errors, and which contained the truths of Shaiva Siddhanta teachings. He is a celebrated figure in Shaiva literary and monastic history, taking initiation at the Dharmapuram monastery and later establishing his own monastery in Benaras.[64] Navalar expresses amazement that Ramalinga, who "lacks the learning of a child," has claimed a similar status.[65] For Navalar, grammatical accuracy was not just a scholarly virtue or an exclusively secular concern, but it was also a sign of sanctity and a prerequisite of sainthood. He asserted that scholarly learning was best exemplified in monastic institutions, making institutional affiliation essential to claims of revelation. Ramalinga was therefore doubly removed from Navalar's criteria for sainthood, producing defective poetry independently of the auspices of established Shaiva institutions.

Turning from his critique of Ramalinga's scholarly credentials, Navalar questions Ramalinga's reputation as a thaumaturge, ridiculing his claim to have lit a lamp using water as fuel. He cites a verse of Ramalinga's from *Tiruvaruṭpā:* "Oh friends of famed Chennai, listen to what I say! I lit a lamp with water, as if it were oil, in front of god."[66] Navalar then cites two other verses recounting this event, one from Velayuda Mudaliyar's *Tiruvaruṭpā Varalāṟu,* and the other Chidambara Swami's prefatory verse to *Tiruvaruṭpā.* He questions whether these two supporters saw Ramalinga light the lamp with water, or if they just heard him say that he did. Navalar focuses on the prefatory verse, which praises the power of Ramalinga's path by citing "the event when water had power to fuel a lamp's flame." The verse is attributed to "Chidambara Swamigal, of the Madurai Tirugnanasambanda Swamigal Monastery, the renowned seat of religious teachers of pure Shaiva Siddhanta based on the Vedas and Agamas."[67] This is one of the only references in *Tiruvaruṭpā* that links the work to monastic authority. Navalar seeks to question this connection, asking with some derision, which monastery does Chidambara Swami head? Navalar raises the possibility that Chidambara Swami did not actually write the verse himself, implying that it was Ramalinga or his followers who wrote it.[68] Navalar is clearly eager to cast doubt on that monastic connection, asking "people of the world" to examine these things.

Navalar then challenges Ramalinga to demonstrate the truth of Shaivism by repeating this miracle in front of a large crowd of people, both Shaiva and non-Shaiva, rather than "advertising it to friends in Chennai in verse." He contrasts Ramalinga with Naminandi Adigal, who used water to fuel lamps in a Shiva temple at Tiruvarur, to the consternation of Jains who had refused to provide him with ghee as fuel.[69] According to Navalar, for Ramalinga to verify his claim that his verses are *aruṭpā,* he would need to do no less than perform a public miracle.[70] Here, Navalar seeks to weaken Ramalinga's claims by casting doubt on his miracles, recognizing that stories of Ramalinga's extraordinary capabilities were contributing to his emerging authority and reputation as a Shaiva saint. He does not deny outright the possibility of the performance of miracles, stating quite clearly that Naminandi Adigal did indeed perform a miracle in public. Thus, we should not see Navalar's polemic as an attempt to thoroughly rationalize or disenchant Shaiva tradition. However, he restricts evidence for these miracles to the canonical past, dismissing the possibility of new revelations. Here Navalar clearly subscribes to a Protestant notion of revelation, as described by Yelle: "Many Protestants insisted further that, with the Passion, all miracles, magic, and mystery ceased, and the obscurely figurative language of both the pagan oracles and Jewish rituals was replaced by the illuminated 'plain speech' of the Gospel."[71] Ramalinga's verses announced the occurrence of miracles and the accessibility of Shiva in the present, presenting a challenge to a Protestant model of tradition that was increasingly coming to define elite, cosmopolitan expressions of Hinduism.

Ramalinga's claim that he frequently had direct interactions with Shiva was essential for his bid for authority, because he remained outside established Shaiva institutional power. Navalar thus seeks to undermine Ramalinga's accounts of his personal interactions with Shiva. He ask his readers to consider the following verse from the *Tiruvaruṭpā:* "My master and guru dances in the radiant hall, destroying darkness. My lord revealed his form which is divine grace, his beautiful smile on his bright face, and distinctly touched me with his precious hands. He opened his jewel-like mouth, came close, spoke, and entered inside me. This is something new!"[72] Navalar estimates that there are about two hundred verses in *Tiruvaruṭpā* in which Ramalinga claims direct experience of Shiva. Navalar asserts that these verses glorify Ramalinga, not Shiva. He points out that the benedictory verse by Ramalinga's "nephew" Ponneri Sundaram Pillai suggests that Ramalinga is an incarnation of Shiva himself. He challenges Ramalinga to glorify Shiva by performing miracles in public and by attacking other religious traditions. He contends that instead of these public displays, Ramalinga and his followers "hide" Shiva and announce that Ramalinga himself has risen up, bestowing grace.[73] Although Navalar does not mention precisely which "other religions" Ramalinga should attack, given Navalar's own activities, it is likely that he has in mind Ramalinga's silence about Christianity.

Navalar next recounts an episode in which a brahman priest at the prestigious Chidambaram Nataraja temple took on Ramalinga as his guru. The priest was suffering from some sort of illness, and he appealed to Ramalinga for help. According to Navalar's account, Ramalinga promised to heal him but abandoned him instead, and the priest eventually died. Navalar notes that "even after he had died, Ramalinga told the world in *Tiruvaruṭpā* that he had cured the man, didn't he?" He continues, "This priest, born of a lineage of such high caste, character, and education that they refuse to bow down even to the exalted Shankaracharya Swamis, he fell at Ramalinga's feet, taking him as his teacher, and Ramalinga did not cure him."[74] Navalar finishes his account implying that it was inappropriate, and ultimately foolish, for someone of such high caste to become a devotee of Ramalinga.

Navalar's critique is consistent with his support of caste hierarchies. He fears that Ramalinga's teachings and community of followers blur these caste practices, noting that Ramalinga had won the support of a few priests who had sided with Ramalinga and had rejected the recitation of the *Tēvāram* in temples.[75] These critiques express caste tensions between Navalar and his followers, on the one hand,

and Ramalinga and some of his closest acolytes, on the other. Navalar and the monastic leaders who supported him were high-caste *vellalars*, while Ramalinga's inner circle was composed of middle-caste groups who aspired to higher *vellalar* status.[76] Venkatachalapathy points to these caste tensions, noting that the Navalar camp referred to Ramalinga as "Ramalinga the accountant," a reference to his middle-caste background.[77] Ramalinga's accommodating formulation of Shaivism minimized the importance of caste, and in the case of his almshouse, and his verses published after his death, he was highly critical of caste. Ramalinga's vision for Shaivism was caste inclusive, and Navalar feared that Ramalinga would attract not only the poor and "ignorant" masses, but also upper-caste Shaivas, even those at the center of Tamil Shaivism, the Chidambaram Nataraja temple. His popularity, then, posed challenges to Tamil Shaiva caste structures, supporting claims to authority advanced by middle-caste groups.

It is unclear where Navalar learned the details of the Chidambaram priest episode. He mentions a number of other incidents that cannot be traced to the 1867 text, indicating that Ramalinga's legend went beyond that publication. These episodes provide interesting clues about Ramalinga's emerging hagiography. For example, Navalar reports that "for many years, Ramalinga's followers have entered every place, temple, home, and street, declaring that Ramalinga learned alchemy from Shiva himself; that he produced six large portions of gold through alchemy; that he would use that gold to build a town called 'Parvatipuram'; that he would build a golden hall there, which will spread the fame of Shiva, who will come to that very place and perform his dance; that they will feed all those who are hungry; that they will heal all the sick; and that they will teach all those who desire education." Navalar notes that the town is unfinished, and asks why they have not accomplished these things. He writes that Ramalinga made a promise to Chidambaram priests, in front of many people at the temple, in June–July 1866, that he would use his gold made with alchemy to donate two hundred thousand rupees for their purification ceremony. Navalar notes that the payment has still not been made. He ridicules Ramalinga, asking why, if he knows alchemy, does he "roam from town to town, begging for money and rice? . . . Why were copies of his *Tiruvaruṭpā* produced through the subscriptions of others?"[78]

Some features of Navalar's description, such as alchemical knowledge and the power to heal the sick, highlight tantric and siddha influences that were largely absent in the 1867 publication, but which dominated later publications of Ramalinga's verses. Navalar goes on to mention two additional stories that Ramalinga's followers tell about Ramalinga, stories that bring out more clearly Ramalinga's legend as an accomplished siddha with extraordinary powers. In the first, two of his students had come from Chennai to have *darshan* of Ramalinga. After meeting, Ramalinga gave them a magical pill that allowed them to fly. According to Navalar's account, they claimed to have taken this pill and flew back to Chennai at twice the height of a coconut tree, arriving in less than an hour.

In the next story, Ramalinga was speaking to a few officials in Chidambaram. Ramalinga suddenly moved a short distance away from them, explaining that his wife had just died in Chennai, rendering him impure. Three days later, news came from Chennai confirming the report.[79] While Navalar goes on to ridicule these stories, they suggest that Ramalinga's popularity at this time was at least partly founded on hagiographical accounts of his extraordinary powers.

Navalar asks his readers to conclude that Ramalinga is a fraud. "The poverty of one who calls himself an alchemist; the disease of one who calls himself a doctor . . . the poisoned, flawed knowledge of one who calls himself a wise man; don't all these reveal his words as lies?"[80] Embedded in Navalar's critique, however, is confirmation of Ramalinga's influence among the "people of the world" and a grudging acknowledgment that he has won the patronage of wealthy benefactors. Some people considered his verses equal to the most revered Shaiva works, and they appear to have begun to neglect these established works. Navalar asks his readers to carefully consider the truth of his tract, urging them to take hold of "the true texts of the *Tēvāram,* etc., recite them with faith and understanding according to custom, and attain salvation."[81] Navalar's concern, then, is not just with Ramalinga's students, but perhaps more importantly with his wealthy supporters, priestly following, and a general public that Navalar was himself courting. He hopes that these Shaivas will realize their folly and again respect established forms of ritual and authority.

Navalar ends his polemic with an episode that emphasizes the superiority of monastic scholasticism and the inferior learning of Ramalinga and his students. The incident was a confrontation between two of Ramalinga's followers, Velayuda Mudaliyar and Muthusami Mudaliyar, and a supporter of Navalar's position, Ramasami Pillai. Navalar describes Pillai as a disciple of the Tiruvavadudurai monastery, an expert in grammar, literature, and Shaiva Siddhanta texts, and a "trusty scholarly advisor" to the head of the Madurai Tirugnanasambanda Swamigal Monastery. Pillai sent Navalar a letter describing the dispute, and Navalar published it in his tract for the benefit of the "general public." According to Pillai's letter, the encounter began when Muttusami Mudaliyar arrived at the monastery in Madurai, worshiped at a small temple there, and announced that Velayuda Mudaliyar, Ramalinga's "first student" and a great scholar of grammar, literature, Vedanta, and Siddhanta, would arrive the next day for worship. He asked if there was a copy of *Tiruvaruṭpā* at the monastery. Informed that there was no copy, he offered to send one from Chennai, and he recited some poems from *Tiruvaruṭpā.* At this point Ramasami Pillai protested the visitor's provocations. Pillai notes in an aside that the prior year he had "chased away" a mendicant who came extolling Ramalinga's interactions with Shiva, his knowledge of alchemy, and his lighting a lamp fueled with water. Muttusami Mudaliyar tried to engage Pillai in debate about Navalar's objections to *Tiruvaruṭpā,* but Pillai refused to be baited, waiting to debate Velayuda Mudaliyar directly.[82]

When Velayuda Mudaliyar arrived at the temple two days later, Ramasami Pillai greeted him before testing his knowledge of Shaiva Siddhanta doctrine. According to Pillai, Velayuda Mudaliyar was only able to respond to his questions with a basic level of detail that demonstrated little understanding. Pillai then moved onto the issue of *aruṭpā,* noting that of the twelve sections of *Tirumuṟai,* the tenth, the *Tirumantiram,* and the eleventh, a compilation of works, do not have the proper form or high quality to qualify them as *aruṭpā.* The remainder of the works of the *Tirumuṟai* are *aruṭpā* and as such are sung in temples and at festivals. Pillai continues, "Ramalinga, wearing sacred ash and *rudraksha* beads, has given his verses the name '*Tiruvaruṭpā*' and divided them into *muṟai.* Is this proper?" Velayuda Mudaliyar and Muthusami Mudaliyar responded that the five canonical works were not called "Tiruvaruṭpā" in Chennai, claiming regional differences in naming these works. Pillai ridicules them for this view, suggests that they inquire about this matter at monasteries, which will confirm their error, and asks "what sort of Shaiva tradition do you follow?" Pillai then tells them that they must have gotten confused and changed the name of Ramalinga's poems from "street verses of confusion" to "verses of divine grace." At this point, Velayuda Mudaliyar and his companion declined to answer any further questions, got up, and left.[83]

Ramasami Pillai mocks Ramalinga by calling his verses "terumaruṭpā," "street verses of confusion," instead of "tiruvaruṭpā," "verses of divine grace." This clever play on words was to become emblematic of the position of Navalar's camp, and the debate became known as the "aruṭpā/maruṭpā" debate.[84] Pillai's appellation suggests that Ramalinga composed his poems in ignorance or with malice, and led astray those who were moved by them. Even more revealing was his replacement of *tiru,* which means holy or auspicious, with *teru,* the street. By referring to Ramalinga's poems as "street verses," Pillai characterizes them as common, public, pedestrian, unlearned, simple, and easily accessible. He insists that Ramalinga's verses were not in the same class as the elite literature of Shaiva tradition, celebrated by monasteries and sung in temples. As such, he rejects that Ramalinga's poems were "aruṭpā," suitable for temple ritual and worthy of esteem by educated Shaivas.

It is not clear, though, that Ramalinga would have rejected the "street" character of his poems, even in this period when he presented himself as a conventional Shaiva saint. In the 1867 verses, he celebrated the most accessible features of Shaivism, and in the same year he announced his almshouse to the poor. For Ramalinga, bhakti was not an elite genre, but one through which he could reach a broad audience with a popular message of equality. In his later poems, published after his death, Ramalinga abandoned established conventions and explicitly declared that Shiva was to be found on the streets, far from the world of doctrinal debates of the sort that Ramasami Pillai thrust upon Velayuda Mudaliyar. "Oh people of the world, you wander aimlessly, valuing caste, dogma, sects, noisy doctrinal debates, the disputes over lineage. Your wandering is useless, it is destructive and ugly. Stand in the good path of justice. The dancer is the only lord. Shiva's play of grace and light is occurring on the street. I call out: the right time has come."[85] For Ramalinga, the street was the new site of Shiva's activity, available to all "people of the world," regardless of caste or sect.

For those upholding monastic authority and privilege, however, the common qualities of the street were distinct from those of the divine. For Navalar and other monastic authorities, the presence of Shiva's grace was found in doctrinal and devotional literature and institutions that were best exemplified in monasteries, and, less adequately, in temples. Indeed, it was in the highly regulated private space of monasteries that Shaiva authority could be most tightly controlled. For Navalar, the semipublic nature of temples made them contested sites subject to influence from the "streets," as evidenced by his criticism of priests who followed Ramalinga and by his long-standing conflicts with Shaiva temples over the proper forms of ritual performance. For Navalar, Ramalinga, and others who were redefining Shaivism, these spatial distinctions demarcated distinct spheres of authority, possibility, corruption, and danger.

With his critique of Ramalinga, Navalar sought to reign in Ramalinga's emerging fame as a Shaiva saint who wielded extraordinary powers and composed poems worthy of the Shaiva canon. He worried that the printing of *Tiruvaruṭpā* would advance Ramalinga's claims of sainthood and accelerate the popularity of Ramalinga's poems and their ritual use. His worries were well founded: by 1899, Ramalinga's verses were being included in published compilations of the *Tēvāram*.[86] By insisting that revelation be testified by scripture, Navalar counters Ramalinga's notion of tradition as alive, flexible, and subject to change. He depicts Ramalinga as unlearned, an outsider to established institutions, and incapable of matching the literary standards of the Shaiva canon. Navalar's drew on emerging cosmopolitan notions of tradition in formulating a Shaivism that grounded authority exclusively in texts, located revelation in an ancient past, and resisted contemporary claims of miracles or of new revelations.

A NEW REVELATION: A RESPONSE FROM THE RAMALINGA CAMP

Ramalinga never directly participated in the dispute, but his closest followers did. The first published contribution to the debate was Shanmugam Pillai's 1868 "Tiruvaruṭpā Tūṣaṇa Parikāram," "Antidote to the Slander of *Tiruvaruṭpā*," which I analyze in detail below.[87] Velayuda Mudaliyar also wrote a lengthy response to Navalar's critiques in 1969.[88] The content of their responses adhere closely to Ramalinga's views of canon, revelation, the possibility of miracles, and the living character of Shaiva tradition.

In early 1868, Shanmugam Pillai attended one of Navalar's lectures in Chennai. According to Pillai, the lecture was advertised as a discussion of Shaiva initiation practices, but it was instead a sustained attack on Ramalinga. Pillai wrote a response called "Antidote to the Slander of *Tiruvaruṭpā*," which was published in January/February 1868.[89] In his response, Pillai summarizes Navalar's critical comments, which are almost identical to those in the tract that Navalar would publish the following year. According to Pillai's account, Navalar began his lecture by outlining the criteria for inclusion in the category of *aruṭpā;* he attacked Ramalinga for claiming to have performed miracles; he questioned Ramalinga's scholarly credentials; and he warned that Ramalinga was preying on "simple people."[90] Pillai's account indicates that within a year of the publication of *Tiruvaruṭpā,* the dispute between the two camps was under way. It also confirms that Navalar was indeed the author of the "Critique of the Pseudo-Divine Verses," as that publication precisely reiterated the criticisms that he was expressing in public lectures.

Pillai begins his response by questioning whether Navalar's attack on Ramalinga reflects Agamic sensibilities and scholarly learning. He cites two verses from the *Tirukkuṟaḷ:* "Virtue is acting without malice, envy, anger, and slander," and "Strive to learn, and after attaining faultless learning, put it into practice." Pillai suggests that Navalar does not know the meaning of these verses.[91] The *Tirukkuṟaḷ* is a popular work of ethics, consisting of concise verses that outline everyday behavior and wisdom. It is an accessible non-Shaiva text with no apparent sectarian loyalty. Pillai's quotation of this popular work signals a significant departure from the scholastic works that Navalar cites.

Pillai then questions Navalar's insistence that only five works qualify as *aruṭpā.* He asks where in the *Periya Purāṇam* Cekkilar says that the other four works can also have the name *aruṭpā.* He continues,

> Perhaps the authors of those five works appeared in front of Navalar, telling him that their works can be called "*aruṭpā,*" but no other works have the appropriate qualities so are not qualified to be called "*aruṭpā.*" Or did Shiva himself appear in front of Navalar to tell him this? Or did Navalar hear this directly from a voice from the heavens? Or did he receive Shiva's grace and become a knower of the past, present and future? Did he take on a human body that is endowed with the divine perfection of omniscience, and then declare that other than *Tēvāram, Tiruvācakam,* etc., no other texts have the splendor to be called "*aruṭpā*"? I've never known temerity like Navalar's.[92]

Pillai questions Navalar's authority to limit *aruṭpā* to only five works. He discounts the authority of Shaiva scholarly and theological traditions, highlighting that the most authoritative sources of Shaiva authority are Shiva himself and the Shaiva poet-saints, and they never expressed Navalar's position. He asserts that any texts with the appropriate characteristics should qualify as *aruṭpā.* When Pillai points out that Navalar does not know the past, present, and future, he implies that it is indeed possible for works of *aruṭpā* to be composed in the present and the future, not only in the past. By refusing to limit *aruṭpā* to revered texts composed in the past, he rejects Navalar's position that *aruṭpā* is a closed category of texts.

Pillai describes the characteristics that would qualify a work to be *aruṭpā*. He rejects that a poet needs to embody faultless virtue. He cites a verse from *Tiruvācakam,* in which Manikkavacakar describes himself as a flawed human being whose focus on Shiva wavers:

> Oh, my dead heart! There's none like you! You don't dance; you have no affection for the anklet of the dancer [i.e., Shiva's feet]; you don't sing, your body melting with devotion; you don't get excited [at the thought of Shiva]; you don't serve him; you don't place his flower-like feet on your head, and you don't even garland them. You don't search for him on every street. You are indifferent. Your actions confound me.[93]

Pillai also includes a verse of Tayumanavar, a revered eighteenth-century Shaiva poet: "When I reflect on things, my heart is frightened, and I can't sleep. Even if I escape this birth, what will happen in my next birth?" Pillai includes these verses from Shaiva poet-saints as evidence that in addition to all the joy expressed in their works, the Shaiva poet-saints also sang poems expressing their doubts, fears, and fickleness, in order that they might receive Shiva's grace. Pillai links Shiva's grace not with the scholarly accomplishments celebrated by Navalar, but with a humility that opposes presumptions of superiority.[94]

In these initial pages of his response to Navalar, Pillai draws on a specific set of texts to advance his argument. He cites Shaiva bhakti works themselves rather than the scholastic works that Navalar draws on. This allows Pillai to emphasize the parallels between Ramalinga and the Shaiva saints, particularly the human imperfections to which all Shaiva saints admit. Moreover, by citing Tayumanavar, a Shaiva poet whose writings are not part of the *Tirumuṟai* nor on Navalar's list of *aruṭpā,* Pillai extends the category of *aruṭpā* to a relatively recent figure. He points out that Navalar does not consider even the *Tirumantiram* to be *aruṭpā,* even though it is part of the *Tirumuṛai;* has a form similar to that of *Periya Purāṇam;* and its author, Tirumular, is one of the Shaiva saints extolled in the *Periya Purāṇam.* He asks, "who is qualified to attack in this way, looking at texts written by wise people and saying that only some can bestow grace, and others cannot?" He contrasts Navalar, who in his arrogance decides which poems are *aruṭpā* and which are not, and poet-saints like Sambandar, who shows the way to god by expressing their doubts and suffering.[95] He characterizes Navalar's attempt to limit the category of *aruṭpā* as an act of hubris. Although Pillai does not explicitly mention Ramalinga in this passage, he certainly considers Ramalinga to be akin to the poet-saints, and so the underlying contrast he draws is between Ramalinga and Navalar, between the wise, humble poet-saint and the worldly, arrogant scholar.

Pillai argues that many works share the characteristics of *aruṭpā,* not just the five that Navalar lists. He cites a verse that he attributes to the female saint

Auvaiyar: "*Tirukkuṟaḷ*, the four Vedas, the speech of the three Tamil saints [i.e., the *Tēvāram*], *Tirukkovaiyar, Tiruvācakam*, Tirumular's words [i.e., *Tirumantiram*], understand that all of these are the same." Pillai criticizes Navalar's attempts to disparage some saints and points out that Navalar teaches "high and low." He contrasts Navalar's attitude to a position of "great virtue" and humility, which entails seeing that all the poems of saints who have received Shiva's full grace are *aruṭpā*. Pillai continues, "Why, then, is Navalar now declaring that the work which has been published with the name 'Tiruvaruṭpā' is not deserving of the title of a new scripture, and moreover that the wisdom and experiences in that scripture are lies? Are such experiences [of Shiva] impossible for everyone in this present time? Or can one dare say that they are only impossible for Navalar?"[96] Pillai asserts that new experiences of Shiva are possible, and he explains Navalar's rejection of this possibility as an indication of Navalar's own lack of Shiva's grace.

Pillai attests that Ramalinga has indeed received the nectar of bliss from Shiva. He affirms that Ramalinga has performed many miracles, demonstrating that he is dear to Shiva; that he received Shiva's grace; that Shiva took pains to come to Ramalinga and embraced him; and that he deserves the title "benevolent one with the splendor of grace." He also extolls the literary quality of Ramalinga's poems, citing the following verse as an example: "Wanting to see you, Vishnu and Brahma abandoned their dignity and assumed animal forms, but they couldn't fathom you, benevolent one. I am a cruel man, with a heart as coarse as a husk of grain. Without any principles, I'm not able to know you. Oh pure one who dances in the hall, in your grace, manifest yourself to me. Otherwise, it will be impossible for me."[97] Pillai asserts that "when reading this verse aloud, it is clear that *Tiruvaruṭpā* has the same literary fineness that is exemplified in the *Tēvāram* and *Tiruvācakam*." Thus, Pillai argues, Ramalinga's work conveys not only the experience of Shiva's grace but also the literary qualities of the finest Tamil Shaiva bhakti works. He extols Ramalinga's statements that he is not worthy of Shiva's grace, seeing this humility as itself evidence of grace. Pillai cites Ramalinga's performance of miracles as further evidence of Shiva's grace, and asserts that Navalar, in denying Ramalinga's extraordinary abilities, also denies the power of grace. Pillai addresses Navalar's demand that Ramalinga perform miracles in public, pointing out that no one saw the saint Tirumular abandon his body, and that other Shaiva saints did not publicize their miracles. He notes that Chidambara Swami, head of the Madurai monastery, praised Ramalinga in a verse that exclaims the miracle of the water lamp, invoking monastic support for Ramalinga's abilities. He calls Navalar's denial of Ramalinga's miracles a "great sin," comparing Navalar to people of other religions who question the power of Shiva's grace.[98]

Pillai was certainly aware of the irony of comparing Navalar to other critics of Shaivism. After all, much of Navalar's polemical writing was directed against missionary critics of Shaivism and Hinduism, and Navalar criticized Ramalinga precisely for not attacking other religious traditions. Pillai writes that Navalar, in his polemical lecture, warned that Christians would ridicule attempts to claim canonical status for Ramalinga's poems, which would bring all other Shaiva works into disrepute.[99] If Pillai has accurately represented Navalar's position, it provides evidence that Navalar forged his new vision of Shaivism with an eye to the sensibilities of missionaries and other Westerners. Pillai responds that Christians and people of other religions are not Shaivas and so they can say what they want, and that Navalar should instead be concerned about what he is saying. Pillai's response indicates that Ramalinga and his followers had little desire to engage with Christians or to resist missionary evangelization. Pillai does not see Christians as a threat, and instead he viewed Navalar's attack as a more serious challenge to Ramalinga's teaching. He concludes by questioning Navalar's integrity, honesty, and closeness to Shiva. He reasons that because *Tiruvaruṭpā* facilitates experiences of grace, Navalar's polemic against it indicates that Navalar does not recognize Shiva's grace. He worries that Navalar is incurring great sin in opposing Ramalinga and "prays to Navalar's lotus feet" that Navalar joins the path of grace.[100]

Pillai's response adhered closely to the conception of Shaiva tradition that Ramalinga expressed in his poems. Contrary to Navalar's view of tradition, which paralleled emerging cosmopolitan redefinitions of Hinduism, Ramalinga and his followers asserted a Shaiva tradition that was inclusive and flexible. Pillai argued for a diffuse conception of Shaiva authority, one which did not depend on scholastic traditions of interpretation that were composed in the context of monastic institutions and established lineages of authority. He also promoted a radically different view of modernity, one receptive to the performance of miracles and the direct experience of Shiva. Pillai asserted these views by engaging with revered canonical literature, presenting a comparison of Ramalinga's poems and feats with those of the Shaiva saints. In other words, by ignoring the well-established traditions of Shaiva scholasticism that Navalar holds as the gatekeepers of authority, Pillai engaged in an interpretive enterprise, advancing his own reading of Shaiva tradition.

CONCLUSION

The debate between the Ramalinga and Navalar camps was most explicitly over the status of Ramalinga's verses and the authority wielded by Ramalinga. More broadly, it was about two contrasting visions for Shaivism. Navalar indicated this when he asked Ramalinga's followers, "what sort of Shaiva tradition do you follow?"[101] In his defense of Ramalinga, Shanmugam Pillai similarly asks, "what sort of Siddhantam" does Navalar where "Siddhantam" functions as a synecdoche for Shaiva doctrine.[102] Both camps, then, acknowledge that their debate was over the shape of Shaiva tradition, canon, and authority. Both stressed the continuities of their visions within Shaiva traditions. Navalar saw himself as carrying on the work of monastery-based Shaiva scholars, who in past centuries compiled, interpreted, and authorized the corpus of Shaiva literature. Ramalinga, on the other hand, bypassed this scholarly tradition by emphasizing links to the canonical poet-saints themselves. If Navalar was authorizing canon, Ramalinga was creating new canon, yet both situated their projects within Shaivism. They were right to highlight their links to past texts and traditions, and both were products of long-standing Shaiva traditions of education. However, they also innovated in important ways, and both of their projects were modern in the sense that I have been using the term. That is, both Ramalinga and Navalar were aware of the unique challenges of their present; both innovated in strategic ways that responded to those challenges; and both oriented their actions in anticipation of future trends. By looking at these two leaders together, it becomes clear that there was no single, monolithic, or perhaps even hegemonic, expression of modernity in Tamil Shaivism in their time.

The antipathy between the two camps derived in part from the very different ways that they conceived of tradition, history, and revelation. Navalar's sense of tradition reflected Protestant insistence that the miraculous was confined to a revered past. His denial that miracles or revelation could occur in the present posed a radical, temporal break between an enchanted past tradition and a rational present. Navalar and other cosmopolitan reformers insisted that this sacred past required translation in the present, which consisted of explanation in rational terms. For Navalar, scholarly traditions supported by established Shaiva institutions were required to perform this work of translation. He used publishing to advance this project, making available the teachings and messages of canonical works at the same time that he drew the boundaries of canon and its criteria for inclusion.

From the perspective of Ramalinga, however, there was no radical, temporal break with the past. Past tradition was not an object of authority to be interpreted from a radically different present. Rather, Ramalinga expressed a "lived" relationship with tradition, emphasizing the contemporaneity of himself and tradition. He described how the *nāyaṉmār* appeared to him, spoke to him, and inspired him. Rather than assuming a critical break with the past, Ramalinga claimed to be part of the assembly of Shaiva poet-saints. In promoting the most accessible aspects of Shaiva tradition, and in dismissing the importance of scholastic learning, he disputed Navalar's emphasis on the necessity of established, elite mediators. His poems describe his close, personal interactions with Shiva and suggest the accessibility of Shiva to all worshipers. He conceived of tradition as flexible, allowing new experiences of revelation and expression of canon.

Ramalinga's vision of a living tradition, a new revelation, and the immediate presence of Shiva was grounded in Shaiva literary and devotional traditions that were more than a thousand years old. His conception of the past, it seems to me, was more consistent with enduring Shaiva notions than was Navalar's formulation, which imposed a radical break with the past and thus with prior Shaiva tradition. Ironically, perhaps, it was Ramalinga's "traditional" notion of a flexible tradition that more easily accommodated innovation and change. In other words, Ramalinga's "traditional" orientation promoted creativity and innovation, while Navalar's "modern" formulation valued stasis. We might in this case consider reversing the usual dichotomy between static tradition and dynamic modernity.

The dispute between the two groups also reflects the very different positions of authority that they occupied. Navalar wrote from the dais of the powerful Tiruvavadudurai monastery, and he defended the hierarchies that characterized established Shaivism. He supported the ritual hegemony of brahmans, and he promoted the scholarly authority of high-caste *vellalar*s. Ramalinga, on the other hand, stood outside those halls of established Shaiva institutional power, and he advanced a notion of tradition that challenged those established powers. He boasted of having no human preceptor, and he identified with no lineage of contemporary worldly authority, instead placing himself in the line of Shaiva saints. The success of Ramalinga and his followers in effectively spreading their message is best testified by his many followers during his lifetime and afterward, and also by Navalar's response. Navalar's polemic presents important details of Ramalinga's emerging reputation as a saint capable of miraculous feats, and of the ritual employment of Ramalinga's verses in temples. Navalar's criticisms and ridicule of Ramalinga belie the very real threat that Ramalinga posed to Navalar and his vision of Shaivism.

Ramalinga's innovations drew on prior Shaiva traditions, but his vision was not simply a survival from the past. He and his followers were not blind to the shifts in authority and knowledge taking place in South Asian society. As we have seen, their sense of a tradition that is alive and open to new revelations allowed for radical innovations to Shaiva tradition. They developed a new ideology of charity that extended Shaiva ritual transaction to the anonymous poor. They exploited a newly available technology, print, to advance a vision of Shaivism that they hoped would have appeal across class and caste divisions. They conceived of bhakti works as living texts, pointing to Ramalinga's experiences and writings as evidence of the continuity of Tamil Shaiva devotional traditions and of Shiva's grace in the world. As we will see in the next chapter, their vision of a flexible and open tradition enabled a new configuration of yoga powers and religious community. Their articulation of a new Shaivism, and the appeal of their vision to people of varied castes, classes, and traditions, suggests that while they drew on established Shaiva idioms and models, they were not traditionalists stubbornly clinging to the past. Instead, they deliberately formulated a vision that could respond to the challenges of their time.

There are important conclusions to draw from Ramalinga's success. First, while new assertions of the dominating authority of scripture and the location of all revelation in the distant past were gaining prominence, particularly in urban colonial settings, these were not the only important ways that tradition was being reformulated. There was much potential for Hindu leaders on the margins of power to advance ideas of tradition that were less tied to cosmopolitan notions, but which were nevertheless timely, persuasive, and inspirational. Second, these divergent visions often came into conflict. In the case of the *aruṭpā-maruṭpā* conflict, no clear "winner" emerged. Navalar's scholarly legacy is well established, since he was a pioneer in the editing and publication of classical Tamil works. His vision of a systematized Shaivism certainly has its threads of continuity today, where, in temples like the Minakshi temple in Madurai, priests attend Agamic schools that seek to ensure that temple ritual is performed according to the Agamas.[103] But his vision never gained prominence outside of elite, scholarly circles.

Ramalinga's legacy, on the other hand, is more wide ranging. He is respected in literary spheres for his verse writing. He was appropriated by Tamil nationalists in the twentieth century as an ideological forefather because of his critiques of caste. Tamils of many castes and classes continue to revere his verses and sing them in ritual contexts. Groups in India and abroad perpetuate his vision and carry on his work, especially his outreach to the poor. His formulation of tradition has proved to be the more popular one, and in many ways the more modern one. When we look for the origins of modern Hinduism, we need to look beyond cosmopolitan reformers. We also need to look at figures like Ramalinga.

6

The Modernity of Yoga Powers in Colonial India

If Ramalinga's 1867 verses emphasized his place in a lineage of Shaiva bhakti poet-saints, poems published after his death led his followers and others to include him among the antinomian Tamil siddhas. The publication of the sixth *Tirumuṟai* in 1885, more than a decade after his death, was to significantly reconfigure his literary corpus and his Shaiva legacy. These verses were explicitly critical of cornerstones of established Shaivism, such as ritual practices, caste hierarchies, and textual elitism. The critical spirit of these poems, along with Ramalinga's claim to wield supernatural powers, contributed to his reputation as siddha, a poet who juxtaposed social critiques with miraculous claims. In these poems, Ramalinga was not seeking Shaiva respectability and, indeed, many aspects of their message is hardly recognizable as Shaiva. In this chapter I focus on these poems, and on this Ramalinga—Ramalinga the siddha.

It is as siddha that Ramalinga's status as a modern religious leader seems to be most ambiguous. In the poems of the sixth *Tirumuṟai,* Ramalinga ridicules the Vedas and Agamas; calls for the abolishing of caste; and promotes a community that is open to all, regardless of caste or class. He also speaks openly of his acquisition of supernatural powers, and he promises these powers and eternal life to anyone who joins him. If his egalitarianism appears to align with dominant conceptions of modernity, his promotion of the miraculous is contrary to those rationalizing processes that are central to those dominant conceptions.

This ambiguity lies at the heart of this chapter. I argue that the apparent contrast between a "modern" value like egalitarianism and a "traditional" belief in the miraculous only arises as a problem when we attempt to universalize Western modernity. An analysis of Ramalinga's project in terms of Western modernity may lead us to try to disentangle his project into "traditional" and "modern" features, assigning the miraculous to past tradition and his egalitarianism to modern forces, perhaps mediated by missionary or colonial agents.[1] I reject that approach for at least two reasons. First, the diversity of influences on Ramalinga—Shaiva, cosmopolitan, Western, missionary—are so complex, intertwined, and ambiguous, that it is impossible to untangle them in a clear way. Second, Ramalinga's promotion of the miraculous and egalitarianism were not two features that sat uncomfortably together. Instead, his invocation of the miraculous was a primary strategy through which he built his community and advanced his egalitarian teachings. He democratized the miraculous, promising extraordinary powers and immortality to a range of worshipers, regardless of caste or class.

This chapter argues that the combination of Ramalinga's egalitarianism and his promise of the extraordinary resulted in a powerful expression of enchanted modernity that was salient, even transformative, in his own time, and that combination continues to shape Hindu traditions today. As Peter Pels has noted, although scholars have "acknowledged the existence of magic *in* modernity, this acknowledgement was rarely accompanied by theoretical statements that reflected on the ways in which magic *belongs to* modernity."[2] I consider Ramalinga's promotion of miracles to "belong" to modernity, because it presented an innovative vision for thinking about liberation, ethics, community, and society, a vision that responded to his changing world. His formulation drew from a range of institutions and ideologies around him, and the changes he initiated remain influential in Tamil Shaiva discourse. My position requires us to understand his modernity in ways that do not emphasize the characteristics of a Western rationalism, and here he differs significantly from cosmopolitan reform figures who actively sought to adhere to the standards of Western modernity. It is precisely because Ramalinga did not adhere to Western notions of rationality that he has been excluded in narratives of Hindu modernization. By including Ramalinga's teachings in narratives of religious change in nineteenth-century South Asia, I advance a more pluralistic understanding of the emergence of Hindu modernity.

HISTORICIZING THE MIRACLES OF YOGA

The most popular accounts of yogic power among Tamil-speaking communities are narratives of the exploits of the siddhas. Tamil siddhas are Shaiva yogis and authors who claim to have gained extraordinary powers, *siddhis,* through their practice of austerities and also in their consumption of powerful medicines.[3] The Tamil siddhas are noteworthy not only for their possession of magical powers, but also for their trenchant critiques of everyday Hindu practices, such as the worship of icons of the gods in temples, mediation of brahman priests in rituals, and hierarchies of caste.[4] Their writings have often been shunned by established

Shaiva institutions, and until recently they have been relegated to the margins of Tamil religiosity.

In 1860s South Asia, there were various, and contradictory, ways that a number of groups and authors viewed Tamil siddhas and yogis, more broadly. Works of the Tamil siddhas were among the most frequent to appear in the early decades of Tamil book publishing, indicating that there was keen interest in siddha writings among Tamil readers. By 1870, many siddha texts had found their way into print, including works attributed to Agastya, Bhogar, Akappey Cittar, Konganar, Katuveli Cittar, Pulippani, Teraiyar, Civavakkiyar, and Uromarisi. These works included critiques of orthodox ritual and caste, and they also focused on a number of areas of practice such as astrology, medicine, alchemy, mantras, and other magical ritual formulae.[5] This period saw not just the publication of siddha texts but also the composition of new siddha works. In his study of the siddha Bhogar's 7,000-verse text, Layne Little posits that the work was at least partly composed just prior to its publication in 1888, noting that it mentions technological innovations such as parachutes and trains, refers to Rome and China, and includes English words.[6] It seems clear that many Tamils were editing, producing, and reading works attributed to the siddhas in the period of Ramalinga's activity.

Some European Orientalists and Christian missionaries praised siddha works as examples of Hindu monotheism, and they extolled the common anti-ritual sentiment expressed in these writings as an indigenous critique of idol worship and priestly corruption. In an 1871 work, Charles E. Gover described South Indian Hinduism as having an early "authentic" layer that was monotheistic, against caste, and looked very much like Christianity. According to Gover, this early "folk" layer was later corrupted by brahman priests who introduced superstitious beliefs and idol worship. Gover asserted that the Tamil siddhas exemplify this early tradition, expressing the purity of South India Hinduism in writings that were against caste, idol worship, and ritual.[7] This perception that the siddhas articulated a sort of proto-Christian Hinduism may have led to the popularity of siddha works among Tamil Christians. In an 1839 report on the contents of the Mackenzie Manuscripts, the Rev. William Taylor provided some notes about a manuscript of siddha Civavakkiyar's poems. Taylor remarks that because the work strongly criticizes brahmanic ritual, "I was told some years ago that the ascetics (or Pandarams)[brahman priests] of the Saiva class, seek after copies of this poem with avidity, and uniformly destroy every copy they find. It is by consequence rather scarce; and chiefly preserved by native Christians."[8] The social and ritual critiques of the siddhas aligned with Protestant critiques of Hindu worship and won Christian admirers.

If Christians and some Hindu readers were propagating the texts and teachings of the siddhas, many Hindu leaders in the nineteenth century disparaged siddhas or yogis as superstitious embarrassments to an essentially rational tradition.

Dayananda Saraswati extolled the Vedas as works that eschewed ritual and promoted monotheism and a sense of reason. In his *Satyarth Prakash,* Saraswati celebrates the principles that Vedic sages developed through "refined reason."[9] Saraswati speaks out strongly against Hindu traditions that he viewed as contrary to reason, such as astrology, alchemy, and healing. "As regards small pox goddess [sic], incantations, charms, mystic symbols and other magical devices, suffice it to say that they are all superstition."[10] He also objects to a range of important ritual practices, for example, *shraddha* funerary rites, which are "against the teaching of the Vedas and the reason [sic]."[11] Reformers like Saraswati singled out for critique practices that had no textual sanction, practices that were not coincidentally often popular among lower-caste Hindus.

Cosmopolitan reformers like Saraswati employed a specific notion of rationality that they drew from Western discourses. Brian Hatcher links Rammohan Roy's sense of rationality to European views, noting that Roy "was among the first to creatively engage both the Upanishads and the classical tradition of Advaita Vedānta associated with Śankarācārya (ca. eighth century C.E.) from a perspective of Enlightenment rationality."[12] As Robert Yelle points out, this sense of "rationality," which was monotheistic and ritually minimalistic, was largely based on Protestant traditions. "While drawing on indigenous sources, Rammohan Roy's and Dayananda Saraswati's views appear to owe more to their encounter with Protestantism and their desire to reformulate Hinduism as a more rational, simple form of devotion, suitable for modern modes of living."[13] The rationality of these reform leaders was one that replayed Protestant critiques of Catholicism, rejecting the worship of images, polytheism, and the plethora of rituals that make up everyday Hindu practice.

Saraswati's critiques of Hindu traditions extended to the attribution of extraordinary powers, *siddhis,* to accomplished sages and yogis.[14] In *Satyarth Prakash,* he defines ignorance in the following way: "To believe the . . . decaying body to be permanent . . . with the view to keep it on for ever by means of psychic energy or the influence of Yoga . . . is the first phase of ignorance."[15] He rejects the possibility that human beings can possess extraordinary powers or attain immortality, asserting that there has never been a person "who could change the order of nature set up by God. There will never be such a person. . . . No yogi or master of occult powers can alter it [God's law]."[16] Saraswati also recoils at the tantric links to yogic powers.[17] He derides tantric priests who announce their great power, perform murder rituals to kill an enemy, but then secretly hire men to poison their victim.[18] Saraswati rejects the miracles of yoga as contrary to reason and for their tantric associations.

For Saraswati, the powers are tools of deceit that dishonest people use to exploit the gullibility of the uneducated masses. His objections were partly based on class and caste prejudices. Like other reformers, he worked to establish a Hinduism based on elite, Sanskrit works, and his criticisms were directed toward practices and beliefs prevalent among the lower classes and castes. This elitist aspect of the modernizing project of Hindu reform parallels those in Europe, as described by Michael Saler. "From the eighteenth through the twenty-first centuries, elites have tended to associate wonders with the disreputable no less than the irrational, and during this period the self-conscious celebration of wonders and marvels has gravitated from elite to 'popular' and then 'mass' culture."[19] Thus, Saraswati disparages Kabir, a low-caste Hindu poet-saint whose popularity crosses caste boundaries. For Saraswati, Kabir was a fraud who deceived ignorant people, especially from lower castes, and who criticized the Vedas after his efforts to gain a Vedic education were rebuffed by brahman pandits.[20] Swaminarayan, the founder of a nineteenth-century devotional Hindu community that remains popular today, claimed miraculous powers in order to swindle "ignorant, simple and artless people."[21] Thus, we must see in this reform critique of *siddhis* not a process of objective rationalization, but the employment of a Protestant notion of rationality to advance a high-caste vision of Hinduism by attacking practices that were common across classes and castes.

It is the rationalizing projects of reform figures like Dayananda Saraswati and Arumuga Navalar that have received the most attention by scholars of nineteenth-century Hinduism. Ramalinga's project thus presents us with a "minority history" in the sense that Dipesh Chakrabarty describes it. "Such 'minor' pasts are those experiences of the past that always have to be assigned to an 'inferior' or 'marginal' position as they are translated into the academic historian's language." These are pasts "that the 'rationality' of the historian's methods necessarily makes 'minor' or 'inferior,' as something 'non-rational' in the course of, and as a result of, its own operation." For Chakrabarty, these histories offer the potential to challenge those dominant histories, and thus to "cast doubt on the 'major.'"[22]

The "major" history that concerns me here is the scholarly narrative of Hindu innovation and modernization in the nineteenth century, with its almost exclusive focus on cosmopolitan reform expressions of Hinduism that adhered to Western criteria of rationality. As we have seen, Yelle noted that Roy and Dayananda utilized Protestant rationality to produce a Hinduism "suitable for modern modes of living." For Hatcher, Roy employed Enlightenment rationality to fashion a Hinduism that "fit the spiritual needs of his generation. Rammohan's efforts during the 1820s to articulate a rational and modern form of Vedantic theism culminated in the creation of the Brāhmo Samāj in 1828, an organization and later a broad movement that would have immense influence across India." As Hatcher points out, though, this influence was largely limited to a bourgeois class of Hindus.[23] I do not want to unfairly critique Hatcher's and Yelle's outstanding works, both of which are important contributions to the study of religion in colonial India. I simply want to suggest that there were other projects to reshape Hinduism along lines that did not accord with Protestant rationality, but which nevertheless "fit the spiritual needs" of the nineteenth century. Ramalinga's promotion of the miraculous was one such project, and I argue here that it was as modern as those reform traditions that opposed him.

RAMALINGA'S ACQUISITION OF THE *SIDDHIS*

Ramalinga and his followers deliberated carefully over the sort of public persona they would project with the publication of verses in 1867. The editor of the 1867 work, Toluvur Velayuda Mudaliyar, pointedly noted that he possessed many of Ramalinga's poems that he would withhold from publication. He allocated these poems to a sixth chapter to be published in the future. "With regard to the sixth *Tirumuṟai,* which the great one [Ramalinga] gave us through his grace—there are those who decided that fate has determined that is not yet time for their publication. Enough said. I'll now describe the publication of the other five *Muṟai.*"[24] Mudaliyar's statement suggests that there was debate among Ramalinga's followers about whether to publish these more radical verses. By including only the most conventional poems in the 1867 publication, Ramalinga's followers chose to present him as a respectable Shaiva saint rather than a controversial siddha poet.

This sixth book was first published nearly twenty years later in 1885.[25] It is the longest of all six sections, with 2,551 verses of a total of 5,817 verses in all six sections, or about 44% of his verse writings.[26] This indicates that far from being marginal or secondary to Ramalinga's thinking and teaching, these radical ideas were central to his vision of a new religious society. The date of their composition is not clear, though given that Velayuda Mudaliyar seemed to have some in his possession in 1867, we can assume that they were not all written in the last years of Ramalinga's life.

Velayuda Mudaliyar, editor of the prior five chapters, did not contribute to the 1885 publication. His non-participation may indicate that he disputed the publication, as the poems of the sixth chapter would certainly undermine his goal to present Ramalinga as a conventional Shaiva saint. R. Venkatesan suggests that Ramalinga's "middle caste" supporters, which included Velayuda Mudaliyar as well as some of his financial patrons, were seeking to establish their position within established Shaivism. He argues that they therefore resisted the publication of verses that directly criticized established Shaiva practices and norms.[27] The title page of the sixth chapter states that it was published at the request of two "honorable members" of Ramalinga's "Society of the True Path." It states that "the goal of those who dare to publish this is to make it available for the general use of those of the Vadalur, that is Parvatipuram, almshouse. It is not for others."[28] The editors seem to have been responding to some controversy, or at least sensitivity over the verses, by clearly stating that work was only for those in the organization left by Ramalinga. However, they also would post the book to interested buyers: "Anyone who wants the book can send the book price and postage costs by money orders to: . . . " The volume was therefore both esoteric and freely available to anyone who could afford the somewhat extravagant price of three rupees and eight annas.

The title page lists the author of the work as "Ramalinga Swamigal." As a title, Swami indicates a high level of spiritual attainment and religious authority. When the 1867 edition of *Tiruvaruṭpā* was nearing publication, Ramalinga explicitly directed his followers not to call him "Swami" in the publication, hinting at some controversy.[29] It is no accident that this title appears on the sixth chapter of verses, which makes a strong claim to Ramalinga's extraordinary attainments. In this gesture we see a significant departure from the goals of the 1867 publication. If that earlier publication sought to establish Ramalinga in the lineage of Shaiva poet-saints, the publication of the sixth chapter cemented his status as a miracle-worker and vocal critic of established Shaivism.

Largely because of the poems of the sixth chapter, Tamils today often consider Ramalinga to be the latest in a line of Shaiva siddhas. Popular books that focus on Ramalinga's powers and status as a siddha reflect the contemporary popularity of both Ramalinga and the Tamil siddhas.[30] Scholars follow suit, with Stuart Blackburn tracing a siddha tradition from Kannada Virashaiva poetry to Civavakkiyar to Ramalinga, and Raj Gautaman noting the debt Ramalinga's sixth book owed to the siddhas.[31] It seems that Ramalinga had direct familiarity with Tamil siddha writings. In his 1882 biography of Ramalinga, Velayuda Mudaliyar wrote that Ramalinga could "recite the contents of the works of Agastia and other Munis," Agastya being a siddha whose authorship is attached to many works on medicine, alchemy, and magical rituals.[32] People began to describe Ramalinga as a siddha soon after his death, if not before, a logical consequence of popular perceptions of Ramalinga as an alchemist and miracle-worker. In the first complete edition of his poetry published in 1892, the title page describes Ramalinga as a "divine, great siddha," a convention followed by subsequent editions. In the biography appended to that edition, P. Ramasami Mudaliyar writes that just prior to his disappearance, Ramalinga told his followers that his body would soon vanish, and he would become a siddha for forty thousand years.[33] Since at least 1899, Ramalinga has been included in collections of siddha poems, such as *Patiṉeṇcittarkaḷ Periya Ñāṉakkōvai* [The eighteen siddhas' garland of great knowledge].[34]

In his own writings, Ramalinga does not refer to himself as a siddha. He does, however, frequently claim to possess the *siddhis,* which is the basic criterion for inclusion among the siddhas. The 1885 publication is replete with Ramalinga's claims that he received miraculous powers and other boons from Shiva. These powers and boons include the acquisition of a golden body, the ability to raise the dead, divine ambrosia, the *siddhis,* and immortality. Although Ramalinga's closest followers hesitated to publicize the siddha elements of his writing, Ramalinga himself announces often and with no ambiguity his attainment of the *siddhis.* He credits Shiva with bestowing the powers on him: "You brought my heart to life, and gave me the boon of immortality. You gave me all the limitless *siddhis.* You gave me, a slave, your great compassion. Such is your way!" (3848). In describing the *siddhis* as a gift from Shiva, Ramalinga departs from classical yoga traditions, which consider the *siddhis* to be markers of ethical, physical, and mental accomplishments that are earned, not bestowed by god. Ramalinga's characterization of the *siddhis* as a gift from Shiva indicates his dedication to a bhakti framework that is less pronounced in Shaiva tantra and largely absent in classical yoga.

Ramalinga frequently juxtaposes his depravity and the *siddhis*, employing a further bhakti trope that highlights the greatness of the divine in comparison to human imperfection. In his poem "Peṟṟa Pēṟṟiṉai Viyattal," or "Amazement about the great boon that was received" (3842–3851), he consistently cites his moral deficiencies. "I'm an insignificant person. What can I do? I'm lower than a dog who roams around the bazaar" (3844). "I'm below everyone, more insignificant than everyone else. Who will be patient with my faults?" (3845). The answer to this last question is Shiva, of course. "There is no one as degraded as me, yet you raised me up to the amazement of everyone. You graced me with a golden body, an unblemished heart, complete knowledge, wealth, the powers (*siddhis*) capable of doing anything one thinks of, and great rapture. Oh lord without equal! I proclaim: such is your grace" (3849). In these poems, Ramalinga departs from tantric Shaiva narratives of the acquisition of *siddhis*, which stress the eminence of the recipient.[35] An important consequence of Ramalinga's positioning of the *siddhis* in a bhakti framework is that he makes them compatible with human imperfection, effectively expanding their accessibility to all sincere devotees.

What are the powers that Ramalinga receives? He mentions a variety of extraordinary gifts: a golden body, perfect cognition, riches (presumably acquired through extraordinary means), and great joy. He describes Shiva's gift of ambrosia (*amirtam*), which he links to immortality (4960), eternal knowledge (4909), bliss (3693), freedom from bondage (3693), the Universal Path (3696), and clarity of mind (5489). Ramalinga considers immortality to be the most important of all of Shiva's boons, and he consistently emphasizes that he has transcended death. This claim was dramatically manifested when, in the last days of his life, he went into his residence, which he called "The House of Siddhi" (*citti vaḷākam*), locked the door, and never emerged. His followers assert that he did not die.[36]

The list of Shiva's boons indicates that Ramalinga was drawing on diverse sources and traditions. His specific characterization of the *siddhis* evokes Shaiva tantric traditions more than they do classical yoga. The *siddhis* frequently appear in Shaiva tantric texts from the fifth to sixth century.[37] This corpus of texts views the *siddhis* as instruments of amusement and enjoyment that are thoroughly worldly in their application and benefits. Rather than describing the attainment of *siddhis* through ethical purification and ascetic discipline as in classical yoga, tantric works outline mantra-based rituals for attaining *siddhis*, including immortality, the power of flight, and sexual enjoyment of women in "subterranean paradises."[38] Ramalinga's account of the *siddhis* contains some of this tantric flavor. He describes them as "countless" powers that he commands "at all times in the world and the heavens" (4961). With the *siddhis* one can do "everything one can imagine" (3849). Ramalinga associates the *siddhis* with pleasure, worldly action, and play or sport, exclaiming to his reader that "the holy day when we play with the *siddhis* has dawned" (4906); he uses the *siddhis* to "dance in every world" (3692).

Others boons confirm this tantric influence and suggest other sources of inspiration. Ramalinga claims that Shiva "gave me a youthful, golden body that never perishes" (3869), suggesting Tamil siddha alchemical and medical influences.[39] As we have seen, hagiographies of Ramalinga refer to his alchemical powers, and Navalar reported that Ramalinga himself claimed to be able to produce gold. Tamil siddhas are frequently attributed with alchemical powers, an attribution that is consistent with pan-Indian siddha traditions.[40] The claim to have undergone a perfection of cognitive processes and to have received clarity of mind evokes classical yoga goals. Finally, "great joy" (3849) is a central promise of Tamil Shaiva bhakti. While it includes some of the resonances of material pleasure, it also points to a transcendent joy that surpasses the possibilities of materiality. Thus, Ramalinga described his extraordinary powers in ways that have precedence in Shaiva traditions that characterize much of Ramalinga's thinking: yoga, bhakti, tantra, and siddha.

An additional point of difference with yoga and tantric traditions, but more in line with siddha traditions, is that Ramalinga consistently links the *siddhis* to liberation. In the *Yoga Sutras,* Patanjali advises that the attainment of the *siddhis* is not the final stage of yogic accomplishment, but that one must be dispassionate toward the powers and go beyond them, pointing to the dangers of pride and attachments due to these "enticements of the gods."[41] Somadeva Vasudeva notes that in Shaiva tantric traditions, the *siddhis* are associated with enjoyment more than they are with liberation. "When Śaiva religious activities are classified teleologically into the pair of those that are conducive to liberation (*mokṣa, mukti*) and those that are conducive to experience or enjoyment (*bhoga, bhukti*), the latter goal is often synonymous with the *siddhi.*"[42]

Ramalinga, however, generally describes the *siddhis* as a feature of liberation. He praises Shiva: "you destroyed the cruel bonds of illusion, karma and arrogance that afflicted me. You turned my heart into a holy temple; you gave me all the *siddhis;* you turned my body into a golden body, and fed me fresh ambrosia" (3866). Ramalinga regularly speaks of the acquisition of the *siddhis* alongside other soteriological accomplishments, suggesting their equality. "I realized that the state of Shiva (*civam*) is unified, and at the very moment I realized this, I reached a state of true understanding. And lo and behold, I received all the true *siddhis,* which are the fruits of devotion to the dancer in the hall of Chidambaram" (5499). While other Hindu traditions clearly consider the *siddhis* to be derivative or auxiliary to liberation, or even obstacles to liberation, for Ramalinga the *siddhis* are part of liberation, and the pleasures of the *siddhis* are consistent with the joy of liberation.

Ramalinga's incorporation of the *siddhis* into a bhakti framework made the *siddhis* a powerful tool in his nineteenth-century context. He cannot take credit for this particular innovation, however. Rather, as David Shulman notes, Tayumanavar had similarly sought to integrate aspects of yoga and bhakti traditions about a century and a half before Ramalinga wrote his poems. Shulman notes that Tayumanavar was influenced by classical yoga and especially by medieval tantric yoga traditions that emphasize "magical transformation of the body and world in the direction of immortality, physical and psychic power, alchemical effects, and antinomian attitudes towards social order."[43] Tayumanavar sought the *siddhis* and alchemical knowledge, and also yogic equanimity. He emphasized that the *siddhis* fall short of true realization, however, which he conceived as a state of mental control and contemplative tranquility.[44] Ramalinga, unlike Tayumanavar, placed the *siddhis* at center stage and made them part of his soteriological goals. By lowering the intellectual and practical demands for the *siddhis,* he made their attainment a possibility for any sincere Shaiva worshiper.

What is missing from Ramalinga's claim to have received the *siddhis,* and from his specific description of the character of these powers, is any rationalizing sensibility that we saw at work among cosmopolitan reformers. His claim to possess powers was directly contrary to reformist rationalities that sought to locate the miracles of Hindu traditions in the past, and that recoiled at the attribution of extraordinary powers to any living person. As we will see in the next section, however, this does not mean that Ramalinga was in no way influenced by cosmopolitan discourses.

RAMALINGA'S PROMOTION OF THE *SIDDHIS*: THE SOCIETY OF THE TRUE PATH

By dropping yoga's demand that the *siddhis* can only be achieved after rigorous physical and mental practice, and tantra's demand for esoteric ritual knowledge, Ramalinga was able to introduce a community of devoted householders who would all possess the *siddhis,* most importantly, the boon of immortality. This democratization of the *siddhis* was consistent with other features of his teachings and reflected his vision for social transformation of his world. Here I examine Ramalinga's voluntary society and his promotion of the *siddhis* to Shaivas of a broad range of castes and classes.

In 1865, Ramalinga established the "Camaraca Veta Caṉmārka Caṅkam," the Society of the True Path that is Common to All Scripture.[45] He conceived of his society as an organization that would embody his teachings, which he called the "True Path," and which would put those teachings into practice to effect social change. The society was at the center of a broad range of institutions and initiatives. An 1867 announcement states that the members intended to establish a number of branches that would be part of the society, including those specializing in medicine, textual study, service, development, ritual worship, law, and yoga.[46] It is not clear whether the society successfully established these branches. They did, as we have seen, establish an almshouse in 1867 to enact this ideology of ritual giving. In 1872 they finished construction of a temple, the "Cattiya Ñāṉa Capai" (Temple of True Knowledge), that housed an image of god as fire that they called "aruṭperuñjōti," "The Great Light of Grace."[47] The temple and almshouse served as the center of worship for the community during Ramalinga's lifetime, and they remain in use today.

The society had a formal, if loose, structure. Two fliers that announced the opening of the almshouse in 1867 give some indication of its organization. One was signed by "M. Appasamy Chetty, a member of the Society of the True Path, on the command of Chidambaram Ramalinga Pillai, head of the Almshouse of Unity."[48] Membership seems to have been deliberately taken and recognized by others of the society. The second announcement was signed by the "Members of the Society of Unity," indicating that the society consisted of a group of members that acted in a concerted way.[49] One of the few pieces of evidence that gives us detailed information of the society membership is a list of those who made financial contributions toward the establishment of a journal called "Caṉmārkka Vivēka Virutti [The Nature of the Wisdom of the True Path]."[50] The list, dated from 1867, includes forty-nine names, their places of residence, and amount contributed. A variety of towns are named, most in the Pondicherry-Cuddalore-Vadalur-Chidambaram region, with little representation from Chennai. The caste composition includes a range of communities, including brahmans (Aiyars), merchants (Naidu, Chetty, Reddy), Mudaliyars, Pillais, at least one Muslim (Kadhar Sahib), and a number of names with no caste marker, which may indicate dalit castes, such as Velayudam, Arumugam, and Arangasamy.[51] It seems clear that at least to some degree, Ramalinga's society successfully transcended the caste distinctions that he attacked so forcefully.

Ramalinga declared himself to be the indisputable human leader of his Society of the True Path, stating that he was chosen by Shiva himself to spearhead a new movement. He writes of the public nature of this selection, where Shiva singles out Ramalinga as the special recipient of his grace in conspicuous public displays. He sings that Shiva "crowned" him "with all the world looking on," a clear gesture toward his leadership claims (4166). "All the flawless people of the world, they really saw this. He of the hall of the lord raised lowly me above the realm of words with brilliant light and gave me the nectar of grace" (4825). It is not quite clear who, precisely, Ramalinga refers to as witnesses to these acts of grace, and perhaps the ambiguity of this reference would allow any followers to consider themselves part of this audience.

Ramalinga's founding of a voluntary society appears to have been influenced by cosmopolitan models of religious organization. Ulrike Stark notes the proliferation of such associations in North India after the 1857 rebellion. These associations "emulated British models," allowing "educated Indians to actively participate in the grand 'project' of modernity." They advanced "a civilising project based on notions of individual morality and merit, civic participation, public service and social reform."[52] Ramalinga's society embodied this sort of project, as an association of like-minded individuals who would implement his social and ethical vision of nonviolence, compassion, and social inclusivity. Individuals could join on a voluntary basis, in contrast to established Shaiva forms of inclusion based on lineage and caste. This elective society internalized important features of Western discourses of religion, namely, the notion that religion is a matter of individual choice; that religious communities should advance social change; an assertion that all worshipers, regardless of caste, have access to god; and the emphasis on personal conscience and ethics as central features of a religious community.[53]

Ramalinga's verses in the sixth volume of *Tiruvaruṭpā* emphasized compassion and nonviolence as central features of his society. Ramalinga reports that Shiva instructed him: "All those who have compassion are part of the True Path. Join with them here, come and enjoy, playing on the subtle path of good grace" (4163). Ramalinga makes nonviolence the central criterion for inclusion in his society, singing, "My guru [Shiva] directed me: 'Shun those who perpetuate killing; all others are part of your clan. You are the head of my clan, oh son! Act so that the Unified, True Path of Pure Shaivism, which destroys delusion, will flourish'" (4159). When Ramalinga condemns killing, he particularly has in mind meat-eating, asserting that Shiva told him that "those who perpetual killing and enjoy eating flesh are cruel people" (4162). He directs his followers to show compassion to meat-eaters, but also to avoid associating with them (4162). In defining the boundaries of his community through individual ethical behavior, Ramalinga departs from tantric and siddha paths that highlight technical skill and alchemical knowledge. He also departs from established Shaiva traditions of his day, which made caste a central criterion for community belonging and for religious authority. Ramalinga's community was ideally open to all, but because vegetarian and nonvegetarian diets have caste associations in South India, brahmans and vegetarian *vellalar*s would have found it easiest to meet his dietary demands.

If Ramalinga's society shared the social and ethical objectives, and the form, of many cosmopolitan reform societies, his emphasis on the miraculous was a point of radical difference. Stark notes that voluntary associations in the period sought to advance scientific knowledge. The group that was the focus of her study, Jalsah-e Tahzib, described their first objective as undertaking "the necessary efforts in giving currency to useful arts and sciences," signaling their dedication to advancing scientific rationalism in Indian society.[54] Ramalinga outlined a goal that directly challenged this rationalism: he based his leadership credentials on his possession of the *siddhis,* and he promised that those who joined his society would themselves acquire supernatural powers and initiate Shiva's physical coming to raise the dead to life.

Ramalinga invites his followers to share in Shiva's grace and the *siddhis* through him. He describes a present world characterized by the proliferation of the extraordinary. "The light of grace is flourishing, the darkness of night is disappearing, my heart is overflowing, auspicious things are happening, a golden hue is everywhere, the woman who is the *siddhis* is mating" (3758). The *siddhis* are thus not just individual achievements, as in classical yoga or tantric traditions, but they are divine gifts that can be shared and enjoyed collectively. Ramalinga gives his own attainment of the *siddhis* an evangelistic imperative, emphasizing that Shiva favored him so that Ramalinga would carry Shiva's message to the world. "My father gave to me, a person of this world, the ability to see the entire world and all worlds. I will continue to pursue my path, making all beings join the society of the True Path" (5514). Indeed, here Ramalinga claims to employ the *siddhis* to recruit members to his society.

Ramalinga enticed his audience with promises that they, too, could receive grace and extraordinary powers from Shiva. He warns them of their impending deaths and offers his society as a path to immortality. "Thinking, I have honor and connections, you rejoice proudly here. You don't know the secret place. Haven't you heard the news that angry Yama, the god of death, is coming? Don't you think even a little bit about your relatives who have died?" (5573). In his poem "Tiruvuntiyār," "They Who Play the Holy Game," Ramalinga invites a companion to join in and "play the game." "Play the game of *unti*, chanting 'I saw my father, and attained the boon of immortality.' Play the game, chanting 'I can perform all the *siddhis*.' Play the game, chanting 'I gained liberation, and with that liberation I gained the siddhi of knowledge.' Play the game, chanting 'I am a siddha'" (4903–4904). He promises that playing the game will remove his listeners from the sorrows of the world and will deliver to them the highest powers imaginable.

What game is Ramalinga playing? It appears to have at least two components. One is conventional devotion to Shiva. "So that even people who are old with wrinkles will attain youth, so that the dead will rise again, the accomplished one, capable of depicting and doing everything, performs the dance of knowledge. This is the time he is coming! You shall attain this boon. Dissolving, the heart melting, your eyes widening, think joyously inside of god of the dance of compassion" (5583). Ramalinga suggests that his followers will receive Shiva's extraordinary boons through quite ordinary cognitive and emotional registers of Shaiva worship. "Thinking of him, experiencing him, your heart melting, full of love for him, your body wet with your tears . . . praise him, people of the world, and you can live a life without dying" (5576).

However, according to Ramalinga, conventional modes of bhakti worship are not enough to secure immortality. One must also join Ramalinga's community, the Society of The True Path. "Oh you who are dear to me, come here and join the Society of the True Path! You can live, praised by the entire world of pleasures. You can obtain divinity and the *siddhis*, capable of all actions" (5580). Ramalinga claims that his society's True Path is the only one that will lead to immortality. "Take on bodies that are indestructible in the three times. . . . People of the world, see that the auspicious opportunity is here and now. This is the time of the coming of my father, the great lord of the light of grace . . . come and attain the True Path, the imperishable holy path" (5586). "People of the world, up until now, you haven't known the truth. Now follow the True Path of Unity and realize deep truths. Accept my father's grace, and you will receive the boon of immortality. You will have bliss" (5579). In a "confidential" circular dated April 27, 1870, Ramalinga tells his followers that their society will flourish once "we receive wisdom, and from that day on, our dead friends, relatives, neighbors, youth, children, sons and daughters, men, and women, all of them will be revived."[55] Ramalinga offers physical, bodily immortality not only to those who join his path, but even to their dead loved ones.

Ramalinga's promise of the *siddhis* to those who join him is consistent with the way that yoga, tantra, and siddha traditions have utilized the *siddhis* as enticements for centuries.[56] Tamil siddha medical traditions today continue to search for powerful medicines that might bestow immortality, while tantric traditions detail techniques to bring the world under one's control for the sake of pleasure and power. Ramalinga follows these traditions, but he significantly reduces the threshold of expertise required, offering the *siddhis* through a relatively simple path of virtuous action, bhakti, and dedication to his True Path. This is consistent with his larger project of making the highest goals of Shaivism accessible to ordinary worshipers and of establishing a broad community of householders. To this end, he found an ideal organizational model in emerging voluntary associations, which brought together like-minded individuals who shared an ethical orientation and pursued their goals in concert. He was not, then, limited by a "traditional" orientation but drew liberally from a variety of teachings and models that were available to him.

RAMALINGA'S CRITIQUES OF CASTE, SCRIPTURE, AND ESTABLISHED TRADITIONS

In addition to his literary contributions, Ramalinga is probably best known today for his attacks on caste and established religious traditions. As we have seen in prior chapters, his early poems hinted at a critical attitude toward elite, exclusionary Shaiva practices. The sixth volume of verses gives explicit voice to these critiques and sets out his vision for an alternative to established Shaivism, one that would include a range of castes and classes.

It seems clear that Ramalinga was drawing on Tamil siddha traditions in formulating these critiques. Kamil Zvelebil describes the writings of the Tamil siddhas as "a protest, sometimes expressed in very strong terms, against the formalities of life and religion; rough handling of priests and brahmins in general; denial of the religious practices and beliefs of brahmanism, and not only that: an opposition against the generally pan-Indian social doctrine and religious practice; protest against the abuses of temple-rule; emphasis on the purity of character."[57] Although Ramalinga does not single out brahmans for critique, he shares this siddha spirit of protest against elite practices. His attacks centered most on the non-brahman, *vellalar* institutions that dominated Shaivism; the scholastic traditions of those institutions; and the textual and ritual elitism associated with them. Ramalinga's attacks on social hierarchy, and his emphasis on *siddhis* and immortality, clearly indicate that his central ethical positions were influenced by siddha traditions. It is likely that contemporary debates also informed Ramalinga's critiques, as a variety of colonial, reformist, and missionary leaders engaged in acrimonious exchanges about caste, scriptural authority, and ritual practice.

In these poems, Ramalinga attacks religious traditions that were prevalent in his day, distinguishing his society from established traditions. He most often refers to other religious traditions as "matam" or "camayam," terms that are most often today translated as "religion."[58] When he uses these terms, he does not have in mind a group of world religions and does not describe a comprehensive phenomenon. Thus, the term "religion," taken in the modern sense, to translate his use of *matam* or *camayam,* is misleading. I will leave the terms untranslated or occasionally translate both as "tradition." Ramalinga uses these terms to refer to specific traditions that were active around him or that he knew through Tamil literature. He never refers to his True Path as a *matam* or *camayam,* consistently calling it a path, a "neṟi." He describes *matam* and *camayam* only in negative terms, pointing to "the troubles of *matam* and *camayam*" (3319), "a sinful path of *camayam* and *matam*" (3696), "nauseating *matam*" (3709), and "foolish *matam*" (5592).

Ramalinga speaks of all religious traditions other than his own as *matam* and *camayam.* He writes that Shiva told him that "all the heads of *matam,* such as Brahma, Shiva, Vishnu, the other gods, the famed Buddha and Mahavira, they are just a gang of small children, who appeared in the heavens, saw a little bit of god's light, and played around in heaven and earth like they're drunk" (4178). Here Ramalinga's conception of religious community is not derived from a World Religions discourse, but draws from a Shaiva literary world in which Shaiva traditions vied for preeminence with Vaishnava, Buddhist, and Jain traditions, as described in the *Tēvāram* and *Periya Purāṇam.* His critiques of a range of traditions reveal an attitude of exclusivity that is contrary to common perceptions of Ramalinga as an ecumenical unifier.

Ramalinga defines his path against Buddhist, Jain, and other Hindu paths, but I have not found references to Christianity or Islam in his writings. This does not mean that he was unaware of these traditions, or even that he was not influenced by them. Islam had a significant presence in his region at the time he wrote, and the impact of Christian missions was extensive. However, as I have argued throughout these pages, it is difficult to posit specific influences of these traditions in the absence of clear evidence. His conception of the religious landscape of central Tamil Nadu was shaped by the traditional Tamil Shaiva literature that he knew, including the canonical bhakti works of the *Tēvāram* and the *Periya Purāṇam*. We might posit that the world that he lived in was distinct from the world that he described in his writings. This, however, was not the case. His writings on hunger responded to an environment of food shortages and even famine. Likewise, his writings on caste and the failings of other traditions express his concern for the society in which he lived. His most sustained critiques refer to specific aspects of Hindu traditions that were influential in his time and place. Why he chose to forgo direct reference to Christianity and Islam in his writings is something of a mystery. In any case, this sets him apart from Navalar and from other cosmopolitan reformers of his day, for whom Islam and especially Christianity provided important points of orientation in their redefinition of Hindu traditions.

For the most part, when Ramalinga refers to other, competing religious traditions, he has in mind Hindu concepts and practices, indicating that his primary foils are Hindu traditions. He distinguishes his "True Path" from these opposing traditions. "Oh lord, you revealed to me that all this is child's play: communities of *camayam*, bound together by their excess karma; their traditions of learning; the paths set out in those traditions; their images of deities; and their gods. . . . The traditions of learning that talk about the four castes (*varuṇa*), the stages of life (*āciramam*), established practices of conduct (*ācāram*), etc., all this is child's play" (4173–4174). The language of *varuṇa, āciramam,* and *ācāram* confirms that Ramalinga's criticisms are directed to the exclusionary, caste-based, elite practices and texts of Hindu traditions. Thus, he frequently links *matam* and *camayam* with *cāti* or caste. He addresses Shiva: "You taught me long ago that the rubbish piles of shastras, which distinguish many paths according to caste and *camayam*, are worthless. I realized this truth only today, through your love and grace. I am now on the path of unity which is praised by the learned" (5515). He condemns a variety of Hindu practices and traditions as "possession-dancing," including "caste, lineage, *camayam, matam,* initiation, caste conduct" (5508). This linking of caste with *matam* and *camayan* indicates that Ramalinga's critiques were directed toward Hindu traditions, most pointedly the Shaiva traditions of the mathas that dominated religious intellectual life in the Kaveri Delta. However, he was not an advocate for ritual practices and theologies associated with low-caste communities. His characterization above of elite elements of Hindu teachings as "possession-dancing," a practice associated with lower castes, reveals his own rejection of low-caste practices.

Ramalinga blames the proliferation of gods and sects for confusion, conflict, and death. He condemns "those who think there are many gods, those who profess many ways to reach god, those who exclaim the various, false scholarly disciplines, those who admire the many false traditions" (4726). His frequent references to religious controversy appear to reflect his historical milieu, in which conflict was a major feature of interactions between traditions. He writes that Shiva told him that "the beings of the vast earth, they don't realize that all the various religious traditions are crazy spirit-possession and child's play. They perpetuate all sorts of division and conflicts everywhere. They perish, their lives wasted" (3677). Ramalinga claims that Shiva told him that "a destructive path, consisting of the many religious traditions, has thus far prevailed. People of the world haven't known the refined path, and they have kept dying. Until now, they have been living in darkness" (3696). The proliferation of false traditions leads to a variety of social ills and, ultimately, death.

For Ramalinga, there is nothing to redeem, reform, or save from these traditions, so he pushes for their elimination in favor of his True Path. Shiva urges Ramalinga: "you go and steer them away from the diseased path. Lead them to the excellent path, the Pure True Path, which is the public path that bestows the heavenly, fresh ambrosia" (3696). Ramalinga's True Path is not an elite path that is limited to those of particular castes or with particular intellectual achievements, but it is a "public path" accessible to all. Shiva grants extraordinary boons only to those on Ramalinga's path, so Ramalinga presents the choice between his path and established paths as a choice between life and death. "Oh people of the world! . . . Why will you not accept the great boon of immorality? . . . Do you take joy in disease and old age? . . . There is just one excellent, true path. Look, it destroys disease, old age and death. Know this: in this very birth, you can achieve eternal life. You will quickly receive the highest bliss" (5600). As we have seen, Ramalinga even presents his potential followers with the prospect that their adherence to his teachings will lead Shiva to appear in Vadalur and raise the dead. Ramalinga's aspiration for his path was that it would transcend conflict and division between people, and usher in a new age of harmony and eternal life.

In addition to his attacks on caste and established traditions, Ramalinga also criticizes the elite texts of Shaivism, the Vedas and Agamas that reformers like Roy, Saraswati, and Navalar extolled as the basis of a reformed Hinduism. He is not always dismissive, at times writing that the Vedas reveal the truth of Shiva. For example, he calls Shiva "the god of Chidambaram who is praised by the Vedas as unity and diversity" (5510); "the highest of the jewels of the four Vedas" (3693); and the "light which is the apex of the greatness of the Agamas" (3700). However, just as often Ramalinga advances trenchant critiques of these texts. Shiva tells Ramalinga: "I'm telling you: the extant Vedas and Agamas are deceptive. If you see that they are false, both at the level of the meaning of words and as literature, then the truth of the Vedas and Agamas will be clear to you: you'll realize that the Vedas and Agamas, famous throughout the world, are lies" (4177). The problem, it seems, is not that canonical Hindu works are wrong in some fundamental way, but that they are mysterious and difficult to understand, and therefore mislead people and create conflict. "You engage in useless debate about the Vedas and Agamas. You don't know the fruit of the Vedas and Agamas. They speak mystifyingly about the truth which is in plain view. What use are they?" (5516). In an interesting reversal of the elite character and audience of Hindu canonical works, Ramalinga calls the study of the four Vedas, the Agamas, and shastras "bazaar education," contrasting this with his Pure True Path, which teaches the "knowledge of immortality" (4955). Again, the target of his criticisms are elite Shaiva traditions represented by the mathas in his milieu, the same traditions vehemently defended and promoted by Navalar. Ramalinga mocks "you great ones who think themselves greater than the Great One, you provoke conflicts, dirtying yourselves. You quote all sorts of false texts, taken from various traditions, and shout 'My God, My God,' not realizing that there is only one God. What will you do when your material body dies? You don't know the way to make the fragile body immortal" (5570). According to Ramalinga, the danger of choosing any path that emphasizes textual learning is death itself. It is perhaps for this reason that Ramalinga dropped "Veda" from the name of his society in 1872, suggesting that his rejection of textual elitism increased toward the end of his life.[59] In his critiques of texts, he never mentions the writings of the Tamil Shaiva saints, to which, as we have seen, he owed a great debt and in many ways used as a model for his own writings.

Ramalinga asserts that Shiva's grace and immortality could be gained only through direct, personal experience of Shiva, not through the Vedas and Agamas. He describes encounters with Shiva in sensory, and especially visual, terms. This assertion is consistent with his claims that he had frequent, close interactions with Shiva in the form of conversations, physical encounters, and direct sightings. After dismissing canonical texts as "child's play," Ramalinga reports: "You, my true guru, declared to me, open your eyes!" (4174). This contrast of the eyes with texts is a common refrain in his poems. "People speak about various treatises, from Vedagamas, Puranas, and Itihasas, to magical texts (*intiracālam*), they think that only those texts that confuse are trickery. Oh jewel, wise preceptor, catcher of my heart, you told me, 'my son, you must realize that all texts are trickery; view all activity with the light of my grace" (4176). Ramalinga equates esteemed works of Hindu traditions, the Vedas and Agamas, with magical texts that most orthodox Shaivas would view with suspicion. Ramalinga invites all listeners to join his society, where one can find truth by "viewing" all things, illuminated by Shiva's light.

Ramalinga described such encounters with Shiva in physical terms, not as interior or imaginative visions. He did not limit these encounters to individual interactions. In a circular addressed to everyone with some connection to his society, he announces that Shiva will appear before them all together. He instructs that they should not cremate their dead, but bury them. "Have complete faith that the dead will be resurrected and will return to us. Don't feel sorrow or cry out loud, but keep the god of Chidambaram in mind." He warns his audience to cease performing any rites for the dead, and he promises that if they do what he says, then Shiva will appear in the almshouse at Parvatipuram and will instruct them how to develop the society and the almshouse. Shiva will at that time resurrect those who belonged to the society. He will also resurrect others, even those who opposed the society, but they will not be allowed to join the society.[60] The price for immortality is in this case not insignificant, as the rejection of mortuary rites would mark a radical break from established community norms. The rewards of this break are likewise immense. By rejecting textual learning, Ramalinga also spurned the authority of Shaiva traditions of learning that favored high-caste communities embedded in positions of power. This rejection was consistent with other aspects of his teachings, which clearly display his sympathies with the poor, the hungry, and ordinary worshipers. What he required from his followers was not a high-caste birth or technical knowledge, but the courage to resist social and ritual conventions.

The sources that inspired Ramalinga's Society of the True Path appear to be varied. His juxtaposition of social critique with claims to miraculous powers strongly suggest the influence of siddha writings. At the same time, the organizational structure of his voluntary society does not appear to have been drawn from siddha models. As T.N. Ganapathy observes, "The songs of the Tamil Siddhas do not show any trace of collective thinking; the Tamil Siddhas are not system-builders. . . . They relied only on the individual's effort for the attainment of liberation."[61] Likewise, Eleanor Zelliot writes of bhakti poets that "no specific social movement for an egalitarian society arose from the bhaktas."[62] Siddha and bhakti poets wrote as individuals and did not advance alternative social configurations. Ramalinga, on the other hand, founded a community based on siddha modes of critique and claims to immortality. It is likely that in this he was influenced by new models of religious community that developed in cosmopolitan India through engagement between European and Indian traditions.

We should not, though, describe Ramalinga's Society as a "mixture" of tradition and modernity, with siddha traditions contributing traditional, magical features and Western models providing a modern form of community. The sources of influence are too complex, too "entangled," to sustain such a simple account. In many ways, my discussion so far is already an oversimplification of Ramalinga's sources of influence. It is clear that siddha traditions in his time were in flux, with the publication of new compilations, composition of new works, and redefinition of siddha ideals as representing a monotheistic, Protestantized Hindu past. The pedigree of his claim to be able to raise the dead is unclear, but it does suggest the possibility of Christian influence. It is also likely that Ramalinga was more familiar with voluntary societies that were burgeoning in urban centers under Hindu and Muslim leadership than he was with associational culture in Europe. This is to say that in Ramalinga's time, siddha works were not "purely" Shaiva, and voluntary societies in India were not just "Western." To speak in terms of the encounter of two distinct societies, one modern and the other traditional, oversimplifies the complex webs of influence and interactions that characterized Ramalinga's world. It also discounts the creative potential of Shaiva traditions. What we can say, I think, is that Ramalinga's vision was modern, because it participated in the most important debates of his day, presented new configurations of community, anticipated future trends, and envisioned a future that motivated his followers to work to transform their society.

THE "HERE AND NOW" OF RAMALINGA'S PATH

Ramalinga's poems of the sixth volume are characterized by a heightened sense of immediacy. He focuses on the present, consistently emphasizing the newness of his path and his break from prior traditions. He celebrates this newness, something that set him apart from reform thinkers who imagined their projects as a return to an idealized past. Ramalinga hoped that his society would destroy the old and would usher in a new age. This gave his writings an urgency, even an apocalyptic character. In these poems, a distinct human audience comes into focus. While he addressed his earlier poems to his own heart or to Shiva himself, in these later poems he frequently addresses present and potential followers, the people of the world. His stress on the importance of the here and now, and his heightened concern to speak to a human audience, mark his teachings as modern in the sense that I have been using the term. That is, his vision was timely, broke from the past, addressed current challenges, innovated, motivated his followers to transform their world, and anticipated future directions for Hindu traditions. Like other aspects of his teachings, his sense of time, place, and audience drew from a variety of influences, Indian and Western, and it also displays elements that appear to have been Ramalinga's own innovations.

One of the primary distinctions he makes between his path and other traditions is that his is new and timely, and others are old and past. He attributes his ideas to his ongoing dialogue with Shiva. "Oh unmatched Nataraja, my precious teacher. You said, 'the multitude of paths appeared, lacking good qualities, and some disappeared. People of the world joined them, and lived in ignorance and distress. My son, this is the holy path, the path of grace that destroys distress and creates all good things. Strive to establish the wisdom of this public path which enables one to drink the cool ambrosia'" (3698). Ramalinga's task is to destroy past tradition, especially those elite traditions that valued caste distinctions and textual authority. He offers instead a "public path" that is accessible to everyone. He is keenly aware of the monumental challenge he set himself, given the power of established Shaiva institutions and the embedded character of caste and ritual practices. His alliance with Shiva is necessary—it is only Shiva's miraculous intervention that is capable of bringing about such an epochal shift, away from the troubles of caste, religious conflict, and death toward a universal community that enjoys immortality. He makes frequent reference to the transformative, miraculous character of the "cool ambrosia" that Shiva gave to him, describing it as "fresh" or "new" (3866, 5572). Given the persistence and pervasiveness of caste and religious hierarchies, Ramalinga could perhaps only envision the concrete realization of his teachings in miraculous terms. Victory would require the *siddhis,* ambrosia, and the direct intervention of Shiva.

Ramalinga spoke of Shiva's appearance in concrete spatial terms. He directed his followers to bury their dead in anticipation of their revival when Shiva appears at Parvatipuram. Such specific references to Shiva's physical return are consistent with his early poems, which provide precise detail of his encounters with Shiva. He promises members of his society that they will gain the same sort of direct, physical access to Shiva. "This is indeed the auspicious time when my matchless father is coming to the Northern Chidambaram which is famous as Cittipuram of abundant light. He comes in order to perform the five functions of god which are just a trifle to him, and to establish himself in me, who am overjoyed at his refuge" (5575). Ramalinga refers to the area of his temple and almshouse as "Northern Chidambaram," and "Cittipuram," the "town of the *siddhis,*" is the place of his residence. In promising the imminent arrival of Shiva and the raising of the dead, Ramalinga was offering a narrative of hope for an extraordinary new stage of society.

Another spatial dimension of his narrative is his assertion that Shiva appears on the "street." "Oh people of the world, you wander aimlessly, valuing caste, dogma, sects, noisy doctrinal debates, and disputes over lineage. Your wandering is useless, it is destructive and ugly. Stand in the good path of justice. The dancer is the only lord. The play (*viḷaiyāṭal*) of grace and light is occurring on the street. I call out: the right time has come" (5566). The "play" of grace and light is a clear reference to Shiva's activity, which is often described as a form of play, as in the popular text *Tiruviḷaiyāṭal Purāṇam* [Divine play], which narrates sixty-four episodes of Shiva's activity. Ramalinga insists that Shiva's play is "on the street," in public for all to see, to experience, to access. This provocative imagery of Shiva in the street distinguishes Ramalinga's vision from that of traditions which located Shiva in obscure, elite textual knowledge, or in temples that limited access to particular caste communities. He draws on broader South Asian conceptions, where the street carries the resonance of a public space that does not exclude based on caste. Chakrabarty describes the street, the bazaar, and the fair as paradigmatic spaces in South Asia that are "outside" private spaces of regulation and control. This public space is "exposed. . . . It is not subject to a single sense of (enclosing) rules and ritual defining a community." The street is marked by unfamiliarity, danger, potential and possibilities. Because it is a public, accessible space, it "provides a venue for linkage across communities."[63] Ramalinga's announcement that Shiva is available on the street highlights his accessibility. Ramalinga's public Shiva contrasts sharply with worship at established Shaiva temple centers like Chidambaram, which in Ramalinga's time excluded people of certain castes. For Ramalinga, Shiva's revelation is available to everyone, not limited and controlled by a Shaiva elite.

In at least one verse, Ramalinga plays on this distinction between public and cloistered manifestations of Shiva. The term "potu" designates "public" things, but it is also the name for the inner chamber of Chidambaram, one of the most highly controlled abodes of Shiva, which in Ramalinga's time was not open to worship by dalit castes. Ramalinga sings, "I realized that all living beings are equivalent to that revered hall (*potu*) where you perform your sacred dance. . . . I sing these public songs [*potuppāṭṭu,* which can also mean 'songs of the Hall of Chidambaram'], so that the tender sprouts of the pure True Path flourish" (5426). By asserting that all living beings are revered sites of Shiva's sacred dance, Ramalinga universalizes the private space of Chidambaram by extending it to all the world's beings. This move epitomizes the accessibility of his True Path: he opens up the sacred hall of Chidambaram to all beings.

Ramalinga not only writes of the "here" of his revelation but also of the "now." He speaks to his listeners with a sense of urgency. "See that this is the time when our god will rise up and grace the world, in order to quickly destroy all the foolish *matam* which brings no benefits to the world, and in order that the unique True Path, which is without errors, is established everywhere. Like people sleeping who wake and rise up, all the dead are appearing and rising up. This has already begun. Come quickly and learn!" (5592) He urges people not to delay from joining his path, cautioning them to put their doubts aside. "Don't wonder, 'what is the time of clarification, when god of the light of grace will come, so that the entire world will rejoice and attain bliss for immeasurable time?' O people of the world, this is that luminous time, when the dead will rise" (5584). The danger of delay is death, which can strike at any moment. "If you delay even a little bit, thinking 'we'll come to that later,' then the great sin that is death will come. Behold! You can't delay that, even a little bit. Except for the members of the Society of the True Path, there is no one in any world who is capable of fighting against that and delaying it" (5599).

Ramalinga appears to acknowledge the radical character of his claims, and he urges people not to doubt his words. "Our kin who live in the four directions, don't despise my words as lies" (5532). He reassures his audience that Shiva's coming is imminent, and the immense benefits of joining his society will be immediate. "Don't despair, wondering which day will our father come, he who rules all? Don't worry at all. I told the truth directly: he will appear on this very day and come" (5533). Those who join his path will immediately enjoy its benefits, including the *siddhis*. "All the glittering sects and religions are full of lies. Don't join them. Know that god is one. Know and worship the dance of the hall. Today all the *siddhis* will truly come [to you]" (5595). Ramalinga's promises were not general or vague, but specific as to the place and time of Shiva's appearance: Parvatipuram today, or at least in the very near future. Ramalinga's sense of time was not the homogenous time of Western modernity but a sense of the special nature of the present. His emphasis on the conquering of death was itself a conquering of history, an abolishing of the progression of life and death.

The immediacy of Ramalinga's message is accentuated by the emergence of a clear, human audience in these poems. Instead of addressing Shiva, or his own heart, as he does in his earlier poems, here he speaks to his contemporaries, those who are in his society and especially those whom he asks to join him. He speaks to "those close to me who are spread in the four directions" (5532), and he asks "you are dear to me, come here and join the Society of the True Path!" (5584). Most often, he addresses "people of the world" (*ulakīr*), signifying a broad, general audience of listeners not distinguished by caste or class. He often couches this form of address as a sort of warning, describing his audience as "people of the world that deludes" (5598) and "people of the world of unbearable strain" (5569). He invites "you of this earth" to join him at Cittipuram (5574). His effort to address a broad, inclusive audience is consistent with his goal to create a truly universal community.

Ramalinga's invocation of "people of the world" has parallels in North Indian devotional literature. Christian Lee Novetzke notes the Marathi poet Namdev's use of "loka" to address a broad audience of listeners. He describes this "loka" as a "public," asserting that such referential practices seek to unify an audience "unmarked by caste, class, or gender," but they also divide, as "the creation of shared publics is also always a creation of differences between different publics."[64] Ramalinga's invocation of people of the world, equivalent to Namdev's "loka," performs similar work, even if the sense of a public is so diffuse it seems difficult to define as such. He does, however, clearly divide those who join him and those who do not. Members of his society will be blessed with immortal life, and those who reject his teaching will be relegated to death. Ramalinga writes that Shiva told him: "Those who kill beings and eat flesh, they are not close to us. They are outcasts. Until they approach your desirable true path, do no more than dispel their hunger. Don't sympathize with them or speak courteously to them. Don't give them friendly assistance. This is my command" (4160). Contrary to his professed ideal to establish a universal society, Ramalinga's writings enforce divisions among the "people of the world" whom he addresses.

Ramalinga's sense of place also has precedents in Tamil Shaiva bhakti and siddha traditions. Bhakti poet-saints such as the authors of the *Tēvāram* sung at length about Shiva as a living presence at local temples and towns. Siddha poets spoke of the street as a site of divine "play," not of public impurity. Pattinattar wrote of Shiva: "He walked the street in the habit of a mendicant-devotee, searched and found me and said: 'Share your alms with me.' Hearing this I fell at his feet."[65] Pampatti siddha links his anti-caste stance with accessible, public spaces.

> We shall kindle the fire in the rift among castes
> We shall plant our staff in open market places
> We shall play and dance on the crossroads and in the streets
> We shall establish friendships in undesirable houses . . .
> This is what you do and say o dancing snake.[66]

Ramalinga's sense of the "here" is thus attested in the Shaiva poems that influenced him most significantly.

Ramalinga's sense of time is more difficult to trace. Some aspects align with notions of time and history in Western modernity as described by Reinhart Koselleck. These include "the knowledge that one is living in a period of transition in which it becomes harder and harder to reconcile established traditions with necessary innovations."[67] Ramalinga's rejection of the established Shaiva traditions and deliberate embrace of change mark him out as "modern" in Koselleck's terms. Likewise, his desire to destroy all prior traditions and establish a new community conforms to a "true present" in Marshall Berman's summary of Paul de Man's formulation. The "full power of the idea of modernity lay in a 'desire to wipe out whatever came earlier,' so as to achieve 'a radically new departure, a point that could be a true present.'"[68] Or, his rejection of past community and his aspiration for a future with a radically different configuration of society conforms to S.N. Eisenstadt's assertion that the redefinition of communities is a central aspect of modernization. This is especially the case for the consideration of belonging to wider, nonlocal communities, such as Ramalinga's voluntary society open to people of all castes and classes.[69] In other ways, though, he departs from Western modernity's sense of time. He displays little sense of the openness or changeability of the future; of the "nonsimultaneity of diverse but, in a chronological sense, simultaneous histories"; or of historical perspective.[70] Most importantly, for Ramalinga, divinity pervades time, and in his claims to immortality, he contends that death, probably the greatest marker of time, can be overcome, departing from a modern Western insistence that rationality should prevail in the flow of history.

Ramalinga's modernity, however, should not be denied or confirmed through establishing his departures from, or alignment with, characteristics of Western modernity. Instead, his project was modern because it exhibited an acute awareness of contemporary challenges; it responded to those challenges in innovative ways; it sought to transform the world; it was influential; and it anticipated future directions of Hindu traditions. Ramalinga's sense of time and place challenged Shaiva notions that regulated community based on caste, and he attacked past traditions in order to open up space for new possibilities. The newness of his vision is not undermined by the presence of divinity or the *siddhis*, or the promise of immortality. These features are essential to his project, and their removal would not have made his project more modern. The whole package was modern, and the sense of the miraculous was central to that modernness, in the way I have defined it here. Ramalinga's authority rested on his claim that he had direct experience of Shiva, and that Shiva granted him the power to perform miracles. He enticed followers by offering them the promise of the *siddhis* and immortality. His insistence that Shiva was in the here and now reassured his audience that they, too, could enjoy the fruits of Shiva's grace. These aspects of his teachings were not anachronistic but spoke to the most vital concerns of his time, and presaged the emergence of later expressions of Hindu traditions. By considering the modern apart from a list of features that describe Western modernity, we can include even these most enchanted aspects of Ramalinga's teachings as part of the narrative, or more accurately narratives, of the emergence of modern Hinduism. The timeliness of Ramalinga's message demands that we do just that.

CONCLUSION

Ramalinga's claims and promises of miraculous powers and immortality drew on prior Tamil siddha traditions. Testimonies about his life and disappearance followed narratives of the extraordinary exploits of gurus, yogis, and siddhas that have filled Hindu literature for millennia. Those traditions of yoga, or of the siddhas, are not static but are ever-changing, and Ramalinga was very much a siddha of the middle decades of the nineteenth century. He drew from a range of contemporary sources in imagining a voluntary society that would embody this extraordinary promise, which he hoped would respond to contemporary challenges in the world around him. His was a period of radical change, when colonial and especially missionary networks and institutions were increasingly providing ideologies and avenues for social egalitarianism. Within this context, he celebrated the most accessible features and most egalitarian teachings of Shaiva traditions. He considered the possibility of the miraculous central to this project. Most importantly, he gave the miraculous a communal character, founding a society open to all that would enjoy Shiva's extraordinary boons. He thus offered an organized alternative to both established Shaiva traditions and new expressions of reform Hinduism that were taking shape in the cosmopolitan centers.

When we consider a figure like Ramalinga to be crucial to the story of the emergence of modern forms of Hinduism, we challenge narratives that insist that Western rationality is necessary to all expressions of modernity. Notions of modernity need not only entail the emergence of rationality. After all, religion continues to be a major force in our world, and it shapes this world in crucial ways. We can describe Ramalinga's teachings as modern without having to overlook his emphasis on divine intervention, his promise of the *siddhis,* or his claim to have become immortal. Instead of parsing his message into "traditional" and "modern" aspects, we should rather take his message as a whole, one that achieved such relevance and influence that it invited criticism from powerful Shaiva leaders, motivated worshipers to action, and presaged future directions that a variety of Hindu traditions would take.

If we accept Ramalinga's project as integral to the transformation of nineteenth-century Hinduism, it becomes clear that we need to expand our historiography of modern Hinduism to include a number of features that are more commonly assigned to past "tradition." We should consider Ramalinga's celebration of the miraculous, embodied in an egalitarian society, to be as modern as the Hindu reform pursuit of Protestant rationality. Ramalinga's promise of Shiva's appearance as a living, breathing, tangible god in the here and now inspired audiences of his time as effectively as did the Hindu reform emphasis on an abstract, monotheistic deity. Moreover, Ramalinga's insistence on the possibility, and indeed the necessity, of direct experience of Shiva, and his critique of elite texts and rituals, responded as well to the challenges of his day as did the reform Hindu insistence on the textual authority of the past. Ramalinga's powerful juxtaposition of accessibility, egalitarian community, and the miraculous presaged future directions of Hindu traditions as much, if not more, than did the elite textualism of reform Hinduism.

When we better understand Ramalinga's view of history, the misnomer of calling him a "reformer" becomes clear. He was not interested in reforming established Shaivism in the confidence that human effort can effect a rationalization of established religious practice and theology. He rather professed revolution, seeing his own role as the executer of Shiva's desire to destroy established traditions and establish a radically new community. Thus, Ramalinga was much more a siddha than he was a reformer. He was a critic who pushed the boundaries of the community he grew up in and the larger Shaiva community that dominated religious life in central Tamil Nadu. Ironically, then, his rejection and transcendence of Shaivism itself had a Shaiva siddha character. He articulated an alternative vision that gave ordinary people hope that they, too, could experience the miraculous in their local place and time. The timeliness of his message of the accessibility of the divine, with its critique of caste and elitism, spoke to the hopes and ideals of people across castes and communities.

7

Conclusion

In the preceding pages, I have argued for a fundamental shift in the way we conceptualize the nature of the "modern" in South Asia, and the processes that led to its emergence. Common understandings of modernization in South Asia tend to be structured by a series of linked pairs of opposed concepts: colonial centers versus periphery; the agency of Western culture and its local proxies versus a characterization of non-cosmopolitan actors as passive recipients of change; modernity as a force or pattern that is essentially opposed to and by tradition; and, in the case of India, a Hinduism shaped by reform versus other minority strands of the complex fabric of Indian religiosity. I have proposed, instead, that important projects of modernity were pursued on the periphery by actors deeply embedded in tradition and deploying all its resources as the key means for change, using texts and languages not associated with centralized power or national or global discourses.

My study has implications reaching considerably beyond the local context of its case study, and even beyond India and South Asia. Despite his peripheral location and deep roots in living tradition, Ramalinga, I have argued, was as modern as the protagonists who dominate the drama as it is usually rehearsed. In so doing, I have advanced a broader, less Eurocentric notion of modernity, one which is flexible enough to accommodate a wider range of cases; is not beholden to Western origins or a list of Western-derived characteristics; and does not conform to a narrative of rationalization, Westernization, or even nationalization. I have defined modern actors as those who were aware of the unique challenges of their present, willing to innovate in response to those challenges, and oriented their actions in anticipation of future trends. This broader view has allowed me to highlight the transformative, modernizing capacities of tradition and develop new ways of doing scholarly work that more accurately reflect diverse ways of being modern, and the agency of a greater range of actors, not just for the case of Hindus but for colonized people throughout the world.

I have achieved these goals through a microhistorical approach, focusing on Ramalinga and the projects, writings, and conflicts that marked the last ten years of his life. This case study has been ideal to address the larger questions outlined above. Working in a provincial town in central Tamil Nadu, Ramalinga developed influential and novel ideologies and institutions, finding inspiration in Hindu traditions rather than in Western ideas and models. He drew on Shaiva traditions to develop innovative responses to some of the most pressing concerns in his contemporary world: hunger, caste, ritual exclusion, and poverty. He responded with a new ideology to feed the poor, a new community that cut across distinctions of caste and class, and promises of powers and immortality to ordinary householders. For Ramalinga, Shaiva tradition did not limit the possibilities of innovation, but it expanded them. He saw things that we might associate with tradition—texts, rituals, myths—not as fixtures of the past, but as living presences that "spoke" to him and provided inspiration for new ideas about ritual and community. He worked within Hindu traditions to formulate teachings that were innovative, critical, and responded to the most crucial challenges of his day.

Ramalinga did not engage directly with Western ideas or colonial institutions, but he was, I have argued, as modern as those who did. I have focused on Ramalinga's teachings to demonstrate two things. First, his innovations were at the forefront of Hindu change. He used print technology to promote his messages; he extended charity to the poor; he criticized caste hierarchies; he encouraged the democratization of knowledge and the accessibility of ritual; he wrote devotional poems in everyday language; he argued for the centrality of the charismatic leader/guru; and he offered ordinary Hindus the highest achievements of yoga. Second, his inspiration for these innovations came from Hindu traditions, and from institutions and ideas with varied, "entangled" histories. I have presented a more complex model of Hindu modernization than those that emphasize idioms of dialogue or encounter between Indians and Westerners. In these concluding pages I discuss the broader implications of my study for reconceptualizing modernity and tradition.

MODERN HINDUISM IN THE PROVINCES

The case of Ramalinga provides a vantage point from which I have described an alternate genealogy for modern Hinduism. Ramalinga's teachings do not pursue a Protestant rationality, but they build on the importance of hagiography, the miraculous, the guru, divine authority, and poetry that makes the heart melt. He was inspired by populist strands of Shaiva traditions, and powerful Shaiva institutions were his primary foil. We can at times catch glimpses of the impact of Western discourses and institutions, but these are through lines of influence that were mediated by Indian agents and institutions. On the margins of colonialism, the model of a European-Indian encounter breaks down, and we need to view processes of cultural interaction in much more messy, complicated, and entangled ways.

One might speak of Ramalinga as marginal in two senses. First, he was marginal to the centers of colonial power, establishing his center in a provincial town and never directly engaging with European ideas and discourses. Second, he was marginal to the centers of institutional Shaivism. He worked outside the authority of the powerful non-brahman monasteries of Tamil Shaivism, and he was attacked by institutional stalwarts like Arumuga Navalar. However, to speak of him only as marginal perpetuates a discourse that relegates him, and figures like him, to the periphery of all power, relevance, and even modernity. In his writings, Ramalinga certainly did not view himself in that way. He described himself as Shiva's representative and as the legitimate leader of a new movement. He spoke of Vadalur and its surrounds as a center, the site of new forms of charity to the poor, of new ways of worshiping Shiva, of a new community that would usher in an age of unity, of a set of institutions including a temple and an almshouse, and of Shiva's imminent appearance. For his followers, this was indeed a center, and it continues to be so today for the many who carry on Ramalinga's legacy. The case of Ramalinga reminds us that marginality can encompass different definitions and always depends on one's point of view.

When we shift our focus from the colonial to the provincial center, we are compelled to expand our view of what constituted modernity in the nineteenth century. This move requires us to do away with the usual measure of modernity, that is, the list of characteristics of Western modernity. I have instead characterized the modern in more general terms, including the sense of the uniqueness of the present; the strategic pursuit of innovation in response to challenges of the present; the rethinking of community; and the anticipation of future developments. Ramalinga's modernity is validated by the success of his vision, not only in drawing followers in his day but also because his innovations were part of larger transformations that continue to shape Hindu traditions.

If the case of Ramalinga inspires us to rethink modernity, it also compels us to reconceptualize tradition. Prevalent notions of tradition as static, past-oriented, homogenous, enchanted, and resistant to innovation emerged in the nineteenth century, a product of linked discourses of modernity and tradition. These "antinomies of modernity," as described by Saurabh Dube, consign India to "tradition" and reward the West with "modernity." India becomes a "'never, never land' of endless tradition."[1] We have seen this play out as reform leaders began to conceive of Hindu tradition as a coherent entity grounded in an ancient, glorious, and textual past. Ironically, this new notion of tradition was modern in the sense that I have talked about modernity: it was innovative, strategic, addressed present challenges, and anticipated future trends.

One might suggest that Ramalinga's traditional orientation was a *reaction* to this coproduction of tradition and Western modernity, that is, that he developed his ideas in opposition to the cosmopolitan discourses of Hindu reform. If this were the case, then Western ideas played a far more important role in his projects than I have recognized, even if they functioned primarily as foils against which Ramalinga developed his new ideologies and institutions. Was he carefully and deliberately presenting himself as a traditional figure, distancing himself from explicit statements that would reveal his debt to Western ideas? Was his emphasis on miracles meant as a pointed critique of the Protestant rejection of the possibility of modern miracles, mediated through cosmopolitan Hinduism? Was his attack on the Vedas a response to the textual fetishism of Hindu reformers? Did he neglect to acknowledge Western influences or sources because such acknowledgment would compromise his status as a traditional Shaiva leader?

Although it is impossible to answer these questions with certainty, the evidence presented in his writings does not support the view that his teachings were a reactionary, traditionalist response to cosmopolitan notions of rationality, tradition, and canon. Hindu leaders in Ramalinga's time certainly articulated such traditionalist accounts. These were, however, framed according to Western discourses and therefore very different in their presumptions and content than Ramalinga's orientation to the past.[2] Moreover, Ramalinga explicitly refers to his foils, which were not Western or Hindu reform traditions, but established Hindu traditions that upheld caste hierarchies and exclusionary ritual practices. He never explicitly expresses antipathy toward the cosmopolitan discourses of Hindu reform. The ways that his position ended up opposing those new discourses seem almost accidental, drawing him in as a reluctant participant in debates that were not his primary focus.

Ramalinga's sense of tradition was different from both Hindu reform conceptions of traditions and the traditionalist conceptions that emerged in opposition to Hindu reform. For Ramalinga, tradition, in the sense of the literary, ritual, and theological legacy of Shaivism, was not primarily an orientation toward the past or a coherent entity that valued stasis. Rather, he viewed Shaiva tradition as had many Shaivas before him: as a framework for moral action, ritual practice, and theological understanding, and as a basis for innovation. He neither masked change in the garb of newly conceived "tradition" nor did he view his project as one of recuperation of an idealized past. He embraced innovation and change, and he saw the world around him to be demanding such change. Ramalinga did not need Western modernity to imagine and implement influential and novel expressions of ethics, revelation, and community, because inspiration and the potential for creative change were inscribed into Shaivism.

This does not mean that he worked within a pure Shaiva tradition. Ramalinga himself would agree, I think, that Shaivism always responded to local material and social processes. Ramalinga's innovations addressed the social, economic, material, and technological challenges around him and contributed to debates about egalitarianism, the accessibility of ritual, and the possibility of modern miracles. These precipitants of change were not "external" to his Shaiva tradition. Rather, Ramalinga experienced, and responded to, those changes through Shaiva tradition, advancing novel projects with Shiva's direction that addressed the variety of ills that he saw around him: poverty, malnourishment, elitism, caste, neglect of the poor, religious division, and conflict. Tradition was not a withdrawal into an idealized past but the basis for present action.

Ramalinga viewed Shaivism not as an unchanging reservoir of symbolic and authoritative resources from the past, but as flexible, living texts, ideas, and processes that were open to reinterpretation or even reinvention. That is, he did not draw from the past as a pool of resources, working from a perspective independent of those positions, deciding which to retain and which to reject. Dipesh Chakrabarty calls such a position "decisionism," according to which "the critic is guided by his or her values to choose the most desirable, sane, and wise future for humanity, and looks to the past as a warehouse of resources on which to draw as needed."[3] Chakrabarty rightly questions this position, which assumes the "Lockean fable" that "reason is external to history, and its attainment signals a freedom from any political authority of the past." Avoiding decisionism, we must resist speaking of tradition as a pool of resources that a modern, transcendent actor sifts through and selects from. Tradition is not a resource, any more than modernity is a resource. Yet Chakrabarty also warns against adherence to a strict historicism, such as Marx's evocative "nightmare" of tradition that prevents the possibility of revolutionary change.[4] Such a modernist view, in which tradition is an irresistible force of inertia, fails to recognize that innovation always occurs within, or out of, the continuities of specific traditions.

Once we recognize that traditions also provide space and tools for innovation, it becomes clear that we do not need to choose between a Lockean fable and a Marxian nightmare. Ramalinga was not picking and choosing from a position that transcended Shaivism, because Shaivism itself supplied the orienting ideologies for his projects. Nor was he, however, a passive and helpless subject of Shaivism. Shaivism has always contained contested elements and debates, and Shaiva actors have always exercised their judgment and a degree of freedom in choosing sides, and in developing new Shaiva ideas and models. Ramalinga's experiences, moral judgments, social views, and decisions were conditioned by Shaiva traditions, but Shaivism also offered opportunities for debate, resistance, and innovation. Thus, Ramalinga exercised no less agency than those cosmopolitan leaders who formulated new expressions of reform Hinduism according to a colonial, Protestant rationality. Both worked within limitations and spaces for innovation that were presented by diverse traditions.

When we dispense with a dichotomy between tradition and modernity, we need to change the language with which we speak about both. My delineation of the terms demands some overlap. The "modernity" that accompanied British colonialism was not one of universal, ahistorical rationality but of a very specific historical genealogy with roots in Protestantism. Western modernity was, and indeed remains, a tradition, one whose most uncanny skill is its ability to present itself as universal. Reform Hinduism was, and remains, modern because it is innovative and addresses concerns of the present, but it also draws on traditions of Western modernity, and it maintains continuities with elite Hindu traditions. Thus, reform Hinduism is no less traditional than is Ramalinga's formulation, and no more modern than Ramalinga's modernity.

Does this mean that everything is traditional, and everything is modern? Or as Saurabh Dube asks, "does all this mean that . . . everyone living in the modern age axiomatically counts as a modern?"[5] Perhaps so. Or, perhaps it is closer to the truth to say that nothing is traditional, and nothing is modern, if by those terms we employ a dichotomy between stasis and innovation, between a slavish subjugation to history and a liberating transcendence of history. In my redefinition of these terms, they are not markers that distinguish and order particular actors, movements, ideas, institutions, or practices. Rather, they specify aspects of continuity and change that are shared by actors, movements, et cetera. When we call something traditional, we do not deny it its modernity, because traditions can and do change. Likewise, actors working within traditions innovate, even if they highlight the ideals of continuity or portray their innovations as a return to the past. Modernity is not a decisive shift to objective reason but entails a process in which actors situated in specific traditions develop innovative responses to the conditions that characterize contemporary worlds.

The risk in generalizing too much from the case of Ramalinga is that my view of modernity may be as myopic as those assumed in studies that focus on reform Hinduism, or on instances of clear engagement between Indian and European people and ideas. This is perhaps not a cause for apology, however, since, as Dube points out, modernity is an "idea, ideal, and ideology."[6] That is to say, I hope this book challenges historians of Hinduism to broaden their narratives by including figures like Ramalinga, not as leaders working in a traditional mode that is contrary to modernity, or reacting against modernity, but as innovators who made crucial contributions to modern Hinduism. This shift that I propose does not deny the importance of Europe in thinking about modern Hinduism, but it does question the Eurocentrism that has often defined its narrative. Indeed, there were multiple centers for Hindu innovation, including centers on the margins of colonialism such as that occupied by Ramalinga and his followers. If we accept the heterogeneity of Hinduism in the present, we need to account for this present by documenting and analyzing the diverse histories that have produced it.

GLOSSARY

Agamas	manuals that describe the performance of public and household rites, and temple architecture and iconography
Appar	also called Tirunavukkaracu, one of the poet-saints of the *Tēvāram*
aruḷ	Shiva's grace
aruṭpā	poems of Shiva's grace
aruṭperuñjōti	"The great light of grace," Shiva in the form of light; the central focus of worship at Ramalinga's temple
Arya Samaj	Hindu reform group founded by Dayananda Saraswati
bhakti	devotion
Brahmo Samaj	Hindu reform group founded by Rammohan Roy in 1828
Camaraca Veta Ca̱nmārka Caṅkam	"Society of the True Path that is Common to All Scripture"; Ramalinga's voluntary society of followers, founded in 1865
Camaraca Vēta Tarumaccālai	"Almshouse of the Unity of Scripture"; Ramalinga's almshouse that distributed food to the poor
camayam	established tradition, often translated as "religion"; Ramalinga uses the term to refer to specific Hindu sects that are limited in their teaching
ca̱nmārkkam	"true path"; the path that Ramalinga set out for his followers

Cattiya Ñāṉa Capai	"Temple of True Knowledge"; Ramalinga's temple in Vadalur that was completed in 1872
Cekkilar	twelfth-century Shaiva poet; author of the *Periya Purāṇam*
chattram	South Asian institution that provides accommodation and food to pilgrims and the poor
Chidambaram	famous temple of Shiva as Nataraja, the Lord of Dance
citti vaḷākam	Ramalinga's residence in the last years of his life; the site of his final disappearance
Cuddalore	colonial outpost 35 kilometers from Vadalur
dāna	Hindu practice of ritualized gift-giving
JKO (*Jīva Karuṇya Oḻukkam*)	*The Path of Compassion for Living Beings;* Ramalinga's prose work that describes his ideology of food-giving to the poor
Karunguli	residence of Ramalinga near Vadalur after his return to his birth village area
Karuniga	caste of scribes and bookkeepers; Ramalinga's caste
Manikkavacakar	Tamil Shaiva devotional poet; author of the *Tiruvācakam*
Marudur	village of Ramalinga's birth
maruṭpā	"verses of delusion"; Navalar's name for Ramalinga's poems
matam	established tradition; often translated as "religion" or "sect"
matha	powerful nonbrahman monasteries that dominated Tamil literary and temple practices
Mudaliyar, Irakkam Irattina	one of Ramalinga's closest followers; he frequently corresponded with Ramalinga
Mudaliyar, Toluvur Velayuda	Tamil pandit and one of Ramalinga's close devotees; editor of the first five sections of *Tiruvaruṭpā*
muṟai	path or tradition; section of a larger work or compilation
Murugan	Shaiva god particularly popular in Tamil areas; son of Shiva
nālvar	four most important Tamil Shaiva poet-saints: Sambandar, Appar, Sundarar, and Manikkavacakar
Navalar, Arumuga	Jaffna-born Tamil Shaiva scholar and reformer

nāyaṉmār	sixty-three saints of Tamil Shaivism whose hagiographies are recounted in the *Periya Purāṇam*
pañcāṭcaram	five-syllable mantra in praise of Shiva
Periya Purāṇam	twelfth-century Tamil hagiography of Shaiva saints
Pillai, Shanmugam	follower of Ramalinga; author of a rejoinder to Navalar's polemical attack on Ramalinga
Puranas	writings that recount the activities of gods, sometimes focused on specific temples
Roy, Rammohan	Bengali Hindu reformer; active in early decades of the nineteenth century
Sambandar	one of the poet-saints of the *Tēvāram*
Saraswati, Dayananda	Hindu reformer contemporaneous with Ramalinga
Shaiva Siddhanta	Shaiva ritual and theological tradition
shastra	category of Hindu texts and ideology that advances moral, ritual, and doctrinal prescriptions
siddha	accomplished yogi who has acquired supernatural powers
siddhis	extraordinary powers gained through yogic practice
Sundarar	one of the poet-saints of the *Tēvāram*
Tayumanavar	eighteenth-century Tamil Shaiva poet
Tēvāram	revered poems in the Tamil Shaiva devotional canon; composed by the poet-saints Appar, Sundarar, and Sambandar between the sixth and the ninth centuries C.E.
Tirukkuṟaḷ	popular, nonsectarian Tamil ethical work
Tirumuṟai	Tamil Shaiva devotional canon; name of chapters in Ramalinga's *Tiruvaruṭpā*
tirunīṟu	ash used in Shaiva ritual contexts
Tiruvācakam	Shaiva devotional work by Manikkavacakar
Tiruvaruṭpā	collection of Ramalinga's poems; published in three volumes and six sections
Tiruvavadudurai Adhinam	non-brahman Shaiva monastery that exerted a powerful influence on Tamil literary culture and temples
Tiruviḷaiyāṭal Purāṇam	Shaiva work that narrates sixty-four episodes of Shiva's "games"
Tiruvotriyur	also called "Otri"; Shaiva temple on the outskirts of Chennai

Vadalur	area of Ramalinga's almshouse and temple; also called Parvatipuram
Vedas	ancient Sanskrit works that many Hindus consider to be the most authoritative works in Hindu traditions
vellalar	elite, non-brahman castes; leaders of Tamil scholarly and monastic traditions

NOTES

1 INTRODUCTION: RETHINKING RELIGIOUS CHANGE IN NINETEENTH-CENTURY SOUTH ASIA

1. A good place to start is with the collections J.E. Llewellyn, *Defining Hinduism: A Reader* (New York: Routledge, 2006); and Esther Bloch, Marianne Keppens, and Rajaram Hegde, *Rethinking Religion in India: The Colonial Construction of Hinduism* (London: Routledge, 2010).

2. Tomoko Masuzawa, *The Invention of World Religions, or, How European Universalism Was Preserved in the Language of Pluralism* (Chicago: University of Chicago Press, 2005).

3. Specifically, Hatcher notes that there was an "elective affinity" between the Vedantic theism of Roy and the elite members of the Tattvabodhinı Sabha. Brian A. Hatcher, *Bourgeois Hinduism, or the Faith of the Modern Vedantists: Rare Discourses from Early Colonial Bengal* (New York: Oxford University Press, 2008).

4. *Report on the Census of British India, Taken on the 17th February 1881*, vol. 1 (London: Her Majesty's Stationary Office, 1883), 23.

5. Ibid., 49.

6. Anthony Appiah, *The Ethics of Identity* (Princeton: Princeton University Press, 2005).

7. Peter van der Veer, "Colonial Cosmopolitanism," in *Conceiving Cosmopolitanism: Theory, Context, and Practice*, ed. Steven Vertovec and Robin Cohen (New York: Oxford University Press, 2002), 165.

8. Amiya P. Sen, "Debates within Colonial Hinduism," in *Hinduism in the Modern World*, ed. Brian A. Hatcher (New York: Routledge, 2016), 67.

9. Quoted in Amiya P. Sen, "The Idea of Social Reform and Its Critique among Hindus of Nineteenth Century India," in *Development of Modern Indian Thought and the Social Sciences*, ed. Sabyasachi Bhattacharya (New Delhi: Oxford University Press, 2007), 117.

10. J.N. Farquhar, *Modern Religious Movements in India* (New York: The Macmillan Company, 1915), 1.

11. Paul Hacker, "Aspects of Neo-Hinduism as Contrasted with Surviving Traditional Hinduism," in *Kleine Schriften*, ed. Paul Hacker and Lambert Schmithausen (Wiesbaden: Steiner, 1978), 582, 604.

12. Sen, "Idea of Social Reform," 116–18. For another critique of the "impact" model, see Brian A. Hatcher, "Contemporary Hindu Thought," in *Contemporary Hinduism: Ritual, Culture, and Practice*, ed. Robin Rinehart (Santa Barbara, CA: ABC-CLIO, 2004), 201.

13. Hatcher, "Contemporary Hindu Thought," 201–2.

14. Brian A. Hatcher, *Eclecticism and Modern Hindu Discourse* (New York: Oxford University Press, 1999).

15. Hacker, "Aspects of Neo-Hinduism," 582.

16. Brian A. Hatcher, "Colonial Hinduism," in *The Continuum Companion to Hindu Studies*, ed. Jessica Frazier (New York: Continuum, 2011), 172, 180–81.

17. See, especially, the work of Raymond Williams, including *A New Face of Hinduism: The Swaminarayan Religion* (Cambridge: Cambridge University Press, 1984); *An Introduction to Swaminarayan Hinduism* (Cambridge: Cambridge University Press, 2001); and with Yogi Trivedi, eds., *Swaminarayan Hinduism: Tradition, Adaptation, and Identity* (New York: Oxford University Press, 2016).

18. Anncharlott Eschmann, "Mahima Dharma: An Autochthonous Hindu Reform Movement," in *The Cult of Jagannath and the Regional Tradition of Orissa*, ed. Anncharlott Eschmann, Hermann Kulke, and Gaya Charan Tripathi (New Delhi: Manohar, 1978), 375. See also the important studies of Ishita Bannerjee-Dube: *Religion, Law, and Power: Tales of Time in Eastern India, 1860–2000* (London: Anthem Press, 2007); "Issues of Faith, Enactments of Contest: The Founding of Mahima Dharma in Nineteenth-Century Orissa," in *Jagannath Revisited: Studying Society, Religion, and the State in Orissa*, ed. Hermann Kulke and Burkhard Schnepel (New Delhi: Manohar, 2001); with Johannes Beltz, *Popular Religion and Ascetic Practices: New Studies on Mahima Dharma* (New Delhi: Manohar Publishers & Distributors, 2008).

19. G. Patrick, *Religion and Subaltern Agency* (Madras: University of Madras, 2003); M.S.S. Pandian, "Meanings of 'Colonialism' and 'Nationalism': An Essay on Vaikunda Swamy Cult," *Studies in History* 8, no. 2 (1992): 167–85; James Ponniah, "Alternative Discourses of Kali Yuga in Ayyā Vaḻi," *Nidān* 1 (2014): 65–87.

20. Italics in original. Farquhar, "Modern Religious Movements, 430.

21. Ibid., 430–32.

22. Wilhelm Halbfass, *India and Europe: An Essay in Understanding* (Albany: State University of New York Press, 1988), 217, 228, 220.

23. Arvind Sharma, *Modern Hindu Thought: An Introduction* (New York: Oxford University Press, 2005), 5.

24. Hatcher, "Contemporary Hindu Thought," 202.

25. Hatcher, "Colonial Hinduism."

26. Gavin D. Flood, *An Introduction to Hinduism* (New York: Cambridge University Press, 1996). See also Ariel Glucklich, *The Strides of Vishnu: Hindu Culture in Historical Perspective* (New York: Oxford University Press, 2008); Rachel Fell McDermott, *Sources of Indian Traditions*, 3rd ed. (New York: Columbia University Press, 2014).

27. David Smith, *Hinduism and Modernity* (Malden, MA: Blackwell Pub., 2003), viii, x.

28. Ibid., 40.

29. Sudipta Kaviraj, "Modernity and Politics in India," *Daedalus* 129, no. 1 (2000): 146.

30. Brian A. Hatcher, "Introduction," in *Hinduism in the Modern World,* ed. Brian A. Hatcher (New York: Routledge, 2016), 8.

31. On the project of "provincializing Europe," see Dipesh Chakrabarty, *Provincializing Europe: Postcolonial Thought and Historical Difference* (Princeton: Princeton University Press, 2000).

32. Here I use Ramalinga Swami, which is the most common usage today. Ramalinga Swami's name appears in a variety of forms in the various editions of his writings, so I have simplified these by using "Ramalinga Swami" as author for all editions, while retaining the original name cited in the extended titles for each work. The earliest reference I have found to "Ramalinga Swami" is on the title page of an 1867 edited volume of poems to Shiva, which states that the collection was published "with the permission of Ramalinga Swamigal, renowned for his wise speech, resident of Vadapuliyur, near Karunguli." Suppaiya Desikar, *Caṅkaraṉantāti, Civacaṅkarapatikam* [Poems to Shiva] (Chennai: Kalaratnakaram Accukkutam, 1867).

33. In chapter 3, I provide a close study and analysis of the initial publication of these verses in 1867. See also Richard S. Weiss, "Print, Religion, and Canon in Colonial India: The Publication of Ramalinga Adigal's *Tiruvarutpa,*" *Modern Asian Studies* 49, no. 3 (2015): 650–77.

34. Toluvur Velayuda Mudaliyar, "Tiruvaruṭpā Varalāṟu" [The history of *Tiruvaruṭpā*], in *Citamparam Irāmaliṅkapiḷḷai Avarkaḷ Tiruvāymalarntaruḷiyatiruvaruṭpā* [Chidambaram Ramalinga Pillai's *Tiruvaruṭpā*], ed. Toluvur Velayuda Mudaliyar (Madras: Asiatic Press, 1867), 39–47.

35. P. Ramasami Mudaliyar, "Irāmaliṅkapiḷḷaiyavarkaḷ Carittiraccurukkam [A short account of the life of Ramalinga Pillai]," in *Irāmaliṅkapiḷḷai Avarkaḷ Tiruvāymalarntaruḷiya Tiruvaruṭpāttirumuṟaittiraṭṭu* [Compilation of the sections of Ramalinga Pillai's *Tiruvaruṭpā*], ed. Po. Sundaram Pillai and Kaliyanasundara Mudaliyar (Chennai: Alpiniyan Press, 1892), 3–27.

36. The two most important recent biographies are Dr. M. P. Sivagnanam, *Vaḷḷalār Kaṇṭu Orumaippāṭu* [The universal vision of Vallalar] (Chennai: E. K. S. Books World, 2013); and Uran Adigal, *Irāmaliṅka Aṭikaḷ Varalāṟu* [Biography of Ramalinga Adigal], 3rd ed. (Vadalur: Samarasa Sanmarga Araycchi Nilayam, 2006). Sivagnanam's work received India's National Academy of Letters (Sahitya Akademi) prize for Tamil in 1966. Uran Adigal's biography won a prize from the Tamil Nadu government in 1975, presented by Chief Minister K. M. Karunanidhi. Uran Adigal also includes a condensed biographical account of Ramalinga's life in the introduction to his edition of Ramalinga's verses, Ramalinga Swami, *Tiru Aruṭpā,* ed. Uran Adigal, 2nd ed., 3 vols. (Chennai: Iramalingar Panimandram, 1981).

37. Ramalinga Swami, *Tiru Aruṭpā* [Uran Adigal ed.], 21.

38. Ibid.

39. Mudaliyar, "Irāmaliṅkapiḷḷaiyavarkaḷ," 8.

40. Ibid., 8–10.

41. Ramalinga Swami, "Camaraca Cutta Caṉmārkka Cattiyap Peru Viṇṇappam [Sincere, long petition to god about the pure path of unity]," in *Tiruvaruṭpā, Vacaṉa Pakuti* [*Tiruvaruṭpā,* prose section], ed. A. Balakrishna Pillai (Chennai: Nam Tamilar Patippakam, 2010), 126.

42. Ramalinga Swami, *Citamparam Irāmaliṅkapiḷḷai Avarkaḷ Tiruvāymalarntaruḷiya Tiruvaruṭpā* [Chidambaram Ramalinga Pillai's *Tiruvaruṭpā*], ed. Toluvur Velayuda Mudaliyar (Madras: Asiatic Press, 1867); Ramalinga Swami, *Tiruvaruṭpā Tiruttaṇikai Patikam* [*Tiruvaruṭpā,* poems to Murugan at Tiruttanikai] (Madras: Memorial Press, 1880); Ramalinga Swami, *Citamparam Irāmaliṅkacuvāmikaḷ Tiruvāymalarntaruḷiya Tiruvaruṭpā, Āṟāvatu Tirumuṟai* [Chidambaram Ramalinga Swami's *Tiruvaruṭpā,* sixth section] (Madras: Authikalanithi Press, 1885).

43. Ramalinga Swami, *Citamparam Irāmaliṅka Cuvāmikaḷ Tiruvāymalarntaruḷiya Tiru Aruṭpā* [Chidambaram Ramalinga Swamigal's *Tiruvaruṭpā*], ed. A. Balakrishna Pillai, 2nd ed., 12 vols. (Chennai: Nam Tamilar Patippakam, 2010).

44. Uran Adigal, *Irāmaliṅka Aṭikaḷ Varalāṟu,* 279.

45. Ramalinga Swami, *Tiru Aruṭpā* [Uran Adigal ed.], 30–31.

46. "A New Revelation," *Madras Mail,* July 5, 1871.

47. Verses 3419–3420, Ramalinga Swami, *Tiru Aruṭpā* [Uran Adigal ed.]. All translations from Tamil are my own. Unless otherwise indicated, all references to Ramalinga's verses follow the numbering of Uran Adigal's edition, which has become the standard of citation in contemporary works.

48. Arumuga Navalar (under the name of Mavandur Tiyagesa Mudaliyar), "Pōliyaruṭpā Maṟuppu" [Critique of the pseudo-divine verses], in *Aruṭpā Maruṭpā: Kaṇṭaṉattiraṭṭu* [Verses of divine grace, verses of delusion: a collection of polemical literature], ed. P. Saravanan (Nagarkovil: Kalaccuvatu Patippakam, 2010), 699. The *Tēvāram* is a collection of devotional verses to Shiva that is the earliest and probably the most important part of the Shaiva *Tirumuṟai* canon.

49. Luba Zubkova (Bytchikhina), "Religious Universalism of Ramalinga Swamikal, the Holy Poet of Tamils," *Journal of Tamil Studies* 59 (2001): 93.

50. Charles H. Heimsath, *Indian Nationalism and Hindu Social Reform* (Princeton: Princeton University Press, 1964), 45.

51. V. R. Ramachandra Dikshitar, *Studies in Tamil Literature and History* (London: Luzac & Co., 1930), 124.

52. Kamil Zvelebil, *Tamil Literature* (Wiesbaden: Harrassowitz, 1974), 113.

53. N. Subrahmanian, *History of Tamilnad, A.D. 1565–1956,* 2nd ed. (Madurai, India: Koodal Publishers, 1982), 289.

54. R. Balachandran, "Pioneers of Tamil Literature: Transition to Modernity," *Indian Literature* 49, no. 2 (2005): 181.

55. C. Jesudasan, *International Encyclopaedia of Indian Literature,* vol. 2: *Tamil,* ed. Ganga Ram Garg, rev. ed. (Delhi: Mittal Publications, 1987), 135.

56. Neela Padmanabhan, "Modern Tamil Literature," in *Modern Indian Literature, an Anthology,* ed. K. M. George (New Delhi: Sahitya Akademi, 1992), 378.

57. Sascha Ebeling, *Colonizing the Realm of Words: The Transformation of Tamil Literature in Nineteenth-Century South India* (Albany: State University of New York Press, 2010), 159, 183 n. 136.

58. Sisir Kumar Das, *A History of Indian Literature, 1800–1910: Western Impact,' Indian Response,* ed. Birendra Kumar Bhattacharyya, A History of Indian Literature 8 (New Delhi: Sahitya Akademi, 1991), 152–53.

59. Jean-Luc Racine and Josiane Racine, "Dalit Identities and the Dialectics of Oppression and Emancipation in a Changing India: The Tamil Case and Beyond," *Comparative Studies of South Asia, Africa, and the Middle East* 18, no. 1 (1998): 8.

60. Peter Heehs, *Indian Religions: A Historical Reader of Spiritual Expression and Experience* (New York: New York University Press, 2002), 416.

61. Hacker, "Aspects of Neo-Hinduism," 582, 604.

62. Eugene F. Irschick, *Tamil Revivalism in the 1930s* (Madras: Cre-A, 1986), 82–88. For a more detailed account of the Dravidianist appropriation of Ramalinga, see P. Saravanan's chapter, "Vaḷḷalār: Tirāviṭa Iyakkattiṉ Vēr" [Vallalar: the root of the Dravidian Movement]," in P. Saravanan, *Vāḻaiyaṭi Vāḻaiyeṉa . . . Vaḷḷalār Kaṟṟatum Vaḷḷalāril Peṟṟatum* [The banana doesn't fall far from the tree: the teachings of Vallalar and his heritage] (Chennai: Cantiya Patippakam, 2009), 13–26. For an account of Ramalinga's influence on Maraimalai Adigal, perhaps the leading figure in the reconfiguration of Shaivism along the lines of a Tamil ethnic community, see V. Ravi Vaithees, *Religion, Caste, and Nation in South India: Maraimalai Adigal, the Neo-Saivite Movement, and Tamil Nationalism, 1876–1950* (New Delhi: Oxford University Press, 2015), 199–205.

63. Srilata Raman, "The Spaces in Between: Ramalinga Swamigal (1823–1874), Hunger, and Religion in Colonial India," *History of Religions* 53, no. 1 (2013): 1–27. See also Srilata Raman, "Justifying Filicide: Ramalinga Swamigal, the Periyapurāṇam, and Tamil Religious Modernity," *International Journal of Hindu Studies* 18, no. 1 (2014): 33–66.

64. Raj Gautaman, *Kaṇmūṭi Vaḻakkam Elām Maṇmūṭippōka . . . ! Ci. Irāmaliṅkam (1823–1874)* [C. Ramalinga (1823–1874), who buried ignorant habits], 2nd ed. (Chennai: Tamilini, 2007), 22–27.

65. R. Venkatesan, "Irāmaliṅkam Pāṭalkaḷ Vaḷḷalār Tokuppāṉa Varalāṟu" [The history of the Vallalar compilation of C. Iramalinga's verses], in *Tamiḻ Nūl Tokuppu Varalāṟu* [The history of Tamil text compilation], ed. P. Ilamaran Muttaiya Vellaiyan, J. Sivakumar, and K. Ganesh (Chennai: Puthiya Puthakam Pusuthu, 2010), 86–93.

66. P. Saravanan, *Aruṭpā Maruṭpā: Kaṇṭaṉattiraṭṭu* [Verses of divine grace, verses of delusion: a collection of polemical literature] (Nagarkovil: Kalaccuvatu Patippakam, 2010).

67. Chakrabarty, *Provincializing Europe,* 43.

68. In a passage that accords with much of my argument, Hatcher suggests "the possibility that Sahajanand was not merely almost modern but was in fact modern—we might even say as modern as Rammohan Roy." Brian A. Hatcher, "Situating the Swaminarayan Tradition in the Historiography of Modern Hindu Reform," in *Swaminarayan Hinduism: Tradition, Adaptation, and Identity,* ed. Raymond Brady Williams and Yogi Trivedi (New York: Oxford University Press, 2016), 27.

69. On Ramalinga as a Hindu reformer, see K. S. Mahadevan, "Social Ideals and Patriotism in Tamil Literature (1900–1930)," *Indian Literature* 20, no. 3 (1977): 112; Gautaman, *C. Ramalinga,* 12–13; and C. Paramarthalingam, *Social Reform Movement in Tamil Nadu in the 19th Century with Special Reference to St. Ramalinga* (Madurai: Rajakumari Publications, 1995).

70. Rajeev Bhargava, "Are There Alternative Modernities?" in *Culture, Democracy, and Development in South Asia,* ed. N. N. Vohra (New Delhi: Shipra Publications, 2001), 25.

71. S. N. Eisenstadt, "Multiple Modernities," *Daedalus* 129, no. 1 (2000): 2–3.

72. Ibid., 2, 24.

73. Timothy S. Dobe, "Modern Monks and Global Hinduism," in *Hinduism in the Modern World,* ed. Brian A. Hatcher (New York: Routledge, 2016), 164.

74. Ibid., 169–75.

75. S. Subrahmanyam, "Connected Histories: Notes Towards a Reconfiguration of Early Modern Eurasia," *Modern Asian Studies* 31 (1997): 737.

76. Italics in original. S. Subrahmanyam, "Hearing Voices: Vignettes of Early Modernity in South Asia, 1400–1750," *Daedalus* 127, no. 3 (1998): 99–100.

77. Subrahmanyam, "Connected Histories," 747–48.

78. Ibid., 737–39.

79. Velcheru Narayana Rao, David Dean Shulman, and Sanjay Subrahmanyam, *Textures of Time: Writing History in South India, 1600–1800* (Delhi: Permanent Black, 2001), 264.

80. Sheldon Pollock, "Pretextures of Time," *History and Theory* 46, no. 3 (October 2007): 381.

81. Eisenstadt, "Multiple Modernities," 25.

82. Brian A. Hatcher, "Remembering Rammohan: An Essay on the (Re-)Emergence of Modern Hinduism," *History of Religions* 46, no. 1 (2006): 80.

83. Bjorn Thomassen, "Anthropology and Its Many Modernities: When Concepts Matter," *Journal of the Royal Anthropological Institute* 18 (2012): 170, 173.

84. Critical work has highlighted that Western ideas and rubrics were themselves transformed through colonial encounters. See, for example, Peter van der Veer, *Imperial Encounters: Religion and Modernity in India and Britain* (Princeton: Princeton University Press, 2001).

85. Shalini Randeria, "Entangled Histories of Uneven Modernities: Civil Society, Caste Councils, and Legal Pluralism in Postcolonial India," in *Comparative History and the Quest for Transnationality: Central European Approaches and New Perspectives,* ed. Jürgen Kocka and Heinz-Gerhard Haupt (New York: Berghahn Books, 2009), 80. For an effective utilization of the notion of entangled histories in thinking about colonial religious encounters, see Michael Bergunder, "What Is Religion? The Unexplained Subject Matter of Religious Studies," *Method and Theory in the Study of Religion* 26 (2014): 246–86.

86. van der Veer, "Colonial Cosmopolitanism," 178.

87. Frederick Cooper, *Colonialism in Question: Theory, Knowledge, History* (Berkeley: University of California Press, 2005), 148.

88. Saurabh Dube, "Modernity and Its Enchantments: An Introduction," in *Enchantments of Modernity: Empire, Nation, Globalization,* ed. Saurabh Dube (New Delhi: Routledge, 2009), 2.

89. Anne M. Blackburn, *Locations of Buddhism: Colonialism and Modernity in Sri Lanka* (Chicago: University of Chicago Press, 2010), xii–xv.

2 GIVING TO THE POOR: RAMALINGA'S TRANSFORMATION OF HINDU CHARITY

1. For example, at the important Tirupati temple in South India, the most popular charitable schemes among devotees are those that provide food and medical service to the poor. See Pushpa Sundar, *For God's Sake: Religious Charity and Social Development in India* (New Delhi: Sampradaan Indian Centre for Philanthropy, 2002), 61. Sundar's work provides a good overview of the charitable projects of a range of religious institutions in India.

2. David Kopf, *The Brahmo Samaj and the Shaping of the Modern Indian Mind* (Princeton: Princeton University Press, 1979), 119.

3. Dayananda Saraswati, *An English Translation of the Satyarth Prakash,* trans. Durga Prasad (Lahore: Virjanand Press, 1908), 349.

4. Carey Anthony Watt, *Serving the Nation: Cultures of Service, Association, and Citizenship* (New York: Oxford University Press, 2005). See also Malavika Kasturi, "'All

Gifting Is Sacred': The Sanatana Dharma Sabha Movement, the Reform of Dana and Civil Society in Late Colonial India," *Indian Economic and Social History Review* 47, no. 1 (2010): 107–39. The Arya Samaj provided famine relief in 1897. As this chapter will demonstrate, Lajpat Rai was wrong to assert that with this effort, "the Arya Samaj was the first non-Christian private agency which started a non-official movement for the relief of distress caused by famine." Lajpat Rai, *The Arya Samaj: An Account of Its Origin, Doctrines, and Activities, with a Biographical Sketch of the Founder* (Delhi: Renaissance Publishing House, 1989 [1915]), 212.

5. Carey A. Watt, "Philanthropy and Civilizing Missions in India C. 1820–1960: States, NGOs, and Development," in *Civilizing Missions in Colonial and Postcolonial South Asia: From Improvement to Development*, ed. Watt and Michael Mann (New York: Anthem Press, 2011), 280.

6. Raman, "Spaces in Between." Raman is not alone in this; many commentators on Ramalinga's radical vision of religious community suggest the influence of Christianity. See, for example, Saravanan, *Vāḻaiyaṭi Vāḻaiyeṉa*, 118–21.

7. The term "Protestant Buddhism" was first popularized by Gananath Obeyesekere in his influential essay "Religious Symbolism and Political Change in Ceylon," in *The Two Wheels of Dhamma: Essays on the Theravada Tradition in India and Ceylon*, ed. Gananath Obeyesekere, Frank Reynolds, and Bardwell L. Smith (Chambersburg, PA: American Academy of Religion, 1972). The concept has had extraordinary salience while inviting a number of critiques. For criticisms, see, especially, Charles Hallisey, "Roads Taken and Not Taken in the Study of Theravada Buddhism," in *Curators of the Buddha: The Study of Buddhism under Colonialism*, ed. Donald S. Lopez (Chicago: University of Chicago Press, 1995): 31–61; Stephen Prothero, "Henry Steel Olcott and 'Protestant Buddhism,'" *Journal of the American Academy of Religion* 63, no. 2 (1995): 281–302; and John Clifford Holt, "Sri Lanka's Protestant Buddhism?" *Ethnic Studies Report* 8, no. 2 (1990): 1–8.

8. Farquhar, *Modern Religious Movements*, 1.

9. Ibid., 433. Emphasis in original.

10. Hatcher, "Contemporary Hindu Thought," 201.

11. Ibid.

12. Ibid., 202.

13. Katherine E. Ulrich, "Food Fights: Buddhist, Hindu, and Jain Dietary Polemics in South India," *History of Religions* 46, no. 3 (2007): 228–29.

14. McKim Marriot, "Caste Ranking and Food Transactions: A Matrix Analysis," in *Structure and Change in Indian Society*, ed. Milton B. Singer and Bernard S. Cohn (Chicago: Aldine Pub. Co., 1968): 133–71.

15. Kathleen Iva Koppedrayer, "The Sacred Presence of the Guru: The Velala Lineages of Tiruvavatuturai, Dharmapuram, and Tiruppanantal" (PhD diss., McMaster University, 1990), 41–42.

16. Ibid., 65–68. These endogamous communities are Pillai, Tondaimandalam Mudaliyar, Shaiva Chettiyar, Karkattar Pillai, and Desikar. Glenn E. Yocum, "A Non-Brahman Tamil Saiva Mutt: A Field Study of the Thiruvavaduthurai Adheenam," in *Monastic Life in the Christian and Hindu Traditions: A Comparative Study*, ed. Austin B. Creel and Vasudha Narayanan (Lewiston, N.Y.: Edwin Mellen Press, 1990), 269; and Koppedrayer, "Sacred Presence," 99.

17. Ibid., 25.

18. Ibid., 128.

19. Maria Heim, *Theories of the Gift in South Asia: Hindu, Buddhist, and Jain Reflections on Dāna* (New York: Routledge, 2004), xx.

20. Ibid., 55. Here the Hindu medieval shastric literature differs from ethnographic evidence on *dāna*. Studies by Parry, Raheja, and others have documented that giving among contemporary Hindus is usually a transaction in which the donor is of higher status than the recipient, and the act of giving entails the transfer of impurity from donor to recipient. Jonathan Parry, "The Gift, the Indian Gift, and the 'Indian Gift,'" *Man* 21, no. 3 (September 1986): 453–73; and Gloria Goodwin Raheja, *The Poison in the Gift: Ritual, Prestation, and the Dominant Caste in a North Indian Village* (Chicago: University of Chicago Press, 1988).

21. Koppedrayer, "Sacred Presence," 250, 278.

22. Ibid., 272. Glenn Yocum notes that during his stay at the Tiruvavaduthurai Adheenam in 1984–85, diners were separated according to prestige, with designated seating for initiates, resident scholars, singers of the Tamil devotional work *Tēvāram*, office staff and guests, and school children. Yocum also observes that distinct kitchens in the monastery cooked for different groups: one for the matha head, one for brahmans, and a large kitchen for others. Yocum, "Non-Brahman," 265. Vasudeva Rao, in his study of the Udupi Madhva Matha, a brahman matha in Karnataka, makes similar observations about distinct areas of seating based on caste divisions. Madhva, Smartha, and Sthanika brahmans are fed in the chowki hall; brahman students are fed in the ground-floor bhojanshala; and non-brahmans eat in the first-floor bhojanshala. Vasudeva Rao, *Living Traditions in Contemporary Contexts: The Madhva* Matha *of Udupi* (New Delhi: Orient Longman, 2002), 74–78.

23. Koppedrayer, "Sacred Presence," 326.

24. It is perhaps for this reason that, according to P.V. Kane, many shastric sources contend that giving to beggars is the most inferior of gifts. Pandurang Vaman Kane, *History of Dharmashastra (Ancient and Mediæval Religious and Civil Law in India)*, 2nd ed. (Poona: Bhandarkar Oriental Research Institute, 1968), 2.1:113.

25. Heim, *Theories of the Gift*, 74–79; and Kane, *History of Dharmashastra*, 2.1:116. Kane notes that according to shastric literature, the giving and receiving of *dāna* is dictated by privilege, while giving to the poor is done out of compassion (*dayā*).

26. David James Brick, "The *Dānakāṇḍa* ('Book on Gifting') of the Kṛtyakalpataru: A Critical Edition and Annotated Translation" (PhD diss., The University of Texas at Austin, 2009), 47–49.

27. R. Champakalakshmi, *Religion, Tradition, and Ideology: Pre-Colonial South India* (New Delhi: Oxford University Press, 2011), 296–97.

28. Koppedrayer, "Sacred Presence," 40.

29. Ibid., 234.

30. Michael Christian Linderman, "Charity's Venue: Representing Indian Kingship in the Monumental Pilgrim Rest Houses of the Maratha Rajas of Tanjavur, 1761–1832" (PhD diss., University of Pennsylvania, 2009), 21–22.

31. K. Nambi Arooran, "The Changing Role of Three Saiva Maths in Tanjore District from the Beginning of the 20th Century," in *Changing South Asia*, ed. Kenneth Ballhatchet and David D. Taylor (Hong Kong: Centre of South Asian Studies in the School of Oriental and African Studies, University of London, 1984), 54.

32. Quoted in ibid., 55.

33. Yocum, "Non-Brahman," 265.

34. For a more detailed account of Ramalinga's society, see Richard S. Weiss, "Voluntary Associations and Religious Change in Colonial India: Ramalinga Adigal's 'Society of the True Path,'" *South Asia: Journal of South Asian Studies* 41, no. 1 (2018): 18–32.

35. Verse 3406, Ramalinga Swami, *Tiru Aruṭpā* [Uran Adigal ed.].

36. Uran Adigal, *Irāmaliṅka Aṭikaḷ Varalāṟu,* 367.

37. He later replaces "Veda" with "cutta caṉmārkka," the "pure path." Ramalinga Swami, *Tiru Aruṭpā* [Balakrishna Pillai ed.], 5:108.

38. Thomas Manninezhath, *Harmony of Religions: Vedānta Siddhānta Samarasam of Tāyumānavar* (Delhi: Motilal Banarsidass Publishers, 1993).

39. Verse 3471, Ramalinga Swami, *Tiru Aruṭpā* [Uran Adigal ed.].

40. Ramalinga Swami, *Tiru Aruṭpā* [Balakrishna Pillai ed.], 5:93.

41. Ibid., 5:96–97.

42. A number of handwritten copies of the work were in circulation among his followers prior to publication. Ibid., 2:64 n. 374. It is not clear, however, precisely what the state of the work was between 1867 and 1879. It seems that Ramalinga was still working on the text in 1869. In a letter dated May 11, 1869, between two of Ramalinga's disciples, Irakkam Irattina Mudaliyar asks Shanmuga Pillai whether Ramalinga has completed the work yet. Ramalinga Swami, *Tiru Aruṭpā* [Uran Adigal ed.], 3:485.

43. In this regard the work differed from some of his other writings, which he intended only for the eyes of his close followers.

44. Ramalinga Swami, *Tiru Aruṭpā* [Balakrishna Pillai ed.], 2:64–65.

45. Ibid., 2:66.

46. See, for example, *Tēvāram* 5.64 (2): "thinking of [Shiva], my heart melts"; 2.109 (5): "those whose melting hearts contain the bright light that is [Siva] . . . they receive his grace [aruḷ]"; 6.85 (3): "he [Siva] loves those devotees whose hearts melt, longing [for him]." "Digital Tēvāram," Institut français de Pondichéry; Ecole française d'Extrême-Orient, http://www.ifpindia.org/digitaldb/site/digital_tevaram/INDEX.HTM.

47. Ramalinga Swami, *Tiru Aruṭpā* [Balakrishna Pillai ed.], 2:66.

48. Ibid., 2:68.

49. Ibid.

50. Ibid., 2:69–71.

51. C. J. Fuller, *The Camphor Flame: Popular Hinduism and Society in India* (Princeton: Princeton University Press, 1992), 83–105.

52. Ramalinga Swami, *Tiru Aruṭpā* [Balakrishna Pillai ed.], 2:70.

53. Heim points to a Jain work that asserts that gift transactions should consider the worthiness of the giver, the recipient, the substance of the gift, and the procedure through which the gift is transferred. Heim, *Theories of the Gift,* xvii.

54. Ramalinga Swami, *Tiru Aruṭpā* [Balakrishna Pillai ed.], 2:78.

55. For example, J. M. Nallaswami Pillai, "The Nature of the Jiva," in *Studies in Saiva Siddhanta,* ed. Nallaswami Pillai (Madras: Meykandan Press, 1911): 316–37; and Hilko Wiardo Schomerus and Humphrey Palmer, *Śaiva Siddhānta: An Indian School of Mystical Thought*, English ed. (Delhi: Motilal Banarsidass Publishers, 2000), 46.

56. Ramalinga Swami, *Tiru Aruṭpā* [Balakrishna Pillai ed.], 2:78.

57. Ibid., 2:79–80.

58. Ibid., 2:72.

59. Ibid., 2:91. For disease names I consulted the magisterial T.V. Sambasivam Pillai, *Tamil—English Dictionary of Medicine, Chemistry, Botany, and Allied Sciences (Based on Indian Medical Science)*, 5 vols. (Madras: Government of Tamil Nadu, 1994).

60. See Richard S. Weiss, *Recipes for Immortality: Medicine, Religion, and Community in South India* (New York: Oxford University Press, 2009).

61. On the medical resonances in the text, see Raman, "Spaces in Between," 17–20.

62. Ramalinga Swami, *Tiru Aruṭpā* [Balakrishna Pillai ed.], 2:96–97.

63. Raman, "Spaces in Between."

64. Ramalinga Swami, *Tiru Aruṭpā* [Balakrishna Pillai ed.], 2:72–74.

65. Ibid., 2:83–84.

66. Srilata Raman also makes this observation, pointing out correspondences between Ramalinga's language and the processes described in classical Ayurvedic texts. Raman, "Spaces in Between," 18–20.

67. Ramalinga Swami, *Tiru Aruṭpā* [Balakrishna Pillai ed.], 2:76.

68. Ibid., 2:82–83.

69. Ibid., 2:83.

70. Ibid., 2:85–87. Raman also analyzes this powerful passage. Raman, "Spaces in Between," 14.

71. Raman, "Spaces in Between," 22.

72. Kamil Zvelebil, *The Smile of Murugan: On Tamil Literature of South India* (Leiden: Brill, 1973), 276. For more on the development of prose as a literary form in Tamil, see Ebeling, *Colonizing the Realm of Words*.

73. Ramalinga Swami, ed., *O̲livil Oṭukkam* (Chennai: Mullai Nilayam, 2004 [1851]).

74. Zvelebil, *Smile of Murugan*, 270–71.

75. On Navalar's use of print, see Richard S. Weiss, "Religion and the Emergence of Print in Colonial India: Arumuga Navalar's Publishing Project," *Indian Economic and Social History Review* 53, no. 4 (2016): 473–500.

76. Bernard Bate, "Arumuga Navalar, Saivite Sermons, and the Delimitation of Religion, C. 1850," *Indian Economic and Social History Review* 42, no. 4 (2005): 469–84.

77. Ramalinga Swami, *Tiru Aruṭpā* [Balakrishna Pillai ed.], 2:84–85.

78. Ibid., 2:86.

79. Ibid., 2:92–93.

80. Ramalinga Swami, *Tiru Aruṭpā Urai Naṭaip Pakuti*, 543–44.

81. Ramalinga Swami, *Tiru Aruṭpā* [Balakrishna Pillai ed.], 2:87–88.

82. Ibid., 2:88.

83. Ibid., 2:72.

84. Ibid., 2:84.

85. Ibid., 2:90–91.

86. Verse 4160, Ramalinga Swami, *Tiru Aruṭpā* [Uran Adigal ed.].

87. Raman, "Spaces in Between," 23.

88. Ibid., 25.

89. Ibid., 26.

90. Ibid., 22–23.

91. Henriette Bugge, *Mission and Tamil Society: Social and Religious Change in South India (1840-1900)* (Richmond, Surrey: Curzon Press, 1994), 65; and B.H. Badley, *Indian*

Missionary Directory and Memorial Volume (Lucknow: Methodist Episcopal Church Press, 1876), 174–75.

92. Raman, "Spaces in Between." Besides Tamil literary representations of hunger, one might also look at didactic literature like *Tirukkuraḷ* and *Nālaṭiyār,* which discuss charity to the poor. According to the 1885 *Imperial Gazetteer of India,* Ramalinga's South Arcot district had more Muslims (48,289 or 2.7%) than Christians (39,571 or 2.2%), as well as 5,261 Jains and Buddhists. William Wilson Hunter, *The Imperial Gazetteer of India,* 2nd ed., 14 vols. (London: Trübner and Co., 1885), 1:322.

93. Linderman, "Charity's Venue."

94. Ibid., 1–2.

95. Ibid., 58–59.

96. Hunter, *Imperial Gazetteer,* 1:327.

97. On Raja Serfoji II, see, especially, the work of Savithri Preetha Nair and Indira Peterson. Savithri Preeta Nair, *Raja Serfoji II: Science, Medicine, and Enlightenment in Tanjore* (New Delhi: Routledge, 2012); and Indira Viswanathan Peterson, "The Schools of Serfoji II of Tanjore: Education and Princely Modernity in Early Nineteenth-Century India," in *Trans Colonial Modernities in South Asia,* ed. Michael S. Dodson and Brian A. Hatcher (New York: Routledge, 2012), 15–44.

98. Linderman, "Charity's Venue," 83, 86–88.

99. M.A. Sherring and Edward Storrow, *The History of Protestant Missions in India from Their Commencement in 1706 to 1881* (London: The Religious Tract Society, 1884), 364, 355. On the Leipzig mission's "flexible approach" to caste, see Will Sweetman, "Colonialism All the Way Down? Religion and the Secular in Early Modern Writing on South India," in *Religion and the Secular: Historical and Colonial Formations,* ed. Timothy Fitzgerald (London: Equinox, 2007):117–34.

100. Ramalinga Swami, *Tiru Aruṭpā* [Balakrishna Pillai ed.], 2:82–83, 86, 92–93.

101. On the Tamil siddhas, caste, and medicine, see Weiss, *Recipes for Immortality,* and Kamil Zvelebil, *The Poets of the Powers* (London: Rider, 1973).

102. David Arnold, "Famine in Peasant Consciousness and Peasant Action: Madras, 1876–78," in *Subaltern Studies III: Writings on South Asian History and Society,* ed. Ranajit Guha (Delhi: Oxford University Press, 1984), 67.

103. Ibid., 72.

104. Ibid., 76–78.

105. Ibid., 85–90.

106. Ibid., 98–108.

107. R.A. Dalyell, *Memorandum on the Madras Famine of 1866* (Madras: Information of the Madras Central Famine Relief Committee, 1867), 102, 107.

108. Ibid., 111.

109. Ibid., 89, 114.

110. Ibid., 114–17.

111. Ibid., 92, 98, 165.

112. Ibid., 109–13.

113. Ramalinga Swami, *Tiru Aruṭpā* [Balakrishna Pillai ed.], 2:87.

114. Erica Bornstein, "The Impulse of Philanthropy," *Cultural Anthropology* 24, no. 4 (2009): 643.

115. Ramalinga Swami, *Tiru Aruṭpā* [Balakrishna Pillai ed.], 5:93.
116. Ibid., 2:66.
117. Michel Foucault, "Nietzsche, Genealogy, History," *Semiotexte* 3, no. 1 (1978): 142.

3 THE PUBLICATION OF *TIRUVARUṬPĀ*: THE AUTHORITY OF CANON AND PRINT

1. Chapter five focuses on this debate.

2. Elizabeth L. Eisenstein, *The Printing Press as an Agent of Change: Communications and Cultural Transformations in Early Modern Europe,* 2 vols. (Cambridge: Cambridge University Press, 1979).

3. Ibid., 362–63.

4. Ibid., 353–54.

5. For a critique of Eisenstein along these lines, see A. Pettegree and M. Hall, "The Reformation and the Book: A Reconsideration," *Historical Journal* 47, no. 4 (2004): 785–808.

6. Alexandra Walsham, "Preaching without Speaking: Script, Print, and Religious Dissent," in *The Uses of Script and Print, 1300–1700,* ed. Julia C. Crick and Walsham (Cambridge: Cambridge University Press, 2004), 212. In the same volume, David d'Avray argues that Martin Luther might have done very well without print. See d'Avray, "Printing, Mass Communication, and Religious Reformation: The Middle Ages and After," in ibid., 50–70.

7. On the reformulation of the Tamil literary canon at the end of the nineteenth century, see A. R. Venkatachalapathy, "The Making of a Canon: Literature in Colonial Tamilnadu," in *In Those Days There Was No Coffee: Writings in Cultural History* (New Delhi: Yoda Press, 2006), 88–113. Rafael Klöber examines the history of Shaiva Siddhanta formulations of canon in the nineteenth and twentieth centuries in Klöber, "What is Saiva Siddhanta? Tracing Modern Genealogies and Historicising a Classical Canon," *The Journal of Hindu Studies* 10 (2017): 187–218.

8. Exceptions are Ulrike Stark, "Publishers as Patrons and the Commodification of Hindu Religious Texts in Nineteenth-Century North India," in *Patronage and Popularisation, Pilgrimage and Procession: Channels of Transcultural Translation and Transmission in Early Modern South Asia; Papers in Honour of Monika Horstmann,* ed. Heidi Rika Maria Pauwels (Wiesbaden: Harrassowitz, 2009), 189–203; and Weiss, "Arumuga Navalar's Publishing Project." Works that look at the impact of print on Islam in South Asia include J. B. P. More, *Muslim Identity, Print Culture, and the Dravidian Factor in Tamil Nadu* (Hyderabad: Orient Longman, 2004); Francis Robinson, "Technology and Religious Change—Islam and the Impact of Print," *Modern Asian Studies* 27, no. 1 (1993): 229–51; and C. Ryan Perkins, "From the Mehfil to the Printed Word: Public Debate and Discourse in Late Colonial India," *Indian Economic and Social History Review* 50, no. 1 (2013): 47–76.

9. Long's data for works published between 1853 and 1867 show a greater diversity of content and genres than in the earlier period, but religious and especially Hindu works still represented a significant percentage of all titles published. See Tapti Roy, "Disciplining the Printed Text: Colonial and Nationalist Surveillance of Bengali Literature," in *Texts of Power: Emerging Disciplines in Colonial Bengal,* ed. Partha Chatterjee (Minneapolis: University of Minnesota Press, 1995), 39, 51.

10. About 38% of the total were Christian, 29% Hindu, and 2% Islamic. John Murdoch, *Classified Catalogue of Tamil Printed Books, with Introductory Notices* (Madras: The Christian Vernacular Education Society, 1865), preface, v.

11. Daniel E. White, *From Little London to Little Bengal: Religion, Print, and Modernity in Early British India, 1793–1835* (Baltimore: John Hopkins University Press, 2013), 65.

12. Rammohan Roy, "The Freedom of the Press," in *Makers of Modern India,* ed. Ramachandra Guha (Cambridge: The Belknap Press of Harvard University Press, 2011), 34.

13. J.T.F. Jordens, *Dayananda Sarasvati: His Life and Ideas* (New Delhi: Oxford University Press, 1978), 214–15.

14. John E. Llewellyn, "From Interpretation to Reform: Dayananda's Reading of the Vedas," in *Authority, Anxiety, and Canon: Essays in Vedic Interpretation,* ed. Laurie L. Patton (Albany: State University of New York Press, 1994), 245.

15. On the identification of various Indian leaders with Luther, and the transformation of Protestant notions of subjectivity, see J. Barton Scott, "Luther in the Tropics: Karsandas Mulji and the Colonial 'Reformation' of Hinduism," *Journal of the American Academy of Religion* 83, no. 1 (2015): 181–209.

16. Murdoch, *Classified Catalogue,* 81. An octavo is about 8 × 10 inches (20 × 25 cm). To put the price in perspective, in his 1859 report on the vernacular press in Bengal, James Long estimated that book hawkers around Calcutta earned between six and eight rupees a month. Anindita Ghosh, "An Uncertain 'Coming of the Book': Early Print Cultures in Colonial India," *Book History* 6 (2003): 30.

17. Kanchipuram Sabhapati Mudaliyar, ed., *Periya Purāṇam,* vol. 1 (Chennai: Kalvi Vilakka Press, 1859).

18. Navalar, *Periyapurāṇam,* ii.

19. Weiss, "Arumuga Navalar's Publishing Project."

20. Robert A. Yelle, *The Language of Disenchantment: Protestant Literalism and Colonial Discourse in British India* (New York: Oxford University Press, 2013).

21. Ulrike Stark, *An Empire of Books: The Naval Kishore Press and the Diffusion of the Printed Word in Colonial India* (Ranikhet, India: Permanent Black, 2007), 21–22.

22. "On the Progress and Present State of the Native Press in India," *The Friend of India* 12 (1825): 139.

23. Ghosh, "Uncertain," 24.

24. Murdoch, *Classifed Catalogue,* 118. There were 16 annas in a rupee, and 12 pies in an anna. Octodecimo size is about 4 × 6 inches (10 × 15 cm).

25. Ghosh, "Uncertain," 48.

26. Stuart H. Blackburn, *Print, Folklore, and Nationalism in Colonial South India* (Delhi: Permanent Black, 2003), 90.

27. Stark, *Empire of Books,* 11. Italics in original.

28. This does not mean that all printed works were simply accepted as authoritative. As Adrian Johns has shown, printed works have not always been associated with veracity, let alone canonicity, and the association of print with truth develops through specific histories. Johns, *The Nature of the Book: Print and Knowledge in the Making* (Chicago: University of Chicago Press, 1998). The great Tamil poet-scholar Minakshisundaram Pillai (1815–1876) expressed misgivings about print, warning his star pupil U.V. Swaminatha Iyer that "Print

does not validate everything. People who are not proficient in the [Tamil] language may print anything." Quoted in A. R. Venkatachalapathy, "Reading Practices and Modes of Reading in Colonial Tamil Nadu," *Studies in History* 10, no. 2 (1994): 275.

29. The first volume was published in 1867, the second in 1880, and the third in 1885. Uran Adigal gives a useful sketch of the publication of these three volumes in his introduction to his edition of *Tiruvaruṭpā*. Ramalinga Swami, *Tiru Aruṭpā* [Uran Adigal ed.], 41–53.

30. Brian Stock, *The Implications of Literacy: Written Language and Models of Interpretation in the Eleventh and Twelfth Centuries* (Princeton: Princeton University Press, 1983), 3.

31. Ibid., 90.

32. Ramalinga Swami, *Tiru Aruṭpā* [Balakrishna Pillai ed.], vol. 5.

33. Ibid., 5:30.

34. Ibid., 5:31–32.

35. The verse is from the poem "Tiruvaruṇmuṟaiyīṭu," Ramalinga Swami, *Tiruvaruṭpā* [1867 ed.], Tirumurai 1, 123. This is verse number 2260 in Uran Adigal's edition.

36. Ramalinga Swami, *Tiru Aruṭpā* [Uran Adigal ed.], 61.

37. Velayuda Mudaliyar, "Tiruvaruṭpā Varalāṟu," verse 43.

38. See, for example, the images of Ramalinga's handwritten verses in Uran Adigal's edition of *Tiruvaruṭpā*. Ramalinga Swami, *Tiru Aruṭpā* [Uran Adigal ed.].

39. Ramalinga Swami, *Tiru Aruṭpā* [Balakrishna Pillai ed.], 5:38–39.

40. Ibid., 5:39.

41. Ibid.

42. Ibid.

43. Velayuda Mudaliyar, "Tiruvaruṭpā Varalāṟu," verses 46–48.

44. Ibid., verses 48–53, 57.

45. Cited in Uran Adigal's introduction to his edition of *Tiruvaruṭpā*. See Ramalinga Swami, *Tiru Aruṭpā* [Uran Adigal ed.], 45.

46. Ramalinga Swami, *Tiru Aruṭpā* [Balakrishna Pillai ed.], 9:136, 169.

47. Murdoch, *Classified Catalogue*, xlii.

48. Quoted in Roy, "Disciplining," 55.

49. Copies of the 1867 edition are extant. I consulted a copy held by the Maraimalai Adigal Library in Chennai.

50. Ramalinga Swami, *Tiru Aruṭpā* [Balakrishna Pillai ed.], 59–60.

51. See, for example, M. P. Sivagnanam, *The Universal Vision of Saint Ramalinga: Vallalar Kanda Orumaippadu* (Annamalainagar: Annamalai University, 1987), 136.

52. A. Balakrishna Pillai notes that we know nothing about this verse preface that Ramalinga promised. Ramalinga Swami, *Tiru Aruṭpā* [Balakrishna Pillai ed.], 5:61.

53. Desikar, *Caṅkaraṉantāti*, title page.

54. Ramalinga Swami, *Tiruvaruṭpā* [1867 ed.], title page.

55. Ibid. "Asiatic Press" was a popular name for presses in India, and indeed throughout Asia, from the nineteenth century to the present day. I was not able to find specific information on this Chennai-based "Asiatic Press," but at least a few other Tamil works were published by an Asiatic Press in Chennai at the time, including Teraiyar's *Nīrniṟakkuṟi Neykkuṟic Cāstiraṅkaḷ*, edited by Kanchipuram Sabhapati Mudaliyar (Chennai, 1868); Minakshisundaram Pillai's *Tirunākaikkārōṇap Purāṇam* (Chennai, 1869); Vedanayagam Pillai's *Peṇmatimālaiyum Peṇkalviyum Peṇmāṇamum*, 2nd ed. (Chennai, 1870); and

Tiruvōṟṟiyūr Purāṇam (Madras, 1869), this last work cited in David Shulman, "The Enemy Within: Idealism and Dissent in South Indian Hinduism," in *Orthodoxy, Heterodoxy, and Dissent in India,* ed. S.N. Eisenstadt, Reuven Kahane, and Shulman (Berlin: Mouton, 1984), 54. If all these books were indeed published by the same Asiatic Press, it would indicate that the press did not adhere to a single ideological or sectarian position, as these works include a siddha text, a conventional temple Purana composed by perhaps the most celebrated Tamil poet-scholar of the nineteenth century, and a work on women's reform by a well-known Christian poet and author.

56. Ramalinga Swami, *Tiruvaruṭpā* [1867 ed.], front matter.

57. Stark, "Publishers as Patrons," 193–94.

58. Ramalinga Swami, *Tiruvaruṭpā* [1867 ed.], front matter.

59. For a poignant account of the efforts of authors to win patronage, see A.R. Venkatachalapathy, *The Province of the Book: Scholars, Scribes, and Scribblers in Colonial Tamilnadu* (Ranikhet, India: Permanent Black, 2012). On page 33, Venkatachalapathy specifically describes the prominent role of Chettiyars in the publication of Tamil classics.

60. Murdoch, *Classified Catalogue,* 75–106.

61. Quoted in Roy, "Disciplining," 44.

62. Robert Darnton, "Book Production in British India, 1850–1900," *Book History* 5, no. 1 (2002): 245.

63. Other works from this period that I have seen marked as copyright are the *Periya Purāṇam* and part of the *Tēvāram.* Mudaliyar, *Periya Purāṇam;* and Tirunavukkaracu, *Tēvārappatikattirumuṟaikaḷ,* ed. Kanchipuram Sabhapati Mudaliyar (Chennai: Kalaniti Press; Kalaratnacuram Press, 1866).

64. Murdoch, *Classified Catalogue,* lxii. See also A. R. Venkatachalapathy's discussion of copyright in Tamil publishing in his *Province of the Book,* 184–87.

65. Velayuda Mudaliyar, "Tiruvaruṭpā Varalāṟu," verse 57.

66. Velayuda Mudaliyar includes these details in an account of Ramalinga's life that he wrote for a Theosophical publication, *Hints on Esoteric Theosophy.* This is reproduced in Uran Adigal, *Irāmaliṅka Aṭikaḷ Varalāṟu,* 648–60. Srilata Raman gives a detailed analysis of Velayuda Mudaliyar's work in Raman, "Departure and Prophecy: The Disappearance of Irāmaliṅka Aṭikaḷ in the Early Narratives of His Life," *Indologica Taurinensia* 28 (2002): 179–203. For a brief biography of Mudaliyar, see U.V. Saminatha Iyer, *Piṟkālap Pulavarkaḷ* [Latter-day poets], ed. S. Vaidyanadan (Chennai: U.V. Saminatha Iyer Library, 2000), 288.

67. On the role of pandits in nineteenth-century Tamil publishing, see Blackburn's chapter "Pundits, Publishing, and Protest," in Blackburn, *Print,* 73–124. On pandits, patronage, and printing, see Venkatachalapathy, *Province of the Book;* V. Rajesh, *Manuscripts, Memory, and History: Classical Tamil Literature in Colonial India* (New Delhi: Cambridge University Press, 2014).

68. Blackburn, *Print,* 74–75. On the role of Tamil pandits in the philological work of the College of Fort St. George, see Thomas R. Trautmann, *Languages and Nations: The Dravidian Proof in Colonial Madras* (Berkeley: University of California Press, 2006); and Trautmann, ed., *The Madras School of Orientalism: Producing Knowledge in Colonial South India* (New Delhi: Oxford University Press, 2009).

69. Iyer, *Piṟkālap Pulavarkaḷ,* 145.

70. Ramalinga Swami, *Tiruvaruṭpā* [1867 ed.], title page.

71. Venkatachalapathy, *Province of the Book*, 28–29.

72. Karen Pechilis Prentiss, *The Embodiment of Bhakti* (New York: Oxford University Press, 1999), 143–44; and Indira Viswanathan Peterson, *Poems to Siva: The Hymns of the Tamil Saints* (Princeton: Princeton University Press, 1989).

73. Velayuda Mudaliyar, "Tiruvaruṭpā Varalāṟu," verses 37–39.

74. Indira Peterson translates *Tirumuṟai* as "sacred tradition." Peterson, *Poems to Siva*, 15.

75. Ramalinga Swami, *Tiruvaruṭpā* [1867 ed.], title page.

76. In his "Tiruvaruṭpā Varalāṟu," Velayuda Mudaliyar frequently refers to Ramalinga as "radiant with grace." Velayuda Mudaliyar, "Tiruvaruṭpā Varalāṟu," verses 28, 33, 34, 42, 56, 60, 61.

77. Ibid., verses 34, 35, 36.

78. Navalar, "Critique of the Pseudo-Divine Verses."

79. On *ciṟappuppāyiram* (special preface) conventions in the nineteenth century, see Ebeling, *Colonizing*, 62–73.

80. Ramalinga Swami, *Tiruvaruṭpā* [1867 ed.], front matter.

81. Uran Adigal, *Irāmaliṅka Aṭikaḷ Varalāṟu*. This book won a prize from the Tamil Nadu government in 1975, presented by DMK Chief Minister K. M. Karunanidhi. There is a certain irony in the DMK, the main Dravidianist party, with a history of anti-Hindu agitation, presenting an award for a biography of a Hindu leader. Ramalinga, however, has long been accepted by Dravidianist political leaders because of his anti-caste verses. See Saravanan, *Vāḻaiyaṭi Vāḻaiyeṉa*, 13–26.

82. Uran Adigal, *Irāmaliṅka Aṭikaḷ Varalāṟu*, 303–4.

83. Ramalinga Swami, *Tiruvaruṭpā* [1867 ed.], Tirumurai 2, 141.

84. Arumuga Navalar, "Critique of the Pseudo-Divine Verses."

85. *Madras Mail*, July 5, 1871, 3.

86. See, especially, the poems that were specifically addressed to the *nālvar*. Ramalinga Swami, *Tiruvaruṭpā* [1867 ed.], Tirumurai 4, 33–38.

87. Ibid., back matter.

88. There is no date for this letter, but it is likely that it was written in 1866. Ramalinga Swami, *Tiru Aruṭpā* [Balakrishna Pillai ed.], 5:85.

89. Ramalinga Swami, *Tiruvaruṭpā* [1867 ed.]. Later editions of *Tiruvaruṭpā* diverge from the ordering of verses in the first edition. A. Balakrishna Pillai's edition mostly follows Velayuda Mudaliyar's ordering but reversed the fourth and fifth *Tirumuṟai* and adds six volumes of other writings not included in the original publications, including prose works, letters, and scattered verses. Ramalinga Swami, *Tiru Aruṭpā* [Balakrishna Pillai ed.]. Uran Adigal, in his edition first published in 1972, attempted to order the verses chronologically by matching verses to details of Ramalinga's biography. Ramalinga Swami, *Tiru Aruṭpā* [Uran Adigal ed.]. Auvai C. Duraisami Pillai, in his 1980s edition with commentary, followed Uran Adikal's arrangement of verses. Ramalinga Swami, *Tiruvaruṭpā Mūlamum Uraiyum* [*Tiruvaruṭpā*, Text and Commentary], ed. Auvai C. Duraisami Pillai, 10 vols. (Chidambaram: Annamalai University, 1988). On the various editions of *Tiruvaruṭpā*, see Uran Adigal's introduction in Ramalinga Swami, *Tiru Aruṭpā* [Uran Adigal ed.], 52–58. Also see the useful overview by P. Saravanan, *Navīṉa Nōkkil Vaḷḷalār* [A new perspective on Vallalar] (Nagarkovil: Kalaccuvatu Patippakam, 2010), 216–32.

90. Ramalinga Swami, *Tiruvaruṭpā* [1867 ed.], front matter.

91. Ibid., 1.

92. S.P. Annamalai, *The Life and Teachings of Saint Ramalingar,* 2nd ed. (Bombay: Bharatiya Vidya Bhavan, 1988), 36–38. On the literary virtuosity of Minakshisundaram Pillai, see Ebeling, *Colonizing.*

93. Ramalinga Swami, *Tiruvaruṭpā* [1867 ed.], Tirumurai 2, 15; Ramalinga Swami, *Tiru Aruṭpā* [Uran Adigal ed.], verse 653.

94. Ramalinga Swami, *Tiruvaruṭpā* [1867 ed.], Tirumurai 1, 118; Ramalinga Swami, *Tiru Aruṭpā* [Uran Adigal ed.], verse 2218.

95. Ramalinga Swami, *Tiruvaruṭpā* [1867 ed.], Tirumurai 4, 21; Ramalinga Swami, *Tiru Aruṭpā* [Uran Adigal ed.], verse 3162.

96. Ramalinga Swami, *Tiruvaruṭpā* [1867 ed.], Tirumurai 4, 33–38.

97. Tamil prose was emerging at the time as a literary form and as a form of religious communication, and Ramalinga himself used prose to communicate to his followers. In Shaiva contexts, prose was used as a form of communication between co-religionists or to enter into debate with one's adversaries, but not as speech addressed to Siva.

98. On prosody in the *Tēvāram,* see Peterson, *Poems to Siva.*

99. Ramalinga Swami, *Tiru Aruṭpā* [Balakrishna Pillai ed.], 5:59–60.

100. Ramalinga Swami, *Tiruvaruṭpā Tiruttaṇikai Patikam.*

101. Gros also notes the influence of the *Tēvāram* on Ramalinga. François Gros, "Towards Reading the Tēvāram," in *Deep Rivers: Selected Writings on Tamil Literature,* ed. M. Kannan and Jennifer Clare (Pondicherry; Berkeley: Institut Francais de Pondichery; Tamil Chair, Dept. of South and Southeast Asian Studies, University of California, 2009), 213, 216.

102. One exception is a verse of the poem "Civanēca Veṉpā," in which Ramalinga praises Shiva for cutting through the shackles of caste and bringing light to the world. However, this verse lacks the radical message of social change of verses in the sixth *Tirumuṟai.* Ramalinga Swami, *Tiruvaruṭpā* [1867 ed.], Tirumurai 1, 84; Ramalinga Swami, *Tiru Aruṭpā* [Uran Adigal ed.], verse 1972.

103. Ramalinga Swami, *Citamparam Irāmaliṅkacuvāmikaḷ Tiruvāymalarntaruḷiya Tiruvaruṭpā, Āṟāvatu Tirumuṟai.*

104. Velayuda Mudaliyar, "Tiruvaruṭpā Varalāṟu," verse 45.

105. The exception is the *Tirumantiram* of Tirumular, but this work is very different from the work of other Tamil siddha poets.

4 RAMALINGA'S DEVOTIONAL POEMS: CREATING A HAGIOGRAPHY

1. Zvelebil, *Tamil Literature.*

2. Smith, *Hinduism and Modernity,* 167, 170, 180.

3. Christian Lee Novetzke, "Bhakti and Its Publics," *International Journal of Hindu Studies* 11, no. 3 (2007): 255. Norman Cutler, in his study of Tamil bhakti literature, both Vaishnava and Shaiva, emphasises that bhakti works are defined by "connections" between the poet, the god, and an audience. See Cutler, *Songs of Experience: The Poetics of Tamil Devotion* (Bloomington: Indiana University Press, 1987).

4. Later, in chapter six, I will discuss the more radical of his poems, published in 1885.

5. Zvelebil, *Tamil Literature*, 113.

6. Ebeling, *Colonizing*.

7. Timothy S. Dobe, "Vernacular Vedānta: Autohagiographical Fragments of Rāma Tīrtha's Indo-Persion, Diglossic Mysticism," *International Journal of Hindu Studies* 18, no. 2 (2014): 181–219; Brian A. Hatcher, "Sanskrit Pandits Recall Their Youth: Two Autobiographies from Nineteenth-Century Bengal," *Journal of the American Oriental Society* (2001): 580–92.

8. Dobe, "Vernacular Vedānta," 186. Emphasis in original.

9. Pechilis Prentiss, *Embodiment of Bhakti*, 6.

10. Cutler, *Songs of Experience*, 19, 69.

11. David Shulman, "The Yogi's Human Self: Tāyumāṉavar in the Tamil Mystical Tradition," *Religion* 21 (1991): 55, 64, 68, 69.

12. Karen Pechilis makes a similar observation with respect to the composers of the *Tēvāram*. Pechilis, "Singing a Vow: Devoting Oneself to Shiva through Song," in *Dealing with Deities: The Ritual Vow in South Asia*, ed. Selva J. Raj and William P. Harman (Albany: State University of New York Press, 2006), 150.

13. G. Vanmikanathan, *Pathway to God Trod by Raamalinga Swaamikal* (Bombay: Bharatiya Vidya Bhavan, 1976), 114.

14. Given the large number of citations of Ramalinga's verses in this chapter, I will cite each with an in-text reference to the verse number, following Uran Adigal's numbering of Ramalinga's verses. See Ramalinga Swami, *Tiru Aruṭpā* [Uran Adigal ed.]. This has become the standard, modern notation, which C. Duraisami Pillai follows in his ten-volume commentary, Ramalinga Swami, *Tiruvaruṭpā* [Duraisami Pillai ed.]. I compared text from Uran Adigal's edition with the 1867 edition, and found only differences in the presentation of sandhi shifts and, in a few cases, changes in word order that did not affect meaning. Uran Adigal retained the names of the poems from the 1867 edition, but he changed the order of poems to conform to a rough chronology of Ramalinga's life. Since the original order of poems is not important to my analysis, I have followed Uran Adigal's modern standard for the convenience of readers who want to refer to the Tamil text of the poems.

15. For a close analysis of this feature of Ramalinga's hagiography, see Srilata Raman, "'Unlearnt Knowing' (Ōtātu Uṇartal): The Genealogy of Wisdom in Ramalinga Swamigal (1823–1874) and the Tamil Śaiva Siddhānta," *Journal of Hindu Studies* 10, no. 2 (2017): 145–63.

16. Mudaliyar, "Tiruvaruṭpā Varalāṟu," 8–10; Sivagnanam, *Vaḷḷalār Kaṇṭu Orumaippāṭu*, 42–45.

17. Vanmikanathan, *Pathway to God*, 180.

18. Vanmikanathan interprets Ramalinga's confessions of lust as "vicarious atonement for all the sins of humanity," not as reflections on Ramalinga's personal desire. Ibid., 182.

19. Andrew Bennett, *The Author* (New York: Routledge, 2005), 56–57.

20. In her discussion of mythological references in the *Tēvāram*, Indira Peterson includes many of those pan-Indian myths that Ramalinga frequently cites. Peterson, *Poems to Siva*, 343–48.

21. Indira Viswanathan Peterson, "Singing of a Place: Pilgrimage and Metaphor and Motif in the Tēvāram Songs of the Tamil Śaiva Saints," *Journal of the American Oriental Society* 102, no. 1 (1982): 79.

22. Paranjoti Munivar, *Tiruviḷaiyāṭaṟ Purāṇam*, with commentary of N. M. Vengatasami Nattar, 3 vols. (Chennai: Saiva Siddhanta Publishing Society, 1965), verses 2031–2100.

23. Cekkilar, *Periya Purāṇam eṉṉum Tiruttoṇṭar Purāṇam*, with Commentary of C. K. Subramaniya Mudaliyar, 7 vols. (Coimbatore: Kovai Tamil Sangam, 1975), verses 174–208.

24. Karen Pechilis Prentiss notes that the poets of the *Tēvāram* often present themselves "as imperfect people, bound by the limits of the human condition"; Pechilis Prentiss, *Embodiment of Bhakti*, 50. She suggests that Appar's oscillation between self-degradation and self-assurance point to one of the defining characteristics of bhakti; Pechilis, "Singing a Vow," 151. The poet Manikkavacakar referred to himself as a "dog" in his poems; Zvelebil, *Smile of Murugan*, 205.

25. This scene evokes the imagery of Tamil Ula literature. In these erotic works, the male king or god goes on procession through the city, arousing the desires of those who see him. See Blake Tucker Wentworth, "Yearning for a Dreamed Real: The Procession of the Lord in the Tamil Ulās" (PhD diss., University of Chicago, 2011).

26. Zvelebil, *Smile of Murugan*, 198.

27. Cutler, *Songs of Experience*, 81–110.

28. Peterson, *Poems to Siva*, 54.

29. Ramalinga wrote all these poems on paper. If we follow Uran Adikal's suggestion that Ramalinga began to prefer paper to palm leaves after leaving Chennai in 1857, it is probable that he composed these poems at some point between 1857 and 1867. Ramalinga Swami, *Tiru Aruṭpā* [Uran Adigal ed.].

30. These correspond to verses 3226–3266 of Uran Adikal's edition. Ibid. G. Vanmikanathan has translated a few of these verses into English. See Vanmikanathan, *Pathway to God*, 26–33.

31. On *mālai* as a "hypergenre of poems," see Kamil Zvelebil, *Lexicon of Tamil Literature* (Leiden: E. J. Brill, 1995), 398–99.

32. "Tiru-aruḷ-pā" becomes "Tiruvaruṭpā" after sandhi changes.

33. Peterson, *Poems to Siva*, 54–56.

34. However, instead of Appar's "vācal," opening, Ramalinga uses the synonymous "vāy."

35. The story appears in the *Periya Purāṇam*, verses 2931–3017. See Alastair McGlashan, *The History of the Holy Servants of the Lord Siva: A Translation of the Periya Purāṇam of Cēkkiḻār* (Victoria, BC, Canada: Trafford Publishing, 2006), 252–57.

36. Cutler notes this bhakti convention of the poet addressing his or her heart or mind, but also an audience that overhears the poem. "Not infrequently the bhakti poet addresses his own heart (*neñcu, ullam*), his mind (*manam*), or the 'breath of life' (*uyir*) that animates his body. In these poems the poet is both speaker and addressee, and so it appears that the deity as well as the audience overhears the poet's words." Cutler, *Songs of Experience*, 25.

37. Ramalinga Swami, *Tiru Aruṭpā* [Balakrishna Pillai ed.], 5:35.

38. Ibid., 5:49.

39. Ibid., 5:31–32.

40. Cutler, *Songs of Experience*, 8.

41. On the Otuvar singers of the Tēvāram, see Pechilis, "Singing a Vow"; Peterson, *Poems to Siva*, 57–75.

42. Peterson notes that the *paṇ* or melodies formerly associated with the *Tēvāram* poems have been "irretrievably lost," having been replaced by relatively modern Carnatic *rāga* scales. Peterson, *Poems to Siva*, 59.

43. On meters used by Manikkavacakar, see Zvelebil, *Tamil Literature,* 100. On meter in the *Tēvāram,* see Peterson, *Poems to Siva,* 77–79. See also the invaluable *Digital Tēvāram* of the École française d'Extrême-Orient, at http://www.ifpindia.org/digitaldb/site/digital_tevaram/INDEX.HTM.

44. Velayuda Mudaliyar, "Tiruvaruṭpā Varalāṟu," verses 46–47.

45. Cutler, *Songs of Experience,* 70.

46. Pechilis makes the same argument vis-à-vis contemporary *Tēvāram* recitation. See Pechilis, "Singing a Vow," 151.

47. Peterson, *Poems to Siva,* 59. Velayuda Mutaliyar calls *Tiruvaruṭpā* both a "*shastra* and a *stotra,*" and writes that the multifaceted character of the work was the basis for his decision to split it into six sections, or *Tirumuṟai.* See Velayuda Mudaliyar, "Tiruvaruṭpā Varalāṟu," verses 37–39.

5 THE POLEMICS OF CONFLICTING MODERNITIES

1. The two most informative long studies in English are Devadarshan Niranjan Ambalavanar, "Arumuga Navalar and the Construction of a Caiva Public in Colonial Jaffna" (PhD diss., Harvard University, 2006); and R. F. Young and S. Jebanesan, *The Bible Trembled: The Hindu-Christian Controversies of Nineteenth-Century Ceylon* (Vienna: Sammlung De Nobili, 1995).

2. A. R. Venkatachalapathy, "'Tappai Oppeṉṟu Tāpittalum, Oppait Tappeṉṟu Vātittalum'; Tamiḻil Kaṇṭaṉa Ilakkiyam" ['Establishing wrong as right, and arguing that right is wrong': polemical literature in Tamil], in *Aruṭpā Maruṭpā: Kaṇṭaṉattiraṭṭu* [Verses of divine grace, verses of delusion: a collection of polemical literature], ed. P. Saravanan (Nagarkovil: Kalaccuvatu Patippakam, 2010), 33.

3. Bate, "Arumuga Navalar, Saivite Sermons," 474.

4. Balachandran, "Pioneers of Tamil Literature," 182.

5. Vaithees, *Religion, Caste, and Nation.*

6. David Washbrook, "Economic Depression and the Making of 'Traditional' Society in Colonial India, 1820–1855," *Transactions of the Royal Historical Society* 3 (1993): 239.

7. Ibid., 251.

8. Ibid., 255–58.

9. L. Mani, "Contentious Traditions, the Debate on Sati in Colonial India," *Cultural Critique,* no. 7 (1987): 119–56.

10. Quoted in ibid., 146.

11. Yelle, *Language of Disenchantment,* 77–78.

12. Mani, "Contentious Traditions," 151.

13. Yelle, *Language of Disenchantment.*

14. Rosane Rocher, "The Creation of Anglo-Hindu Law," in *Hinduism and Law: An Introduction,* ed. Timothy Lubin, Donald R. Davis, and Jayanth Krishnan (New York: Cambridge University Press, 2010), 79–80. Robert Yelle has traced the Protestant roots of this emphasis on the authority of texts over orality in Yelle, *Language of Disenchantment,* 71–102.

15. Donald R. Davis, Jr., and Timothy Lubin, "Hinduism and Colonial Law," in *Hinduism in the Modern World,* ed. Brian A. Hatcher (New York: Routledge, 2016), 96–97.

16. Nicholas B. Dirks, *Castes of Mind: Colonialism and the Making of Modern India* (Princeton: Princeton University Press, 2001).

17. Rocher, "Creation," 82–83.

18. Dirks, *Castes of Mind*, 170.

19. Geoffrey A. Oddie, *Imagined Hinduism: British Protestant Missionary Constructions of Hinduism, 1793–1900* (New Delhi: Sage Publications, 2006).

20. Washbrook, "Economic Depression."

21. Mani, "Contentious Traditions"; and Trautmann, *Madras School.*

22. Davis and Lubin, "Hinduism," 98–99.

23. Eisenstein, *Printing Press*, 319.

24. There are many works that point to the role of print in religious debate in colonial India. See Kenneth W. Jones, *Religious Controversy in British India: Dialogues in South Asian Languages* (Albany: State University of New York Press, 1992); Jones, *Socio-Religious Reform Movements in British India* (Cambridge: Cambridge University Press, 1989); Young and Jebanesan, *Bible Trembled;* Richard Fox Young, J. P. V. Somaratna, and Sammlung De Nobili, *Vain Debates: The Buddhist-Christian Controversies of Nineteenth-Century Ceylon* (Vienna: Institute of Indology, University of Vienna, 1996); More, *Muslim Identity*, 113–38; and C. A. Bayly, *Empire and Information: Intelligence Gathering and Social Communication in India, 1780–1870* (New Delhi: Cambridge University Press, 2007).

25. Venkatachalapathy, "Tappai Oppeṉṟu Tāpittalum," 25–26.

26. Ambalavanar, "Arumuga Navalar," 6.

27. The most important of these conflicts was with priests at the Kandasami temple in Nallur, Jaffna, whom Navalar criticized for not following Agamic ritual prescriptions. Ibid., 380–90.

28. Weiss, "Arumuga Navalar's Publishing Project."

29. For a detailed analysis of Navalar's publishing agenda, see ibid.

30. Young and Jebanesan, *Bible Trembled*, 82–83.

31. D. Dennis Hudson, "Arumuga Navalar and the Hindu Renaissance among the Tamils," in *Religious Controversy in British India: Dialogues in South Asian Languages*, ed. Kenneth W. Jones (Albany: State University of New York Press, 1992), 41. Young and Jebanesan, *Bible Trembled*, 124.

32. S. Thananjayarajasingham, *The Educational Activities of Arumuga Navalar* (Colombo: Sri La Sri Arumuga Navalar Sabai, 1974), 18.

33. Navalar, *Periyapurāṇam.*

34. Ibid.

35. Ibid., iii–iv.

36. Weiss, "Arumuga Navalar's Publishing Project."

37. Navalar, *Periyapurāṇam*, i–ii.

38. Dermot Killingley, "Rammohun Roy on the Vedanta Sutras," *Religion* 11, no. 2 (1981): 151–69.

39. Weiss, "Arumuga Navalar's Publishing Project."

40. Ambalavanar, "Arumuga Navalar," 244–45.

41. Ibid., 243.

42. Gauri Viswanathan, "Colonialism and the Construction of Hinduism," in *The Blackwell Companion to Hinduism*, ed. Gavin D. Flood (Malden, MA: Blackwell Pub., 2003), 35–36.

43. Ambalavanar, "Arumuga Navalar," 381.

44. A. R. Venkatachalapathy lists a number of his polemical tracts that attacked non-Agamic worship practices, including critiques of temple practices at the Katirecan temple in Vennarppannai, and the Kandasami temple in Nallur. Venkatachalapathy, "Tappai Oppeṉṟu Tāpittalum," 34.

45. P. Saravanan has collected many of the contributions to the dispute. Saravanan, *Aruṭpā Maruṭpā.*

46. Arumuga Navalar, "Critique of the Pseudo-Divine Verses."

47. Venkatachalapathy, "'Tappai Oppeṉṟu Tāpittalum," 28.

48. Ibid., 37.

49. Shanmugam Pillai, "Tiruvaruṭpā Tūṣaṇa Parikāram" [Antidote to the slander of *Tiruvaruṭpā*], in *Aruṭpā Maruṭpā: Kaṇṭaṉattiraṭṭu* [Verses of divine grace, verses of delusion: a collection of polemical literature], ed. P. Saravanan (Nagarkovil: Kalaccuvatu Patippakam, 2010): 71–82.

50. Arumuga Navalar, "Critique of the Pseudo-Divine Verses," 697. Indira Peterson describes these five works as the *Pañcapurāṇam,* "The five Puranas," and observes that nonbrahman Otuvar singers recite verses from these works as a regular part of Shaiva ritual worship. Peterson, *Poems to Siva,* 60.

51. Cutler, *Songs of Experience,* 96–98.

52. Arumuga Navalar, "Critique of the Pseudo-Divine Verses," 698–99.

53. Ibid., 699.

54. Ibid.

55. Young and Jebanesan, *Bible Trembled,* 190.

56. Here Tamil Shaivism appears to differ from the effects of print on Islamic oral practices. Francis Robinson notes that "print outflanked the oral, person to person, systems for the transmission of knowledge." Robinson, "Technology and Religious Change," 249.

57. Arumuga Navalar, "Critique of the Pseudo-Divine Verses," 699, 708.

58. Navalar, *Periyapurāṇam,* ii.

59. Ambalavanar, "Arumuga Navalar," 77, 253, 390.

60. Dagmar Hellmann-Rajanayagam, "Arumuka Navalar: Religious Reformer or National Leader of Eelam," *Indian Economic and Social History Review* 26, no. 2 (1989): 238.

61. Ramalinga Swami, *Tiru Aruṭpā* [Uran Adigal ed.], verse 2775. I have presented translations and analysis of a few of these verses in chapter four.

62. Arumuga Navalar, "Critique of the Pseudo-Divine Verses," 700.

63. On Navalar's literal reading of Ramalinga's claims, see Raman, "'Unlearnt Knowing.'"

64. Zvelebil, *Lexicon,* 374–75.

65. Arumuga Navalar, "Critique of the Pseudo-Divine Verses," 700–701.

66. Ramalinga Swami, *Tiru Aruṭpā* [Uran Adigal ed.], verse 3028.

67. Ramalinga Swami, *Tiruvaruṭpā* [1867 ed.], front matter.

68. Arumuga Navalar, "Critique of the Pseudo-Divine Verses," 702.

69. The legend of Naminandi Adigal appears in the *Periya Purāṇam,* verses 1866–1897. McGlashan, *History of the Holy Servants,* 167–70.

70. Arumuga Navalar, "Critique of the Pseudo-Divine Verses," 702.

71. Yelle, *Language of Disenchantment,* 18.

72. Ramalinga Swami, *Tiru Aruṭpā* [Uran Adigal ed.], verse 2772.

73. Arumuga Navalar, "Critique of the Pseudo-Divine Verses," 702–4.

74. Ibid., 705.

75. Ibid., 708.

76. R. Venkatesan also notes these caste tensions and points out that these were further exacerbated by tensions between Sri Lankan scholars and those based in Chennai. Venkatesan, "Irāmaliṅkam Pāṭalkaḷ," 88–89.

77. Venkatachalapathy, "Tappai Oppeṉṟu Tāpittalum," 36.

78. Arumuga Navalar, "Critique of the Pseudo-Divine Verses," 706.

79. Ibid., 707. Navalar goes on to question the chastity of Ramalinga's wife, writing that she ran away with another man in Chennai. He taunts Ramalinga: "If it is true that Ramalinga is omniscient . . . why would he have married without knowing beforehand the character of such a woman, then fearing ruin, leave her in Chennai and flee?" (707–8)

80. Ibid., 706.

81. Ibid., 709.

82. Ibid., 710–11.

83. Ibid., 711–13.

84. K. Kailasapathy, *Nāvalar Paṟṟi Kailācapati* [Kailasapathy on Navalar] (Colombo: Kumaran Puttaka Illam, 2005), 33.

85. Ramalinga Swami, *Tiru Aruṭpā* [Uran Adigal ed.], verse 5566.

86. R. Gopalasami Pillai, *Tēvāratōttiratiraṭṭu* [Anthology of *Tēvāram* songs] (Thanjavur: Sri Kirusnavilaca Piras, 1899).

87. Shanmugam Pillai, "Tiruvaruṭpā Tūṣaṇa Parikāram."

88. Toluvur Velayuda Mudaliyar, "Pōliyaruṭpā Maṟuppiṉ Kaṇṭaṉam Allatu Kutarkkāraṇiya Nācamahā Paracu" [Refutation of 'critique of the pseudo-divine verses,' or the great battle ax that destroys the forest of fallacies], in *Aruṭpā Maruṭpā: Kaṇṭaṉattiraṭṭu* [Verses of divine grace, verses of delusion: a collection of polemical literature], ed P. Saravanan (Nagarkovil: Kalaccuvatu Patippakam), 2010.

89. The title of this work is likely a play on the title of one of Navalar's well-known polemical tracts against Christianity, *Caiva Tūṣaṇa Parikāram*, published in 1854.

90. Shanmugam Pillai, "Tiruvaruṭpā Tūṣaṇa Parikāram," 74.

91. Ibid., 76.

92. Ibid.

93. My translation, in consultation with the translation of G.U. Pope. G.U. Pope, translator, *The Tiruvāçagam, or 'Sacred Utterances' of the Tamil Poet, Saint, and Sage Māṇikkavācakar* (Oxford: Clarendon Press, 1900), 58.

94. Shanmugam Pillai, "Tiruvaruṭpā Tūṣaṇa Parikāram," 76–77.

95. Ibid., 77.

96. Ibid., 78–79.

97. Ramalinga Swami, *Tiru Aruṭpā* [Uran Adigal ed.], verse 704.

98. Shanmugam Pillai, "Tiruvaruṭpā Tūṣaṇa Parikāram," 79–81.

99. Ibid., 75.

100. Ibid., 81–82.

101. Arumuga Navalar, "Critique of the Pseudo-Divine Verses," 712.

102. Shanmugam Pillai, "Tiruvaruṭpā Tūṣaṇa Parikāram," 77.

103. C. J. Fuller, *Servants of the Goddess: The Priests of a South Indian Temple,* Cambridge Studies in Social Anthropology (Cambridge: Cambridge University Press, 1984); and Fuller, *The Renewal of the Priesthood: Modernity and Traditionalism in a South Indian Temple* (Princeton: Princeton University Press, 2003).

6 THE MODERNITY OF YOGA POWERS IN COLONIAL INDIA

1. For this sort of characterization, see Padmanabhan, "Modern Tamil Literature," 378.

2. Peter Pels, "Introduction: Magic and Modernity," in *Magic and Modernity: Interfaces of Revelation and Concealment,* ed. Birgit Meyer and Pels (Stanford: Stanford University Press, 2003), 3.

3. On siddha medicine, see Weiss, *Recipes for Immortality.*

4. Probably the best introduction to the Tamil siddhas in English remains Zvelebil, *Poets of the Powers.*

5. Details of these publications can be found in the catalogue of the Roja Muthiah Research Library.

6. Layne Ross Little, "Bowl Full of Sky: Story-Making and the Many Lives of the Siddha Bhogar" (PhD diss., University of California, Berkeley, 2004).

7. Charles E. Gover, *The Folk-Songs of Southern India* (Madras: Higginbotham and Co., 1871). However, Gover neglected to cite any of the Tamil siddha writings that boast about their supernatural powers. He considered the miraculous claims of siddha works to be later brahmanic accretions, to be discarded in order to reconstruct true South Indian religion.

8. Rev. William Taylor, "Fifth Report of Progess Made in the Examination of the Mackenzie Mss., with an Abstract Account of the Works Examined," *Madras Journal of Literature and Science* 23 (1839): 327.

9. Dayananda Saraswati, *Satyarth Prakash,* 541.

10. Ibid., 93.

11. Ibid., 177.

12. Hatcher, *Bourgeois Hinduism,* 4–5.

13. Yelle, *Language of Disenchantment,* 124.

14. Saraswati's attack on yogis shared elements with a more general Hindu reform critique of "priestcraft." As J. Barton Scott notes, the critique of priests came to include "sundry Brahmans, gurus, purohits, pirs, swamis, fakirs, and other figures of religious authority, both institutional and charismatic"; *Spiritual Despots: Modern Hinduism and the Genealogies of Self-Rule* (Chicago: The University of Chicago Press, 2016), 26.

15. Dayananda Saraswati, *Satyarth Prakash,* 256.

16. Ibid., 245.

17. Somadeva Vasudeva explores the association between the siddhis and tantric traditions in Vasudeva, "Powers and Identities: Yoga Powers and the Tantric Śaiva Traditions," in *Yoga Powers: Extraordinary Capacities Attained through Meditation and Concentration,* ed. Knut A. Jacobsen (Leiden: Brill, 2011). We also see this association in narratives of "sinister yogis" that populate Hindu mythologies from Sanskrit epic traditions to oral folk traditions. David Gordon White, *Sinister Yogis* (Chicago: The University of Chicago Press, 2009).

18. Ibid., 354–55.

19. Michael Saler, "Modernity and Enchantment: A Historiographic Review," *The American Historical Review* 111, no. 3 (2006): 704.

20. Dayananda Saraswati, *Satyarth Prakash,* 361.

21. Ibid., 372.

22. Chakrabarty, *Provincializing Europe,* 100–101.

23. Hatcher, *Bourgeois Hinduism,* 4–5.

24. Velayuda Mudaliyar, "Tiruvaruṭpā Varalāṟu," verse 45.

25. Ramalinga Swami, *Tiruvaruṭpā, Āṟāvatu Tirumuṟai.*

26. Here I follow Uran Adigal's compilation of verses. Ramalinga Swami, *Tiru Aruṭpā* [Uran Adigal ed.].

27. Venkatesan, "Irāmaliṅkam Pāṭalkaḷ," 92.

28. Ramalinga Swami, *Tiruvaruṭpā, Āṟāvatu Tirumuṟai,* front matter.

29. Ramalinga Swami, *Tiru Aruṭpā* [Balakrishna Pillai ed.], 5:61.

30. Just a few examples are M. P. Sivagnanam, *Vaḷḷār Kaṇṭa Cāvākkalai* [The art of immortality discovered by Vallalar] (Madurai: Tamil Nadu Kandi Ninaivau Niti, 1970); Uran Adigal, *Tirumūlarum Vaḷḷalārum* [Tirumular and Vallalar] (Vadalur: Samarasa Sanmarga Araycci Nilayam, 2005); Jekata, *Maraṇattai Veṉṟa Makā Cittar Vallaḷar* [Vallalar, the great siddha who conquered death] (Chennai: Ramprasanth, 2006); and P. Kamalakannan, *Aruṭperuñcōti Ñāna Cittar* [The wise siddha of the great light of grace] (Chennai: Vanathi, 2008).

31. Blackburn, *Print,* 161; and Gautaman, *Kaṇmūṭi Vaḻakkam,* 6–7.

32. Raman, "Departure and Prophecy," 184.

33. Mudaliyar, "Irāmaliṅkapiḷḷaiyavarkaḷ," 25.

34. Ramalinga Mudaliyar, ed. *Patiṉeṇcittarkaḷ Periya Ñāṉakkōvai* [The eighteen siddhas' garland of great knowledge] (Chennai: Puracai Sundaravilasa Accukkuda, 1899). A popular edition today appears to be a plagiarized copy of this 1899 edition, since it reproduces precisely the same poems of Ramalinga as in the 1899 edition. See R. Ramanathan, ed., *Cittar Pāṭalkaḷ* [Songs of the siddhas], 9th ed., 2 vols. (Chennai: Pirema Piracuram, 1995 [1959]).

35. Vasudeva, "Powers and Identities," 276.

36. See Srilata Raman's analysis of narratives surrounded Ramalinga's "disappearance." Raman, "Departure and Prophecy."

37. Vasudeva, "Powers and Identities," 265.

38. Ibid., 286–87.

39. On alchemy and the Tamil siddhas, see M. C. Subramaniam, *Cittarkaḷ Iracavātakkalai* [The siddhas' art of alchemy] (Chennai: Tamarai Nulakam, 1985).

40. David Gordon White, *The Alchemical Body: Siddha Traditions in Medieval India* (Chicago: University of Chicago Press, 1996); and Weiss, *Recipes for Immortality.*

41. YS 3.50–51. Patanjali, *Yoga: Discipline of Freedom; The Yoga Sutra Attributed to Patanjali. A Translation of the Text, with Commentary, Introduction, and Glossary of Keywords,* trans. Barbara Stoler Miller (Berkeley: University of California Press, 1996), 72.

42. Vasudeva, "Powers and Identities," 271.

43. Shulman, "Yogi's Human Self," 55.

44. Ibid., 56–57.

45. Uran Adigal, *Irāmaliṅka Aṭikaḷ Varalāṟu,* 279.

46. Ramalinga Swami, *Tiru Aruṭpā Urai Naṭaip Pakuti* [*Tiruvaruṭpā,* prose section] (Vadalur, India: Tiru Arutprakasha Vallalar Teyva Nilaiyam, 2008), 542.

47. Ibid., 548–49.

48. Ibid., 539.

49. Ibid., 542.

50. I have not been able to locate any other evidence of the journal.

51. Ramalinga Swami, *Tiru Aruṭpā Urai Naṭaip Pakuti,* 542–44.

52. Ulrike Stark, "Associational Culture and Civic Engagement in Colonial Lucknow: The Jalsah-E Tahzib," *Indian Economic and Social History Review* 48, no. 1 (2011): 2–4.

53. For more on the specifics of Ramalinga's Society of the True Path, see Weiss, "Voluntary Associations."

54. Stark, "Associational Culture," 8.

55. Ramalinga Swami, *Tiru Aruṭpā Urai Naṭaip Pakuti,* 544.

56. Vasudeva, "Powers and Identities," 290.

57. Zvelebil, *Smile of Murugan,* 218.

58. *Kriyāviṉ Taṟkālat Tamiḻ Akarāti: Tamiḻ-Tamiḻ-Āṅkilam* [The Kriya dictionary of contemporary Tamil: Tamil-Tamil-English], ed. S. Ramakrishnan (Chennai: Cre-A Publishers, 2008).

59. Ramalinga Swami, *Tiru Aruṭpā Urai Naṭaip Pakuti,* 551–52.

60. Ibid., 545–46.

61. T. N. Ganapathy, *The Contribution of Tamil Siddhas to Dravidian Thought* (Kuppam: Prasaranga, Dravidian University, 2008), 5.

62. Eleanor Zelliot, "Caste in Contemporary India," in *Contemporary Hinduism: Ritual, Culture, and Practice,* ed. Robin Rinehart (Santa Barbara, CA: ABC-CLIO, 2004), 260.

63. Dipesh Chakrabarty, "Of Garbage, Modernity, and the Citizen's Gaze," *Economic and Political Weekly,* March 7–14 (1992): 543.

64. Novetzke, "Bhakti and Its Publics," 263, 265.

65. Pattinattar, *St. Pattinatthar in English. Tamil Text with English Translation,* trans. T. N. Ramachandran (Mayiladuthurai: International Institute of Saiva Siddhanta Research, Dharmapura Adhinam, 1990), 55.

66. Zvelebil, *Poets of the Powers,* 118.

67. Reinhart Koselleck, *The Practice of Conceptual History: Timing History, Spacing Concepts,* trans. Todd Samuel Presner and others (Stanford: Stanford University Press, 2002), 168.

68. Quoted in Chakrabarty, *Provincializing Europe,* 244.

69. Eisenstadt, "Multiple Modernities," 4.

70. Koselleck, *Practice of Conceptual History,* 165–67.

7 CONCLUSION

1. Dube, "Modernity," 13.

2. For examples of reactionary Hindu traditionalism, see Mani, "Contentious Traditions"; and Jones, *Socio-Religious Reform Movements.*

3. Chakrabarty, *Provincializing Europe,* 247.

4. Ibid., 244–45.

5. Dube, "Modernity," 9.

6. Ibid., 2.

BIBLIOGRAPHY

Ambalavanar, Devadarshan Niranjan. "Arumuga Navalar and the Construction of a Caiva Public in Colonial Jaffna." PhD diss., Harvard University, 2006.

Annamalai, S. P. *The Life and Teachings of Saint Ramalingar.* 2nd ed. Bombay: Bharatiya Vidya Bhavan, 1988.

Appiah, Anthony. *The Ethics of Identity.* Princeton: Princeton University Press, 2005.

Arnold, David. "Famine in Peasant Consciousness and Peasant Action: Madras, 1876–78." In *Subaltern Studies III: Writings on South Asian History and Society,* edited by Ranajit Guha, 62–115. Delhi: Oxford University Press, 1984.

Badley, B. H. *Indian Missionary Directory and Memorial Volume.* Lucknow: Methodist Episcopal Church Press, 1876.

Balachandran, R. "Pioneers of Tamil Literature: Transition to Modernity." *Indian Literature* 49, no. 2 (2005): 179–84.

Banerjee-Dube, Ishita. "Issues of Faith, Enactments of Contest: The Founding of Mahima Dharma in Nineteenth-Century Orissa." In *Jagannath Revisited: Studying Society, Religion, and the State in Orissa,* edited by Hermann Kulke and Burkhard Schnepel, 149–77. New Delhi: Manohar, 2001.

———. *Religion, Law, and Power: Tales of Time in Eastern India, 1860–2000.* London: Anthem Press, 2007.

———, and Johannes Beltz. *Popular Religion and Ascetic Practices: New Studies on Mahima Dharma.* New Delhi: Manohar Publishers & Distributors, 2008.

Bate, Bernard. "Arumuga Navalar, Saivite Sermons, and the Delimitation of Religion, C. 1850." *Indian Economic and Social History Review* 42, no. 4 (2005): 469–84.

Bayly, C. A. *Empire and Information: Intelligence Gathering and Social Communication in India, 1780–1870.* New Delhi: Cambridge University Press, 2007.

Bennett, Andrew. *The Author.* New York: Routledge, 2005.

Bergunder, Michael. "What Is Religion? The Unexplained Subject Matter of Religious Studies." *Method and Theory in the Study of Religion* 26 (2014): 246–86.

Bhargava, Rajeev. "Are There Alternative Modernities?" In *Culture, Democracy, and Development in South Asia,* edited by N. N. Vohra, 9–26. New Delhi: Shipra Publications, 2001.

Blackburn, Anne M. *Locations of Buddhism: Colonialism and Modernity in Sri Lanka.* Chicago: University of Chicago Press, 2010.

Blackburn, Stuart H. *Print, Folklore, and Nationalism in Colonial South India.* Delhi: Permanent Black, 2003.

Bloch, Esther, Marianne Keppens, and Rajaram Hegde. *Rethinking Religion in India: The Colonial Construction of Hinduism.* London: Routledge, 2010.

Bornstein, Erica. "The Impulse of Philanthropy." *Cultural Anthropology* 24, no. 4 (2009): 622–51.

Brick, David James. "The *Dānakāṇḍa* ('Book on Gifting') of the Kṛtyakalpataru: A Critical Edition and Annotated Translation." PhD diss., The University of Texas at Austin, 2009.

Bugge, Henriette. *Mission and Tamil Society: Social and Religious Change in South India (1840–1900).* Richmond, Surrey: Curzon Press, 1994.

Cekkilar. *Periya Purāṇam eṉṉum Tiruttoṇṭar Purāṇam.* With Commentary of C. K. Subramaniya Mudaliyar. 7 vols. Coimbatore: Kovai Tamil Sangam, 1975.

Chakrabarty, Dipesh. "Of Garbage, Modernity, and the Citizen's Gaze." *Economic and Political Weekly,* March 7–14 (1992): 541–47.

———. *Provincializing Europe: Postcolonial Thought and Historical Difference.* Princeton: Princeton University Press, 2000.

Champakalakshmi, R. *Religion, Tradition, and Ideology: Pre-Colonial South India.* New Delhi: Oxford University Press, 2011.

Cooper, Frederick. *Colonialism in Question: Theory, Knowledge, History.* Berkeley: University of California Press, 2005.

Cutler, Norman. *Songs of Experience: The Poetics of Tamil Devotion.* Bloomington: Indiana University Press, 1987.

d'Avray, David. "Printing, Mass Communication, and Religious Reformation: The Middle Ages and After." In *The Uses of Script and Print, 1300–1700,* edited by Julia C. Crick and Alexandra Walsham, 50–70. Cambridge: Cambridge University Press, 2004.

Dalyell, R. A. *Memorandum on the Madras Famine of 1866.* Madras: Information of the Madras Central Famine Relief Committee, 1867.

Darnton, Robert. "Book Production in British India, 1850–1900." *Book History* 5, no. 1 (2002): 239–62.

Das, Sisir Kumar. *A History of Indian Literature, 1800–1910: Western Impact, Indian Response.* Edited by Birendra Kumar Bhattacharyya. A History of Indian Literature 8. New Delhi: Sahitya Akademi, 1991.

Davis, Jr., Donald R., and Timothy Lubin. "Hinduism and Colonial Law." In *Hinduism in the Modern World,* edited by Brian A. Hatcher, 96–110. New York: Routledge, 2016.

Dayananda Saraswati. *An English Translation of the Satyarth Prakash.* Translated by Durga Prasad. Lahore: Virjanand Press, 1908.

Desikar, Suppaiya. *Caṅkaraṉantāti, Civacaṅkarapatikam [Poems to Shiva].* Chennai: Kalaratnakaram Accukkutam, 1867.

"Digital Tēvāram." Institut français de Pondichéry; Ecole française d'Extrême-Orient, http://www.ifpindia.org/digitaldb/site/digital_tevaram/INDEX.HTM.

Dikshitar, V. R. Ramachandra. *Studies in Tamil Literature and History.* London: Luzac & Co., 1930.

Dirks, Nicholas B. *Castes of Mind: Colonialism and the Making of Modern India.* Princeton: Princeton University Press, 2001.

Dobe, Timothy S. "Modern Monks and Global Hinduism." In *Hinduism in the Modern World,* edited by Brian A. Hatcher, 161–79. New York: Routledge, 2016.

———. "Vernacular Vedānta: Autohagiographical Fragments of Rāma Tīrtha's Indo-Persion, Diglossic Mysticism." *International Journal of Hindu Studies* 18, no. 2 (2014): 181–219.

Dube, Saurabh. "Modernity and Its Enchantments: An Introduction." In *Enchantments of Modernity: Empire, Nation, Globalization,* edited by Saurabh Dube, 1–41. New Delhi: Routledge, 2009.

Ebeling, Sascha. *Colonizing the Realm of Words: The Transformation of Tamil Literature in Nineteenth-Century South India.* Albany: State University of New York Press, 2010.

Eisenstadt, S. N. "Multiple Modernities." *Daedalus* 129, no. 1 (Winter 2000): 1–29.

Eisenstein, Elizabeth L. *The Printing Press as an Agent of Change: Communications and Cultural Transformations in Early Modern Europe.* 2 vols. Cambridge: Cambridge University Press, 1979.

Eschmann, Anncharlott. "Mahima Dharma: An Autochthonous Hindu Reform Movement." In *The Cult of Jagannath and the Regional Tradition of Orissa,* edited by Anncharlott Eschmann, Hermann Kulke and Gaya Charan Tripathi, 375–410. New Delhi: Manohar, 1978.

Farquhar, J. N. *Modern Religious Movements in India.* New York: The Macmillan Company, 1915.

Flood, Gavin D. *An Introduction to Hinduism.* New York: Cambridge University Press, 1996.

Foucault, Michel. "Nietzsche, Genealogy, History." *Semiotexte* 3, no. 1 (1978): 78–94.

Fuller, C. J. *The Camphor Flame: Popular Hinduism and Society in India.* Princeton: Princeton University Press, 1992.

———. *The Renewal of the Priesthood: Modernity and Traditionalism in a South Indian Temple.* Princeton: Princeton University Press, 2003.

———. *Servants of the Goddess: The Priests of a South Indian Temple.* Cambridge Studies in Social Anthropology. Cambridge: Cambridge University Press, 1984.

Ganapathy, T. N. *The Contribution of Tamil Siddhas to Dravidian Thought.* Kuppam: Prasaranga, Dravidian University, 2008.

Gautaman, Raj. *Kaṇmūṭi Vaḻakkam Elām Maṇmūṭippōka . . . ! Ci. Irāmaliṅkam (1823–1874)* [C. Ramalinga (1823–1874), who buried ignorant habits]. 2nd ed. Chennai: Tamilini, 2007.

Ghosh, Anindita. "An Uncertain 'Coming of the Book': Early Print Cultures in Colonial India." *Book History* 6 (2003): 23–55.

Glucklich, Ariel. *The Strides of Vishnu: Hindu Culture in Historical Perspective.* New York: Oxford University Press, 2008.

Gopalasami Pillai, R. *Tēvāratōttiratiraṭṭu* [Anthology of Tevaram songs]. Thanjavur: Sri Kirusnavilaca Piras, 1899.

Gover, Charles E. *The Folk-Songs of Southern India.* Madras: Higginbotham and Co., 1871.
Gros, François. "Towards Reading the Tēvāram." In *Deep Rivers: Selected Writings on Tamil Literature,* edited by M. Kannan and Jennifer Clare, 197–230. Pondicherry; Berkeley: Institut Francais de Pondichery; Tamil Chair, Dept. of South and Southeast Asian Studies, University of California, 2009.
Hacker, Paul. "Aspects of Neo-Hinduism as Contrasted with Surviving Traditional Hinduism." In *Kleine Schriften,* edited by Paul Hacker and Lambert Schmithausen, 580–608. Wiesbaden: Steiner, 1978.
Halbfass, Wilhelm. *India and Europe: An Essay in Understanding.* Albany: State University of New York Press, 1988.
Hallisey, Charles. "Roads Taken and Not Taken in the Study of Theravada Buddhism." In *Curators of the Buddha: The Study of Buddhism under Colonialism,* edited by Donald S. Lopez, 31–61. Chicago: University of Chicago Press, 1995.
Hatcher, Brian A. *Bourgeois Hinduism, or the Faith of the Modern Vedantists: Rare Discourses from Early Colonial Bengal.* New York: Oxford University Press, 2008.
———. "Colonial Hinduism." In *The Continuum Companion to Hindu Studies,* edited by Jessica Frazier, 171–84. New York: Continuum, 2011.
———. "Contemporary Hindu Thought." In *Contemporary Hinduism: Ritual, Culture, and Practice,* edited by Robin Rinehart, 179–211. Santa Barbara, CA: ABC-CLIO, 2004.
———. *Eclecticism and Modern Hindu Discourse.* New York: Oxford University Press, 1999.
———, ed. *Hinduism in the Modern World.* New York: Routledge, 2016.
———. "Introduction." In *Hinduism in the Modern World,* edited by Brian A. Hatcher, 1–11. New York: Routledge, 2016.
———. "Remembering Rammohan: An Essay on the (Re-)Emergence of Modern Hinduism." *History of Religions* 46, no. 1 (August 2006): 50–80.
———. "Sanskrit Pandits Recall Their Youth: Two Autobiographies from Nineteenth-Century Bengal." *Journal of the American Oriental Society* (2001): 580–92.
———. "Situating the Swaminarayan Tradition in the Historiography of Modern Hindu Reform." In *Swaminarayan Hinduism: Tradition, Adaptation, and Identity,* edited by Raymond Brady Williams and Yogi Trivedi, 6–37. New York: Oxford University Press, 2016.
Heehs, Peter. *Indian Religions: A Historical Reader of Spiritual Expression and Experience.* New York: New York University Press, 2002.
Heim, Maria. *Theories of the Gift in South Asia: Hindu, Buddhist, and Jain Reflections on Dāna.* New York: Routledge, 2004.
Heimsath, Charles H. *Indian Nationalism and Hindu Social Reform.* Princeton: Princeton University Press, 1964.
Hellmann-Rajanayagam, Dagmar. "Arumuka Navalar: Religious Reformer or National Leader of Eelam." *Indian Economic and Social History Review* 26, no. 2 (1989): 235–57.
Holt, John Clifford. "Sri Lanka's Protestant Buddhism?" *Ethnic Studies Report* 8, no. 2 (1990): 1–8.
Hudson, D. Dennis. "Arumuga Navalar and the Hindu Renaissance among the Tamils." In *Religious Controversy in British India: Dialogues in South Asian Languages,* edited by Kenneth W. Jones, 27–51. Albany: State University of New York Press, 1992.

Hunter, William Wilson. *The Imperial Gazetteer of India.* 2nd ed. 14 vols. London: Trübner and Co., 1885.

Irschick, Eugene F. *Tamil Revivalism in the 1930s.* Madras: Cre-A, 1986.

Iyer, U.V. Saminatha. *Pir̲kālap Pulavarkaḷ* [Latter-day poets]. Edited by S. Vaidyanadan. Chennai: U.V. Saminatha Iyer Library, 2000.

Jekata. *Maraṇattai Ven̲r̲a Makā Cittar Vallaḷar* [Vallalar, the great siddha who conquered death]. Chennai: Ramprasanth, 2006.

Jesudasan, C. *International Encyclopaedia of Indian Literature.* Vol. 2. *Tamil.* Edited by Ganga Ram Garg. Rev. ed. Delhi: Mittal Publications, 1987.

Johns, Adrian. *The Nature of the Book: Print and Knowledge in the Making.* Chicago: University of Chicago Press, 1998.

Jones, Kenneth W. *Religious Controversy in British India: Dialogues in South Asian Languages.* Albany: State University of New York Press, 1992.

———. *Socio-Religious Reform Movements in British India.* Cambridge: Cambridge University Press, 1989.

Jordens, J.T.F. *Dayananda Sarasvati: His Life and Ideas.* New Delhi: Oxford University Press, 1978.

Kailasapathy, K. *Nāvalar Par̲r̲i Kailācapati* [Kailasapathy on Navalar]. Colombo: Kumaran Puttaka Illam, 2005.

Kamalakannan, P. *Aruṭperuñcōti Ñāna Cittar* [The wise siddha of the great light of grace]. Chennai: Vanathi, 2008.

Kane, Pandurang Vaman. *History of Dharmashastra (Ancient and Mediæval Religious and Civil Law in India).* 2nd ed. Poona: Bhandarkar Oriental Research Institute, 1968.

Kasturi, Malavika. "'All Gifting Is Sacred': The Sanatana Dharma Sabha Movement, the Reform of Dana, and Civil Society in Late Colonial India." *Indian Economic and Social History Review* 47, no. 1 (2010): 107–39.

Kaviraj, Sudipta. "Modernity and Politics in India." *Daedalus* 129, no. 1 (2000): 137–62.

Killingley, Dermot. "Rammohun Roy on the Vedanta Sutras." *Religion* 11, no. 2 (1981): 151–69.

Klöber, Rafael. "What Is Saiva Siddhanta? Tracing Modern Genealogies and Historicising a Classical Canon." *The Journal of Hindu Studies* 10 (2017): 187–218.

Kopf, David. *The Brahmo Samaj and the Shaping of the Modern Indian Mind.* Princeton: Princeton University Press, 1979.

Koppedrayer, Kathleen Iva. "The Sacred Presence of the Guru: The Velala Lineages of Tiruvavatuturai, Dharmapuram, and Tiruppanantal." PhD diss., McMaster University, 1990.

Koselleck, Reinhart. *The Practice of Conceptual History: Timing History, Spacing Concepts.* Translated by Todd Samuel Presner and others. Stanford: Stanford University Press, 2002.

Kriyāvin̲ Tar̲kālat Tamiḻ Akarāti: Tamiḻ-Tamiḻ-Āṅkilam [The Kriya dictionary of contemporary Tamil: Tamil-Tamil-English]. Edited by S. Ramakrishnan. Chennai: Cre-A Publishers, 2008.

Linderman, Michael Christian. "Charity's Venue: Representing Indian Kingship in the Monumental Pilgrim Rest Houses of the Maratha Rajas of Tanjavur, 1761–1832." PhD diss., University of Pennsylvania, 2009.

Little, Layne Ross. "Bowl Full of Sky: Story-Making and the Many Lives of the Siddha Bhogar." PhD diss., University of California, Berkeley, 2004.

Llewellyn, J. E. *Defining Hinduism: A Reader.* New York: Routledge, 2006.

———. "From Interpretation to Reform: Dayananda's Reading of the Vedas." In *Authority, Anxiety, and Canon: Essays in Vedic Interpretation,* edited by Laurie L. Patton, 235–51. Albany: State University of New York Press, 1994.

Mahadevan, K. S. "Social Ideals and Patriotism in Tamil Literature (1900—1930)." *Indian Literature* 20, no. 3 (1977): 111–17.

Mani, L. "Contentious Traditions, the Debate on Sati in Colonial India." *Cultural Critique,* no. 7 (Fall 1987): 119–56.

Manninezhath, Thomas. *Harmony of Religions: Vedānta Siddhānta Samarasam of Tāyumānavar.* Delhi: Motilal Banarsidass Publishers, 1993.

Marriot, McKim. "Caste Ranking and Food Transactions: A Matrix Analysis." In *Structure and Change in Indian Society,* edited by Milton B. Singer and Bernard S. Cohn, 133–71. Chicago: Aldine Pub. Co., 1968.

Masuzawa, Tomoko. *The Invention of World Religions, or, How European Universalism Was Preserved in the Language of Pluralism.* Chicago: University of Chicago Press, 2005.

McDermott, Rachel Fell. *Sources of Indian Traditions.* 3rd ed. New York: Columbia University Press, 2014.

McGlashan, Alastair. *The History of the Holy Servants of the Lord Siva: A Translation of the Periya Purāṇam of Cēkkiḻār.* Victoria, BC, Canada: Trafford Publishing, 2006.

More, J. B. P. *Muslim Identity, Print Culture, and the Dravidian Factor in Tamil Nadu.* Hyderabad: Orient Longman, 2004.

Mudaliyar, Kanchipuram Sabhapati, ed. *Periya Purāṇam.* Vol. 1. Chennai: Kalvi Vilakka Press, 1859.

Mudaliyar, P. Ramasami. "Irāmaliṅkapiḷḷaiyavarkaḷ Carittiraccurukkam" [A short account of the life of Iramalinga Pillai]. In *Irāmaliṅkapiḷḷai Avarkaḷ Tiruvāymalarntaruḷiya Tiruvaruṭpāttirumuṟaittiraṭṭu* [Compilation of the sections of Ramalinga Pillai's Tiruvaruṭpā], edited by Po. Sundaram Pillai and Kaliyanasundara Mudaliyar, 3–27. Chennai: Alpiniyan Press, 1892.

Mudaliyar, Ramalinga, ed. *Patiṉeṇcittarkaḷ Periya Ñāṉakkōvai* [The eighteen siddhas' garland of great knowledge]. Chennai: Puracai Sundaravilasa Accukkuda, 1899.

Mudaliyar, Toluvur Velayuda. "Pōliyaruṭpā Maṟuppiṉ Kaṇṭaṉam Allatu Kutarkkāraṇiya Nācamahā Paracu" [Refutation of 'critique of the pseudo-divine verses,' or the great battle ax that destroys the forest of fallacies]. In *Aruṭpā Maruṭpā: Kaṇṭaṉattiraṭṭu* [Verses of divine grace, verses of delusion: a collection of polemical literature], edited by P. Saravanan, 101–242. Nagarkovil: Kalaccuvatu Patippakam, 2010.

———. "Tiruvaruṭpā Varalāṟu" [The history of *Tiruvaruṭpā*]. In *Citamparam Irāmaliṅkapiḷḷai Avarkaḷ Tiruvāymalarntaruḷiyatiruvaruṭpā* [Chidambaram Ramalinga Pillai's *Tiruvaruṭpā*], edited by Toluvur Velayuda Mudaliyar, 39–47. Madras: Asiatic Press, 1867.

Murdoch, John. *Classified Catalogue of Tamil Printed Books, with Introductory Notices.* Madras: The Christian Vernacular Education Society, 1865.

Nair, Savithri Preeta. *Raja Serfoji II: Science, Medicine, and Enlightenment in Tanjore.* New Delhi: Routledge, 2012.

Nallaswami Pillai, J. M. "The Nature of the Jiva." In *Studies in Saiva Siddhanta,* edited by J. M. Nallaswami Pillai, 316–37. Madras: Meykandan Press, 1911.

Nambi Arooran, K. "The Changing Role of Three Saiva Maths in Tanjore District from the Beginning of the 20th Century." In *Changing South Asia,* edited by Kenneth Ballhatchet and David D. Taylor, 51–58. Hong Kong: Centre of South Asian Studies in the School of Oriental and African Studies, University of London, 1984.

Narayana Rao, Velcheru, David Dean Shulman, and Sanjay Subrahmanyam. *Textures of Time: Writing History in South India, 1600–1800*. Delhi: Permanent Black, 2001.

Navalar, Arumuga. *Periyapurāṇam—Tiruttoṇṭarpurāṇam*. Vannarpannai, Jaffna: Vittiyanupalana Yantiracalai, 1852.

——— (under the name of Mavandur Tiyagesa Mudaliyar). "Pōliyaruṭpā Maṟuppu" [Critique of the pseudo-divine verses]." In *Aruṭpā Maruṭpā: Kaṇṭaṉattiraṭṭu* [Verses of divine grace, verses of delusion: a collection of polemical literature], edited by P. Saravanan, 695–713. Nagarkovil: Kalaccuvatu Patippakam, 2010.

"A New Revelation." *Madras Mail*, July 5, 1871, 1.

Novetzke, Christian Lee. "Bhakti and Its Publics." *International Journal of Hindu Studies* 11, no. 3 (2007): 255–72.

Obeyesekere, Gananath. "Religious Symbolism and Political Change in Ceylon." In *The Two Wheels of Dhamma: Essays on the Theravada Tradition in India and Ceylon*, edited by Gananath Obeyesekere, Frank Reynolds and Bardwell L. Smith, 58–78. Chambersburg, PA: American Academy of Religion, 1972.

Oddie, Geoffrey A. *Imagined Hinduism: British Protestant Missionary Constructions of Hinduism, 1793–1900*. New Delhi: Sage Publications, 2006.

"On the Progress and Present State of the Native Press in India." *The Friend of India* 12 (1825): 138–56.

Padmanabhan, Neela. "Modern Tamil Literature." In *Modern Indian Literature, an Anthology*, edited by K. M. George. New Delhi: Sahitya Akademi, 1992.

Pandian, M.S.S. "Meanings of 'Colonialism' and 'Nationalism': An Essay on Vaikunda Swamy Cult." *Studies in History* 8, no. 2 (1992): 167–85.

Paramarthalingam, C. *Social Reform Movement in Tamil Nadu in the 19th Century with Special Reference to St. Ramalinga*. Madurai: Rajakumari Publications, 1995.

Paranjoti Munivar. *Tiruviḷaiyāṭaṟ Purāṇam*. With commentary of N.M. Vengatasami Nattar. 3 vols. Chennai: Saiva Siddhanta Publishing Society, 1965.

Parry, Jonathan. "The Gift, the Indian Gift, and the 'Indian Gift.'" *Man* 21, no. 3 (September 1986): 453–73.

Patanjali. *Yoga: Discipline of Freedom; The Yoga Sutra Attributed to Patanjali. A Translation of the Text, with Commentary, Introduction, and Glossary of Keywords*. Translated by Barbara Stoler Miller. Berkeley: University of California Press, 1996.

Patrick, G. *Religion and Subaltern Agency*. Madras: University of Madras, 2003.

Pattinattar. *St. Pattinatthar in English. Tamil Text with English Translation*. Translated by T.N. Ramachandran. Mayiladuthurai: International Institute of Saiva Siddhanta Research, Dharmapura Adhinam, 1990.

Pechilis, Karen. "Singing a Vow: Devoting Oneself to Shiva through Song." In *Dealing with Deities: The Ritual Vow in South Asia*, edited by Selva J. Raj and William P. Harman, 147–64. Albany: State University of New York Press, 2006.

Pechilis Prentiss, Karen. *The Embodiment of Bhakti*. New York: Oxford University Press, 1999.

Pels, Peter. "Introduction: Magic and Modernity." In *Magic and Modernity: Interfaces of Revelation and Concealment*, edited by Birgit Meyer and Peter Pels. Stanford: Stanford University Press, 2003.

Perkins, C. Ryan. "From the Mehfil to the Printed Word: Public Debate and Discourse in Late Colonial India." *Indian Economic and Social History Review* 50, no. 1 (2013): 47–76.

Peterson, Indira Viswanathan. *Poems to Siva: The Hymns of the Tamil Saints.* Princeton: Princeton University Press, 1989.

———. "Singing of a Place: Pilgrimage and Metaphor and Motif in the Tēvāram Songs of the Tamil Śaiva Saints." *Journal of the American Oriental Society* 102, no. 1 (1982): 69–90.

———. "The Schools of Serfoji II of Tanjore: Education and Princely Modernity in Early Nineteenth-Century India." In *Trans-Colonial Modernities in South Asia,* edited by Michael S. Dodson and Brian A. Hatcher, 15–44. New York: Routledge, 2012.

Pettegree, A., and M. Hall. "The Reformation and the Book: A Reconsideration." *Historical Journal* 47, no. 4 (December 2004): 785–808.

Pollock, Sheldon. "Pretextures of Time." *History and Theory* 46, no. 3 (October 2007): 364–81.

Ponniah, James. "Alternative Discourses of Kali Yuga in Ayyā Vaḻi." *Nidān* 1 (2014): 65–87.

Pope, G. U., trans. *The Tiruvāçagam, or "Sacred Utterances" of the Tamil Poet, Saint, and Sage Māṇikkavācakar.* Oxford: Clarendon Press, 1900.

Prothero, Stephen. "Henry Steel Olcott and 'Protestant Buddhism.'" *Journal of the American Academy of Religion* 63, no. 2 (Summer 1995): 281–302.

Racine, Jean-Luc, and Josiane Racine. "Dalit Identities and the Dialectics of Oppression and Emancipation in a Changing India: The Tamil Case and Beyond." *Comparative Studies of South Asia, Africa, and the Middle East* 18, no. 1 (1998): 5–19.

Raheja, Gloria Goodwin. *The Poison in the Gift: Ritual, Prestation, and the Dominant Caste in a North Indian Village.* Chicago: University of Chicago Press, 1988.

Rai, Lajpat. *The Arya Samaj: An Account of Its Origin, Doctrines, and Activities, with a Biographical Sketch of the Founder.* Delhi: Renaissance Publishing House, 1989 [1915].

Rajesh, V. *Manuscripts, Memory, and History: Classical Tamil Literature in Colonial India.* New Delhi: Cambridge University Press, 2014.

Ramalinga Swami. "Camaraca Cutta Caṉmārkka Cattiyap Peru Viṇṇappam" [Sincere, long petition to god about the pure path of unity]. In *Tiruvaruṭpā, Vacaṉa Pakuti* [*Tiruvaruṭpā,* prose section], edited by A. Balakrishna Pillai, 120–28. 2nd ed. Chennai: Nam Tamilar Patippakam, 2010.

———. *Citamparam Irāmaliṅka Cuvāmikaḷ Tiruvāymalarntaruḷiya Tiru Aruṭpā* [Chidambaram Ramalinga Swamigal's *Tiruvaruṭpā*]. Edited by A. Balakrishna Pillai. 2nd ed. 12 vols. Chennai: Nam Tamilar Patippakam, 2010.

———. *Citamparam Irāmaliṅkacuvāmikaḷ Tiruvāymalarntaruḷiya Tiruvaruṭpā, Āṟāvatu Tirumuṟai* [Chidambaram Ramalinga Swami's *Tiruvaruṭpā,* sixth section]. Madras: Authikalanithi Press, 1885.

———. *Citamparam Irāmaliṅkapiḷḷai Avarkaḷ Tiruvāymalarntaruḷiya Tiruvaruṭpā* [Chidambaram Ramalinga Pillai's *Tiruvaruṭpā*]. Edited by Toluvur Velayuda Mudaliyar. Madras: Asiatic Press, 1867.

———, ed. *Oḻivil Oṭukkam.* Chennai: Mullai Nilayam, 2004 [1851].

———. *Tiru Aruṭpā.* Edited by Uran Adigal. 2nd ed. 3 vols. Chennai: Iramalingar Panimandram, 1981.

———. *Tiru Aruṭpā Urai Naṭaip Pakuti* [Prose section of *Tiruvaruṭpā*]. Vadalur, India: Tiru Arutprakasha Vallalar Teyva Nilaiyam, 2008.

———. *Tiruvaruṭpā Mūlamum Uraiyum* [*Tiruvaruṭpā,* text and commentary]. Edited by Auvai C. Duraisami Pillai. 10 vols. Chidambaram: Annamalai University, 1988.

———. *Tiruvaruṭpā Tiruttaṇikai Patikam* [*Tiruvaruṭpā,* poems to Murugan at Tiruttanikai]. Madras: Memorial Press, 1880.

Raman, Srilata. "Departure and Prophecy: The Disappearance of Irāmaliṅka Aṭikaḷ in the Early Narratives of His Life." *Indologica Taurinensia* 28 (2002): 179–203.

———. "Justifying Filicide: Ramalinga Swamigal, the Periyapurāṇam, and Tamil Religious Modernity." *International Journal of Hindu Studies* 18, no. 1 (2014): 33–66.

———. "The Spaces in Between: Ramalinga Swamigal (1823–1874), Hunger, and Religion in Colonial India." *History of Religions* 53, no. 1 (August 2013): 1–27.

———. "'Unlearnt Knowing' (Ōtātu Uṇartal): The Genealogy of Wisdom in Ramalinga Swamigal (1823–1874) and the Tamil Śaiva Siddhānta." *Journal of Hindu Studies* 10, no. 2 (2017): 145–63.

Ramanathan, R., ed. *Cittar Pāṭalkaḷ* [Songs of the siddhas]. 9th ed. 2 vols. Chennai: Pirema Piracuram, 1995 [1959].

Randeria, Shalini. "Entangled Histories of Uneven Modernities: Civil Society, Caste Councils, and Legal Pluralism in Postcolonial India." In *Comparative History and the Quest for Transnationality: Central European Approaches and New Perspectives,* edited by Jürgen Kocka and Heinz-Gerhard Haupt, 77–104. New York: Berghahn Books, 2009.

Rao, Vasudeva. *Living Traditions in Contemporary Contexts: The Madhva Matha of Udupi.* New Delhi: Orient Longman, 2002.

Report on the Census of British India, Taken on the 17th February 1881. Vol. 1. London: Her Majesty's Stationary Office, 1883.

Robinson, Francis. "Technology and Religious Change—Islam and the Impact of Print." *Modern Asian Studies* 27, no. 1 (1993): 229–51.

Rocher, Rosane. "The Creation of Anglo-Hindu Law." In *Hinduism and Law: An Introduction,* edited by Timothy Lubin, Donald R. Davis, and Jayanth Krishnan, 78–88. New York: Cambridge University Press, 2010.

Roy, Rammohan. "The Freedom of the Press." In *Makers of Modern India,* edited by Ramachandra Guha, 33–40. Cambridge: The Belknap Press of Harvard University Press, 2011.

Roy, Tapti. "Disciplining the Printed Text: Colonial and Nationalist Surveillance of Bengali Literature." In *Texts of Power: Emerging Disciplines in Colonial Bengal,* edited by Partha Chatterjee, 30–62. Minneapolis: University of Minnesota Press, 1995.

Saler, Michael. "Modernity and Enchantment: A Historiographic Review." *The American Historical Review* 111, no. 3 (2006): 692–716.

Sambasivam Pillai, T. V. *Tamil—English Dictionary of Medicine, Chemistry, Botany, and Allied Sciences (Based on Indian Medical Science).* 5 vols. Madras: Government of Tamil Nadu, 1994.

Saravanan, P. *Aruṭpā Maruṭpā: Kaṇṭaṉattiraṭṭu* [Verses of divine grace, verses of delusion: a collection of polemical literature]. Nagarkovil: Kalaccuvatu Patippakam, 2010.

———. *Navīṉa Nōkkil Vaḷḷalār* [A new perspective on Vallalar]. Nagarkovil: Kalaccuvatu Patippakam, 2010.

———. *Vāḻaiyaṭi Vāḻaiyeṉa . . . Vaḷḷalār Kaṟṟatum Vaḷḷalāril Peṟṟatum* [The banana doesn't fall far from the tree: the teachings of Vallalar and his heritage]. Chennai: Cantiya Patippakam, 2009.

Schomerus, Hilko Wiardo, and Humphrey Palmer. Śaiva Siddhānta: An Indian School of Mystical Thought. English ed. Delhi: Motilal Banarsidass Publishers, 2000.

Scott, J. Barton. "Luther in the Tropics: Karsandas Mulji and the Colonial 'Reformation' of Hinduism." *Journal of the American Academy of Religion* 83, no. 1 (2015): 181–209.

———. *Spiritual Despots: Modern Hinduism and the Genealogies of Self-Rule.* Chicago: The University of Chicago Press, 2016.

Sen, Amiya P. "Debates within Colonial Hinduism." In *Hinduism in the Modern World,* edited by Brian A. Hatcher, 67–79. New York: Routledge, 2016.

———. "The Idea of Social Reform and Its Critique among Hindus of Nineteenth Century India." In *Development of Modern Indian Thought and the Social Sciences,* edited by Sabyasachi Bhattacharya, 107–38. New Delhi: Oxford University Press, 2007.

Shanmugam Pillai. "Tiruvaruṭpā Tūṣaṇa Parikāram" [Antidote to the slander of *Tiruvaruṭpā*]." In *Aruṭpā Maruṭpā: Kaṇṭaṉattiraṭṭu* [Verses of divine grace, verses of delusion: a collection of polemical literature], edited by P. Saravanan, 71–82. Nagarkovil: Kalaccuvatu Patippakam, 2010.

Sharma, Arvind. *Modern Hindu Thought: An Introduction.* New York: Oxford University Press, 2005.

Sherring, M. A., and Edward Storrow. *The History of Protestant Missions in India from Their Commencement in 1706 to 1881.* London: The Religious Tract Society, 1884.

Shulman, David. "The Enemy Within: Idealism and Dissent in South Indian Hinduism." In *Orthodoxy, Heterodoxy, and Dissent in India,* edited by S. N. Eisenstadt, Reuven Kahane, and David Dean Shulman, 11–55. Berlin: Mouton, 1984.

———. "The Yogi's Human Self: Tāyumāṉavar in the Tamil Mystical Tradition." *Religion* 21 (1991): 51–72.

Sivagnanam, M. P. *The Universal Vision of Saint Ramalinga: Vallalar Kanda Orumaippadu.* Annamalainagar: Annamalai University, 1987.

———. *Vaḷḷār Kaṇṭa Cāvākkalai* [The art of immortality discovered by Vallalar]. Madurai: Tamil Nadu Kandi Ninaivau Niti, 1970.

———. *Vaḷḷalār Kaṇṭu Orumaippāṭu* [The universal vision of Vallalar]. Chennai: E. K. S. Books World, 2013.

Smith, David. *Hinduism and Modernity.* Malden, MA: Blackwell Pub., 2003.

Stark, Ulrike. "Associational Culture and Civic Engagement in Colonial Lucknow: The Jalsah-E Tahzib." *Indian Economic and Social History Review* 48, no. 1 (2011): 1–33.

———. *An Empire of Books: The Naval Kishore Press and the Diffusion of the Printed Word in Colonial India.* Ranikhet, India: Permanent Black, 2007.

———. "Publishers as Patrons and the Commodification of Hindu Religious Texts in Nineteenth-Century North India." In *Patronage and Popularisation, Pilgrimage and Procession: Channels of Transcultural Translation and Transmission in Early Modern South Asia; Papers in Honour of Monika Horstmann,* edited by Heidi Rika Maria Pauwels, 189–203. Wiesbaden: Harrassowitz, 2009.

Stock, Brian. *The Implications of Literacy: Written Language and Models of Interpretation in the Eleventh and Twelfth Centuries.* Princeton: Princeton University Press, 1983.

Subrahmanian, N. *History of Tamilnad, A.D. 1565–1956.* 2nd ed. Madurai, India: Koodal Publishers, 1982.

Subrahmanyam, S. "Connected Histories: Notes Towards a Reconfiguration of Early Modern Eurasia." *Modern Asian Studies* 31 (July 1997): 735–62.

———. "Hearing Voices: Vignettes of Early Modernity in South Asia, 1400–1750." *Daedalus* 127, no. 3 (Summer 1998): 75–104.

Subramaniam, M. C. *Cittarkaḷ Iracavātakkalai* [The siddhas' art of alchemy]. Chennai: Tamarai Nulakam, 1985.

Sundar, Pushpa. *For God's Sake: Religious Charity and Social Development in India*. New Delhi: Sampradaan Indian Centre for Philanthropy, 2002.

Sweetman, Will. "Colonialism All the Way Down? Religion and the Secular in Early Modern Writing on South India." In *Religion and the Secular: Historical and Colonial Formations*, edited by Timothy Fitzgerald, 117–34. London: Equinox, 2007.

Taylor, Rev. William. "Fifth Report of Progess Made in the Examination of the Mackenzie Mss., with an Abstract Account of the Works Examined." *Madras Journal of Literature and Science* 23 (1839): 313–75.

Thananjayarajasingham, S. *The Educational Activities of Arumuga Navalar*. Colombo: Sri La Sri Arumuga Navalar Sabai, 1974.

Thomassen, Bjorn. "Anthropology and Its Many Modernities: When Concepts Matter." *Journal of the Royal Anthropological Institute* 18 (2012): 160–78.

Tirunavukkaracu. *Tēvārappatikattirumuṟaikaḷ*. Edited by Kanchipuram Sabhapati Mudaliyar. Chennai: Kalaniti Press; Kalaratnacuram Press, 1866.

Trautmann, Thomas R. *Languages and Nations: The Dravidian Proof in Colonial Madras*. Berkeley: University of California Press, 2006.

———, ed. *The Madras School of Orientalism: Producing Knowledge in Colonial South India*. New Delhi: Oxford University Press, 2009.

Ulrich, Katherine E. "Food Fights: Buddhist, Hindu, and Jain Dietary Polemics in South India." *History of Religions* 46, no. 3 (February 2007): 228–61.

Uran Adigal. *Irāmaliṅka Aṭikaḷ Varalāṟu* [Biography of Ramalinga Adigal]. 3rd ed. Vadalur: Samarasa Sanmarga Araycchi Nilayam, 2006.

———. *Tirumūlarum Vaḷḷalārum* [Tirumular and Vallalar]. Vadalur: Samarasa Sanmarga Araycci Nilayam, 2005.

Vaithees, V. Ravi. *Religion, Caste, and Nation in South India: Maraimalai Adigal, the Neo-Saivite Movement, and Tamil Nationalism, 1876–1950*. New Delhi: Oxford University Press, 2015.

van der Veer, Peter. "Colonial Cosmopolitanism." In *Conceiving Cosmopolitanism: Theory, Context, and Practice*, edited by Steven Vertovec and Robin Cohen, 165–79. New York: Oxford University Press, 2002.

———. *Imperial Encounters: Religion and Modernity in India and Britain*. Princeton: Princeton University Press, 2001.

Vanmikanathan, G. *Pathway to God Trod by Raamalinga Swaamikal*. Bombay: Bharatiya Vidya Bhavan, 1976.

Vasudeva, Somadeva. "Powers and Identities: Yoga Powers and the Tantric Śaiva Traditions." In *Yoga Powers: Extraordinary Capacities Attained through Meditation and Concentration*, edited by Knut A. Jacobsen, 265–302. Leiden: Brill, 2011.

Venkatachalapathy, A. R. "The Making of a Canon: Literature in Colonial Tamilnadu." In *In Those Days There Was No Coffee: Writings in Cultural History*, 88–113. New Delhi: Yoda Press, 2006.

———. *The Province of the Book: Scholars, Scribes, and Scribblers in Colonial Tamilnadu*. Ranikhet, India: Permanent Black, 2012.

———. "Reading Practices and Modes of Reading in Colonial Tamil Nadu." *Studies in History* 10, no. 2 (1994): 273–90.

———. "'Tappai Oppeṉṟu Tāpittalum, Oppait Tappeṉṟu Vātittalum'; Tamiḻil Kaṇṭaṉa Ilakkiyam" ['Establishing wrong as right, and arguing that right is wrong': polemical literature in Tamil]. In *Aruṭpā Maruṭpā: Kaṇṭaṉattiraṭṭu* [Verses of divine grace, verses of delusion: a collection of polemical literature], edited by P. Saravanan, 17–47. Nagarkovil: Kalaccuvatu Patippakam, 2010.

Venkatesan, R. "Irāmaliṅkam Pāṭalkaḷ Vaḷḷalār Tokuppāṉa Varalāṟu" [The history of the Vallalar compilation of C. Iramalinga's verses]. In *Tamiḻ Nūl Tokuppu Varalāṟu* [The history of Tamil text compilation], edited by P. Ilamaran Muttaiya Vellaiyan, J. Sivakumar, and K. Ganesh, 86–93. Chennai: Puthiya Puthakam Pusuthu, 2010.

Viswanathan, Gauri. "Colonialism and the Construction of Hinduism." In *The Blackwell Companion to Hinduism,* edited by Gavin D. Flood, 23–44. Malden, MA: Blackwell Pub., 2003.

Walsham, Alexandra. "Preaching without Speaking: Script, Print, and Religious Dissent." In *The Uses of Script and Print, 1300–1700,* edited by Julia C. Crick and Alexandra Walsham, 211–34. Cambridge: Cambridge University Press, 2004.

Washbrook, David. "Economic Depression and the Making of 'Traditional' Society in Colonial India, 1820–1855." *Transactions of the Royal Historical Society* 3 (1993): 237–63.

Watt, Carey A. "Philanthropy and Civilizing Missions in India C. 1820–1960: States, NGOs, and Development." In *Civilizing Missions in Colonial and Postcolonial South Asia: From Improvement to Development,* edited by Carey Anthony Watt and Michael Mann, 271–316. New York: Anthem Press, 2011.

———. *Serving the Nation: Cultures of Service, Association, and Citizenship.* New York: Oxford University Press, 2005.

Weiss, Richard S. "Accounting for Religious Change: Ramalinga Adigal's Transformation of Hindu Giving in Nineteenth-Century India." *History of Religions* 56, no. 1 (2016): 108–38.

———. "Print, Religion, and Canon in Colonial India: The Publication of Ramalinga Adigal's *Tiruvarutpa.*" *Modern Asian Studies* 49, no. 3 (2015): 650–77.

———. *Recipes for Immortality: Medicine, Religion, and Community in South India.* New York: Oxford University Press, 2009.

———. "Religion and the Emergence of Print in Colonial India: Arumuga Navalar's Publishing Project." *Indian Economic and Social History Review* 53, no. 4 (2016): 473–500.

———. "Voluntary Associations and Religious Change in Colonial India: Ramalinga Adigal's 'Society of the True Path.'" *South Asia: Journal of South Asian Studies* 41, no. 1 (2018): 18–32.

Wentworth, Blake Tucker. "Yearning for a Dreamed Real: The Procession of the Lord in the Tamil Ulās." PhD diss., University of Chicago, 2011.

White, Daniel E. *From Little London to Little Bengal: Religion, Print and Modernity in Early British India, 1793–1835.* Baltimore: John Hopkins University Press, 2013.

White, David Gordon. *The Alchemical Body: Siddha Traditions in Medieval India.* Chicago: University of Chicago Press, 1996.

———. *Sinister Yogis.* Chicago: The University of Chicago Press, 2009.

Williams, Raymond Brady. *An Introduction to Swaminarayan Hinduism.* Cambridge: Cambridge University Press, 2001.

———. *A New Face of Hinduism: The Swaminarayan Religion.* Cambridge: Cambridge University Press, 1984.

———, and Yogi Trivedi, eds. *Swaminarayan Hinduism: Tradition, Adaptation, and Identity.* New York: Oxford University Press, 2016.

Yelle, Robert A. *The Language of Disenchantment: Protestant Literalism and Colonial Discourse in British India.* New York: Oxford University Press, 2013.

Yocum, Glenn E. "A Non-Brahman Tamil Saiva Mutt: A Field Study of the Thiruvavaduthurai Adheenam." In *Monastic Life in the Christian and Hindu Traditions: A Comparative Study,* edited by Austin B. Creel and Vasudha Narayanan, 245–79. Lewiston, N.Y.: Edwin Mellen Press, 1990.

Young, R. F., and S. Jebanesan. *The Bible Trembled: The Hindu-Christian Controversies of Nineteenth-Century Ceylon.* Vienna: Sammlung De Nobili, 1995.

Young, Richard Fox, J. P. V. Somaratna, and Sammlung De Nobili. *Vain Debates: The Buddhist-Christian Controversies of Nineteenth-Century Ceylon.* Vienna: Institute of Indology, University of Vienna, 1996.

Zelliot, Eleanor. "Caste in Contemporary India." In *Contemporary Hinduism: Ritual, Culture, and Practice,* edited by Robin Rinehart, 243–68. Santa Barbara, CA: ABC-CLIO, 2004.

Zubkova (Bytchikhina), Luba. "Religious Universalism of Ramalinga Swamikal, the Holy Poet of Tamils." *Journal of Tamil Studies* 59 (2001): 93–110.

Zvelebil, Kamil. *Lexicon of Tamil Literature.* Leiden: E. J. Brill, 1995.

———. *The Poets of the Powers.* London: Rider, 1973.

———. *The Smile of Murugan: On Tamil Literature of South India.* Leiden: Brill, 1973.

———. *Tamil Literature.* Wiesbaden: Harrassowitz, 1974.

INDEX

acharyas (Shaiva preceptors), 40, 47
Agamas, 87, 102–104, 121, 138–139
Agastya, 124, 128
alchemy, 107, 111, 124, 125, 130, 131, 133
Almshouse of Unity, 34–35, 46–50, 132
Ambalavanar, Darshan, 107–108
ambrosia, 128–130, 138, 141
animal sacrifice, 37, 104
Appar, 68, 87, 89, 90
Appasamy Chetty, M., 132
Arnold, David, 47, 48
Arooran, K. Nambi, 33
aruḷ (grace), 35, 69, 88
aruṭperuñjōti (great light of grace), 132
Arya Samaj, 1, 6, 29, 165n4
Asiatic Press, 61, 172n55
autohagiography, 2, 76–77, 80, 82, 95
Auvaiyar, 57, 117
Ayyavazhi Movement, 8

Balachandran, R., 16, 98
Balakrishna Pillai, A., 14, 57, 60
bazaars, 56, 60, 62, 72, 129, 139, 142
Bennett, Andrew, 80
Berman, Marshall, 145
Bhargava, Rajeev, 19
Bhogar, 124
Bible, 54, 55, 102
Blackburn, Anne, 23–24, 128
Blackburn, Stuart, 56, 64
Bornstein, Erica, 49
Brahmo Samaj, 1, 6, 7, 9, 28, 29, 55, 126
Brick, David, 32
Buddha, 136
Buddhism, 9, 23–24, 46, 136
burying of dead, 11, 17, 139, 142

canon: debates about Shaiva, 71, 103, 113–114, 118–119; fixidity of, 97, 106–107, 109, 114, 119; flexibility of, 86–87, 90, 100; print and, 52–55, 64, 71–72, 100–101; *Tiruvaruṭpā* as, 56, 66–72, 76, 86, 118. *See also Tirumuṟai*
caste: food-giving ideology and, 27, 30–31, 33, 40, 43–44, 47; Navalar's support of, 54, 102–104, 108, 110–111, 120; Ramalinga's, 13, 17, 111; Ramalinga's critiques of, 8, 16, 33, 36–38, 135–138, 142–143; Ramalinga's disregard of, 47, 49, 75, 85, 91, 120, 133, 140; Ramalinga's followers and, 14, 17, 38, 43, 98, 111, 127, 132–133. *See also vellalar*
Cekkilar, 89, 103, 115
Chakrabarty, Dipesh, 18, 126, 142, 152
Champakalakshmi, R., 32
chattrams, 46, 48
Chidambara Swamigal, 67, 68, 109
Chidambaram, 2, 3, 13, 45, 61, 66, 69, 79, 82, 93, 110–112, 132, 142–143
Christian influence on Ramalinga, 17, 42, 45, 46–47, 50, 140
Cikkitti Chettiyar, Mayilai, 62

Citti Vaḷākam (House of Siddhi), 14, 129
Cittipuram, 142, 144
Civarakaciyam, 106
Civavakkiyar, 124, 128
Cooper, Frederick, 22, 23
copyright, 62–64
cremation, 17, 139
"Critique of the Pseudo-Divine Verses," 105–115
Cutler, Norman, 76, 92, 94

dalit, 43, 104, 108, 132, 143
Dalyell, R. A., 48, 49
Damodaram Pillai, 64
dāna (charity), 28, 31–37, 41, 44, 46, 50, 91, 166n20
Dandapani Swamigal, 8
Dandapani Tecikar, C., 106
Das, Sisir Kumar, 16
Davis, Donald, 99–100
Dayananda Saraswati, 1, 6, 10, 28–29, 54, 99, 103, 125–126
de Man, Paul, 145
Dharmapuram monastery, 33, 108
dharmashala (resthouse), 34, 46
Dirks, Nicolas, 100
Dobe, Timothy, 19, 75–76
Dube, Saurabh, 23, 150, 153
Dubiansky, A., 15

Ebeling, Sasha, 16
1881 census, 6–7
Eisenstadt, S. N., 19–20, 145
Eisenstein, Elizabeth, 52–53, 101
entangled histories, 2, 22, 44–51, 140, 149–150
eroticism in Ramalinga's poems, 84, 86

famine, 2, 28, 30, 34, 40, 46–50, 137, 165n4
Farquhar, J. N., 6, 9, 29, 159
five syllable mantra. *See pañcāṭcaram*
Flood, Gavin, 10
folk practices, 104, 124
Fort St. George, College of, 56
Foucault, Michel, 50

Ganapathy, T. N., 140
Gautaman, Raj, 17, 128
gender, 6, 7, 29, 40, 41, 43, 44, 144
Ghosh, Anindita, 55–56
golden body, 39, 128, 129, 130
Göle, Nilüfer, 20
Gover, Charles E., 124

Gros, François, 70
guru, Ramalinga as, 73–74, 110, 146, 149

Hacker, Paul, 7, 9, 17
Halbfass, Wilhelm, 9
Hatcher, Brian, 5, 7, 8, 9, 10, 19, 21, 29–30, 75–76, 125, 126, 159
Heehs, Peter, 16–17
Heim, Maria, 31–32
Heimsath, Charles, 15
Hellmann-Rajanayagam, Dagmar, 108
"History of *Tiruvaruṭpā*," work by Velayudha Mudaliyar, 59, 61–62, 66, 71, 94, 109

immortality, 85–86, 125, 128–129, 131, 134–136, 139–141, 145–146, 149
Irattina Mudaliyar, Irakkam, 57–59, 61, 70, 92
Irschick, Eugene, 17
Islam, 9, 136, 137

Jainism, 32, 46, 136, 167n53
Jalsah-e Tahzib, 133
Jesudasan, C., 16
Jīva Karuṇya Oḻukkam (The Path of Compassion for Living Beings), 28, 35–50

Kabir, 126
Kandasami Pillai, S. M., 59, 60
Kandasami temple, 107
Karkatta caste, 102
Karunguli, 57, 58, 61, 67, 106
Karuniga caste, 13, 165n16
Kaviraj, Sudipta, 10
Killingley, Dermot, 103
Koppedrayer, Kathleen Iva, 32
Koselleck, Reinhart, 145
Kumarakuruparar, 108
Kumarasami Pillai, 58

lamp, miracle of, 67–68, 109, 112, 117. *See also* miracles, Ramalinga's performance of
Leipzig Lutheran mission, 45–47
Linderman, Michael, 33, 46
Little, Layne, 124
Long, James, 53, 62
Lubin, Timothy, 99–100

Mackenzie Manuscripts, 124
Madurai Tirugnanasambanda Swamigal Monastery, 67, 109, 112
Mahavira, 136
Mahima Dharma, 8

Mani, Lata, 99–100
Manikkavacakar, 57, 68, 84, 87, 88, 90, 116
manuscripts, Ramalinga's writings on, 58, 74, 167n42, 177n29
Maraimalai Adigal, 98
Marudur, 13
mathas (Hindu monasteries), 30–34, 43, 64, 96, 104, 137, 139, 150, 166n22
meat-eating, 38, 44, 133
medicine, 39, 47, 123, 124, 132, 135
metrical forms in Ramalinga's poems, 70, 93
Minakshisundaram Pillai, 8, 69, 171n28
minor deities, 37, 85, 104
miracles, Ramalinga's performance of, 68, 89, 107, 109–112, 117, 145. *See also* lamp, miracle of
modernity, conjunctural model of, 19–22
modernity, convergence model of, 19–22, 75, 76
modernity, my definition of, 21
modernities, multiple, 19, 21, 22, 26
Murdoch, John, 53, 55, 60, 62, 64
Murugan, Ramalinga's poems to, 13, 60, 70,78, 85
Muthusami Mudaliyar, 112, 113
Muttiyalammal, 67

Nalvaḻi, 57
nālvar (four Shaiva poet-saints), 68, 70, 87–90, 92, 93, 95
Namdev, 144
name, controversy over Ramalinga's, 61, 66
Naminandi Adigal, 109
Nataraja, in Ramalinga's poems, 2, 82, 84, 110, 111, 141
Navalar, Arumuga, 16, 42, 54, 67, 97–98, 101–121
nāyaṉmār (Shaiva saints), 89, 106, 119
neo-Hinduism, 7, 9, 10, 17
Novetzke, Christian Lee, 74, 144
Nyayaratna, Ramgati, 60

Oḻivil Oṭukkam, 42, 108
Otri. *See* Tiruvotriyur.

Pacchaiyappa School, 13, 54
Padmanabhan, Neela, 16
Pampatti siddha, 144
pamphlet form, 55, 59–60, 72, 105
Panapattiran, 82
pañcāṭcaram (five syllable mantra), 57, 66, 68, 85, 91–92
Parvatipuram, 111, 127, 139, 142, 143
Patanjali, 130
Pattinattar, 144
Pels, Peter, 123
Percival, Peter, 42, 54, 102
Periya Purāṇam, 54, 62, 64, 68, 82, 83, 89, 92, 103, 105, 107, 115, 116, 136, 137
Peterson, Indira, 81, 85, 88, 92
polemical literature in Tamil, 101
Pōliyaruṭpā Maṟuppu. *See* "Critique of the Pseudo-Divine Verses"
polemics, *aruṭpā* – *maruṭpā* (verses of grace – verses of delusion), 97, 105–121
Pollock, Sheldon, 20
possession-dancing, 137–138
Preservation of Knowledge Press, 103
Presidency College, 64
prose, writing in, 14, 24, 35, 42, 54–56, 72, 76, 103, 107, 175n97
Protestant Buddhism, 23, 28, 29, 165n7
Protestant literalism, 55, 56, 76
Protestant rationality, 5, 55, 126, 146, 149, 152
Protestant Reformation, 5, 52–53, 99
provincializing Europe, 11, 18
public: character of Ramalinga's message, 35, 74, 138, 141–144; Navalar's notion of, 107–108, 112; *ulakattār* (people of the world) as, 106–107, 112–114, 132, 134–135, 138, 141, 144. *See also* street character of Ramalinga's poems
Puranas, 54, 69, 81, 82, 85, 139. *See also Periya Purāṇam*, *Tiruviḷaiyāṭal Purāṇam*

Racine, Jean-Luc and Josiane, 16
Rama Tirtha, 19
Ramachandra Dikshitar, 15
Ramakrishna, 15
Ramalinga Swami, biography, 11–15
Raman, Srilata, 17, 28, 30, 39, 42, 45
Ramasami Mudaliyar, P., 13, 128
Ramasami Pillai, 112–113
Randeria, Shalini, 22
Rao, Velcheru Narayana, 20
reform Hinduism, 4–11, 54–56, 98–105, 124–126
resurrection of dead, 68, 128, 133–135, 138–140, 142–143
Rocher, Rosane, 99
Roy, Rammohun, 1, 7, 10, 29, 54, 99, 103, 125, 163n68
rudraksha beads, 85, 113

Sabhapati Pillai, 13
Sabhapati Mudaliyar, Kanchipuram, 13, 54, 64
sacred ash, 70, 79, 85, 89, 91–92, 113
Sahajanand Swami, 18, 163n68. *See also* Swaminarayan
Saler, Michael, 126

Sambandar, 62, 68, 87–90, 116
Saminatha Iyer, U. V., 64
Śaṅkarācārya, 125
Sanskrit, Ramalinga's lack of knowledge of, 13, 39, 70, 81, 87–88, 94, 108
Saravanan, P., 17
Sathyarth Prakash, 28, 125
School of Shaiva Splendor, 103
Selvaraya Mudaliyar, 58, 59, 61, 70
Sen, Amiya, 7
Sen, Keshab Chandra, 6, 9, 28
Serfoji II, Raja, 46
Shaiva Siddhanta, 13, 35, 38, 67, 108, 109, 112, 113, 118
Shanmuga Pillai Reddiyar, 58
Shanmugam Pillai, 105, 114–118
Sharma, Arvind, 9
Sherring, M. A., 47
Shulman, David, 20, 77, 131
siddha medicine. *See* medicine
siddhas: as yogis, 40, 43, 86, 87; influence on Ramalinga, 16, 38–39, 47, 128, 130, 135–136, 140, 144; modernity and, 122–125, 140, 146–147; Ramalinga as, 85, 111–112, 122, 127–131, 146–147; Tamil tradition of, 14, 40, 123–124, 128, 140, 144
siddhis (yogic powers): as reward for following Ramalinga's teachings, 38–39, 131, 133–135, 143; in Hindu traditions, 14, 123; Ramalinga's claim to possess, 127–131
sixth section of *Tiruvaruṭpā*, 70–71, 85, 122, 127–128
Smith, David, 10, 73–74
Society of the True Path, 34–35, 43–44, 49–50, 59, 64, 127, 131–135, 140, 143–144
Somasundara Chettiyar, 62
South Arcot district, 46–48, 169n92
Stark, Ulrike, 56, 62, 132
Stock, Brian, 57
Storrow, Edward, 47
street character of Ramalinga's poems, 113–114, 142, 144
subordinate deities, Hindu, 37
Subrahmanyam, Sanjay, 19, 20
Subramanian, N., 15
Sumangala, Hikkaduve, 23
Sundaram Pillai, Ponneri, 68, 69, 110
Sundarar, 68, 82–83, 87–90
Swaminarayan, 8, 15, 18, 126

Tandavaraya Swamigal, 54
tantra, 24–25, 38–39, 111, 125, 129–131, 135
Tattuva Pirakācam, 106
Taylor, Rev. William, 124
Tayumanavar, 34, 77, 116, 131
Temple of True Knowledge, 14, 34, 91, 93, 132, 142
Tēvāram: Ramalinga's challenge to, 14, 94, 106–107, 110, 112, 114; influence on Ramalinga: 68–70, 81–82, 87–89, 94, 117, 137, 144; publication of, 54, 62, 64; ritual use of, 92–94, 103
Thomassen, Bjorn, 21
Tirukkōvaiyār, 105–106
Tirukkōvaiyār Uṇmai, 105
Tirukkuṟaḷ, 13, 56, 115, 117, 169n92
Tirumantiram, 106, 113, 116–117
Tirumular, 116–117
Tirumuṟai, as sections of *Tiruvaruṭpā*, 66, 67, 71, 127
Tirumuṟai, as Tamil Shaiva canon, 66, 67, 102, 103, 106, 113, 116
Tirunavukkaracu. *See* Appar
tiruniṟu. *See* sacred ash
Tiruvācakam, 57, 82, 87, 88, 90, 103, 105, 106, 115–117
Tiruvavadudurai, 2, 33–34, 54, 64, 102, 106, 112, 120, 166n22. *See also* mathas
Tiruviḷaiyāṭal Purāṇam, 82, 142
Tiruvotriyur, 58, 59, 60, 61, 69, 81, 82, 93, 94
Toṇṭamaṇṭala Catakam, 108
tradition, my definition, 23
tradition, Ramalinga's conception of, 86–91, 95–96, 119–120
True Path, Ramalinga's, 14, 34–35, 43, 44, 131–140, 143

Ulrich, Katherine, 30
urukkam (melting of heart), 35, 36, 83

Vadalur, 2, 3, 14, 45, 79, 93, 127, 132, 138, 150
Vākkuvātam, 55
van der Veer, Peter, 6, 22, 159
Vasudeva, Somadeva, 130
Vedanta, 13, 104, 112
Vedas, Ramalinga's view of, 34, 39, 78, 87–88, 138–139
vegetarianism, 38, 133. *See also* meat-eating
Velayuda Mudaliyar, 59, 64–67, 69, 71, 94, 112–114, 127, 128
vellalars: mathas dominated by, 31–32, 120, 136; Navalar and, 102, 103, 104, 108, 111, 120; Ramalinga's followers as, 43, 49, 133;

Ramalinga's status as, 13, 111; Tamil Shaivism and, 17, 47, 85, 88
Velu Mudaliyar, Puduvai, 59, 68
Venkatachalapathy, A. R., 101, 105, 111
Venkatesan, R., 17, 127
Virashaiva, 128
Vishwanathan, Gauri, 104
Vivekananda, Swami, 1, 9, 10, 29
voluntary society, 131–135, 140

Walsham, Alexandra, 53
Washbrook, David, 98–99
Watt, Carey, 28
World Religions discourse, 5, 55, 136

Yelle, Robert, 99, 109–110, 125, 126
Yoga Sutras, 130
yoga, classical, 129, 130, 131, 134
yogic power. See *siddhis*
yogis, 32, 40, 43, 87, 123–125, 146

Zelliot, Elleanor, 140
Zubkova, Luba, 15
Zvelebil, Kamil, 15, 42, 73, 75, 84, 135

www.ingramcontent.com/pod-product-compliance
Lightning Source LLC
Chambersburg PA
CBHW070804230426
43665CB00017B/2481